SERIAL KILLERS OF THE '70s

Other books in the Profiles in Crime Series

How to Catch a Killer–Katherine Ramsland, PhD

Killer Cults–Stephen Singular

Extreme Killers–Michael Newton

Serial Killers of the '80s–Jane Fritsch

SERIAL KILLERS OF THE '70s

BEHIND A NOTORIOUS DECADE OF DEATH

JANE FRITSCH

An Imprint of Sterling Publishing Co., Inc.
1166 Avenue of the Americas
New York, NY 10036

ISBN 978-1-4549-3938-2
ISBN 978-1-4549-3942-9 (e-book)

Distributed in Canada by Sterling Publishing Co., Inc.
c/o Canadian Manda Group, 664 Annette Street
Toronto, Ontario M6S 2C8, Canada
Distributed in the United Kingdom by GMC Distribution Services
Castle Place, 166 High Street, Lewes, East Sussex BN7 1XU, England
Distributed in Australia by NewSouth Books
University of New South Wales, Sydney, NSW 2052, Australia

For information about custom editions, special sales, and premium and corporate purchases,
please contact Sterling Special Sales at 800-805-5489 or specialsales@sterlingpublishing.com.

Manufactured in the United States of America

2 4 6 8 10 9 7 5 3 1

sterlingpublishing.com

Cover design by David Ter-Avanesyan
Interior design by Gavin Motnyk

CONTENTS

Acknowledgments vii
Introduction ix

1. JUAN CORONA 1

2. DEAN ALLEN CORLL, ELMER WAYNE HENLEY, AND DAVID OWEN BROOKS 19

3. RODNEY ALCALA 32

4. EDMUND KEMPER 47

5. DAVID BERKOWITZ 54

6. TED BUNDY 71

7. VAUGHN GREENWOOD 82

8. HERBERT MULLIN 89

9. THE ZEBRA KILLERS 97

10. KENNETH BIANCHI AND ANGELO BUONO 108

11. PATRICK WAYNE KEARNEY 119

12. CORAL EUGENE WATTS 125

13. WILLIAM BONIN 132

14. JOHN WAYNE GACY 143

EPILOGUE 167

APPENDIX 1. Excerpt from People v. Superior Court (Corona), 30 Cal.3d 193, November 16, 1981 175

APPENDIX 2. Excerpt from Rodney Alcala's appeal before the United States Court of Appeals, argued February 6, 2003 188

APPENDIX 3. Excerpt from John Wayne Gacy's appeal in the United States Court of Appeals, Seventh Circuit, argued March 4, 1993 . . 237

Sources 249

Index 257

Image Credits 265

About the Author 267

ACKNOWLEDGMENTS

With grateful appreciation for the help of William Kunkle, Robert Egan and Greg Bedoe. Thanks also to Jonathan Landman for teaching me how to write; Patricia Garcia for her wise suggestions; Molly Fritsch for her invaluable help with research; and Marilyn Allen for her wise counsel over the years.

INTRODUCTION

The baffling thing about serial killers is how ordinary they seem. How is it possible that someone who holds down a job, pays his bills, and mows his lawn can suddenly turn into Jack the Ripper or John Wayne Gacy—and just as suddenly turn back into an average guy? The ability to switch personalities at will is an essential trait of serial killers, who, until recent decades, were called "mass murderers." That phrase is now used to designate a broader group that includes people like Adam Lanza, who gunned down twenty young children and six adults at the Sandy Hook Elementary School in 2012, or Richard Speck, who killed eight student nurses in their Chicago townhouse one summer night in 1966. The Speck murders—by stabbing and strangulation—were called "the crime of the century." That turned out to be a sadly optimistic view.

Cultural, technological, and labor force changes in the last half of the twentieth century were factors that gave rise to an unusual spate of successive murders. But fascination with serial killers, real and imagined, has a long history. The concept of a ruthless and careful murderer came clearly into focus in the 1880s, when Jack the Ripper terrorized the Whitechapel area of London. Five women who were assumed to be prostitutes walking the streets of the East End slums had their throats slashed and their bodies mutilated by an unknown attacker. The killings ended on November 9, 1880, just as mysteriously as they had started ten weeks earlier.

Jack the Ripper was never caught, but his legacy has been powerful. Chinese media reported in 2019 that a man known as China's Jack the

Ripper had been executed. Gao Chengyong, a fifty-three-year-old, had been convicted of murdering eleven young women and girls from 1988 to 2002 in and around Baiyin, a city of nearly two million people about seven hundred miles west of Beijing. The youngest victim was eight years old. Gao raped and robbed his prey, after which he cut off parts of their reproductive organs "to satisfy his perverted desire to dishonor and sully corpses," the court in Baiyin said.

As in the case of England's Jack the Ripper, women and girls were afraid to walk the streets of Baiyin alone for many years. But the original Jack the Ripper did not have to worry about modern science. Gao, a married father of two who ran a grocery store, was identified as the killer in 2016 after an uncle was arrested on a minor charge and a DNA sample was taken. Gao had raped some of his victims before he killed them, and he violated the bodies of others after they were dead. Investigators had preserved samples from the crime scenes. They saw that the DNA from Gao's uncle was close to a match with the Ripper samples they had saved for decades and quickly matched the samples to Gao.

A DNA solution is not possible in the case of London's Jack the Ripper, but dozens of movies, television shows, and books inspired by the Ripper—or speculating about his identity—have been produced over the years. One of the earliest was *Pandora's Box,* a 1929 black-and-white silent film produced in Germany. In *Murder By Decree,* a 1979 movie starring Christopher Plummer, the fictional Sherlock Holmes investigates the Ripper murders. In *Jack's Back,* a 1988 movie starring James Spader, a Los Angeles serial killer celebrates the Ripper's one hundredth birthday by committing murders similar to his. In *Whitechapel,* a television series that ran from 2009 to 2013, the British actor Rupert Penry-Jones plays a detective investigating modern-day crimes with connections to the Ripper murders. *Jack the Ripper—The Case Reopened* is a 2019 British television production featuring the actress Emilia Fox that re-examines the case. Ripper walking tours in the East End of London—some in the dark of night—remain popular tourist attractions.

In the United States, the understanding of serial murder and why and how it happens has been complicated by a variety of factors, including the nation's vast expanses of open land, societal changes brought on by the Vietnam War, and the push for acceptance of homosexuality, among other factors.

The development of the vast interstate freeway system in the last half of the twentieth century made it possible, and even easy, to travel anonymously for thousands of miles. Hitchhiking was still considered an acceptable way for young people to get from place to place, and it was used by many who had family difficulties at home. Resistance to the war in Vietnam and the military draft contributed to the undermining of the cohesion of the traditional family and made it tempting for an unhappy young person to disappear. Of course, there were no cell phones then to track the location of runaways, and there were few security cameras to monitor their travel or suggest where they might have ended up. The thousands of police departments across the country still used fax machines to communicate with each other.

The 1970s was also a time in the country's history when the notion of gay rights and openly accepted homosexuality was just emerging. A 1969 police raid at the Stonewall Inn, a homosexual bar in Manhattan, led to years of protests and demonstrations that marked the beginning of the gay rights movement. Changes in attitudes and acceptance of homosexuality came more slowly in other parts of the country. Many of John Wayne Gacy's victims, six of whom remain unidentified, were runaways who spent time in an area of Chicago known for its gay bars and restaurants.

Spurred by the troubling cases of the 1970s, the Federal Bureau of Investigation began collecting data about the group of murderers who came to be called serial killers. The FBI created a Behavior Analysis Unit in the 1980s to study these killers and to assist and train local law enforcement agencies and prosecutors. The Gacy murders spurred the creation of a new computer data bank where the Chicago Police Department could store information about missing persons. It was set up to be a first step toward a countrywide system that could be used by investigators to locate people who had disappeared and to help police identify patterns in the cases that might link them.

Gacy, who was found guilty of thirty-three murders in 1980, still holds the record for the most convictions at a trial. Since then, other killers have admitted to—or been suspected of—more murders, but they ended their litigations with guilty pleas to avoid trials and, sometimes, to avoid the possibility of the death penalty. Forensic science, computer data, highway cameras, doorbell cameras, cell phone towers, security cameras at gas stations, credit card data, and security cameras everywhere from the local Walmart to the Dunkin' Donuts can make a pretty persuasive record of a person's life and whereabouts. So for most defendants accused of serial murder in the twenty-first century, there are few options other than a plea of guilty or, at best, a plea of not guilty by reason of insanity.

That plea didn't work for Gacy in 1980. The idea that a person who was mentally incapable of controlling his behavior could commit thirty-three murders in private is hard to grasp. How does a normal guy with a normal-seeming life snap into and out of murderous insanity at just the right moment thirty-three times? Would that person have gone ahead with the killing if a police officer had been standing nearby and watching? In the following decades, psychiatrists and criminologists would delve more deeply into that mystery. And other prolific serial killers would emerge into the light.

1.
JUAN CORONA

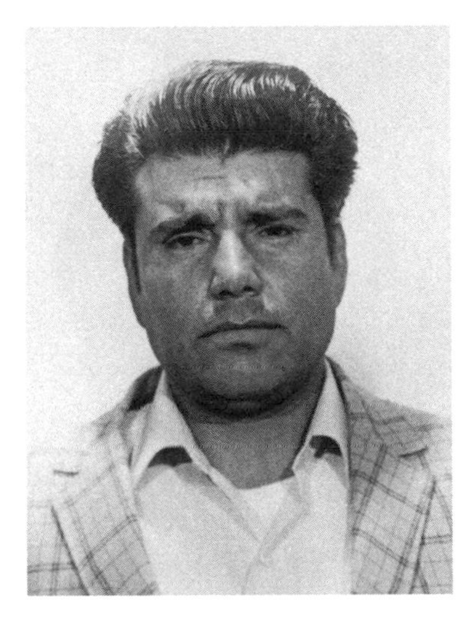

The first sign of anything unusual was the hole in the ground out near the edge of the peach orchard. When the owner circled back at the end of that spring day in 1971, the hole had been filled in. He thought about it over dinner and decided to contact the police. But it wasn't until the next morning that an investigator arrived at the scene in the lush Sacramento Valley to take a look. The spot where the hole had been dug and refilled was, indeed, intriguing. Deputy Sheriff Steve Sizelove and Goro Kagehiro, who had owned the orchard for two decades, picked up shovels. Maybe, they agreed, someone had just dumped some trash and covered it up. That happened sometimes. Even so, they needed to take a look. After a few minutes of careful poking and prodding, they uncovered a shoe. Inside the shoe was a human foot. They had found the first body.

Within a week, the world would be hearing the nightmarish details of what the newspapers and television stations were already calling "the worst multiple murder case in American history." Juan V. Corona, a thirty-seven-year-old contractor who supplied farm laborers to ranches in the area, had been arrested. In less than two weeks, the toll of bodies reached twenty-five. That gave Corona the record for serial murders, but not for long. By the end of the 1970s, more prolific—and more baffling—killers would emerge. Law enforcement officials and psychiatric experts would dive deeply into the subject and come up with a more precise term for people like Corona: serial killer. But in 1971, as investigators began to unearth the shallow graves near a small California town, they had no reason to imagine that the second half of the twentieth century would become known as the "Golden Age of Serial Killers."

The discovery of the first body on May 20, 1971, set off a confounding week for investigators. Juan Corona was on nobody's radar. Sizelove, who had used his car radio to call in reinforcements from the Sutter County Sheriff's Department, watched as the body was carefully unearthed from the shallow grave. He recognized the face as that of a young man he had stopped earlier in the week walking along a highway. His name was Kendall Whitacre, and he was just another of the many vagrants who frequented the area. Sizelove hadn't bothered to file a report on the encounter. Now he could see that there were deep lacerations on the back of Whitacre's head and stab wounds in his chest. Who would want to kill this man in such a vicious way? Why would the killer go to such trouble to bury the body? And why in this particular orchard?

Word spread to the police departments of the nearby towns, and a detective from Marysville gave the sheriff's investigators the first real clue. He remembered that a year or so earlier, a customer had been viciously beaten and cut at the Guadalajara Café, a restaurant owned by a man named Natividad Corona. His younger brother, Juan, had been seen there that night and was known to have violent temper fits. The investigators had their first possible suspect—Juan Vallejo Corona. He had supplied some workers for the peach orchard where the body was found and for the prune orchard on the Sullivan ranch near Yuba City. Investigators found Juan out at the Jack Sullivan Ranch that afternoon and showed him a photograph of Whitacre's body. Juan said he didn't recognize the man. Meanwhile, a worker in another area of the Sullivan ranch noticed a shallow depression in the orchard ground. He asked another worker to take a look. They agreed it was about the size of a shallow grave. In fact, it turned out to be a shallow grave—one of many, as the world would quickly learn. Most of the victims appeared to have been hacked to death with a machete or an axe. One had been shot in the head.

The national media quickly descended on the area as the investigation was unfolding. "COAST MAN SEIZED IN DOZEN KILLINGS" was the headline on the front page of the *New York Times* on May 27, 1971. Television crews rolled into town, and reporters from wire services and all the major newspapers showed up. They brought along rolls of quarters to deposit into pay phones—most with rotary dials—so that they could dictate their stories to rewrite men—mostly men at the time—working on typewriters holding sheets of carbon paper back at the office.

The toll of bodies had reached fifteen, but it was expected to grow. Only two of the victims—itinerant farmworkers—had been identified, but it seemed likely to investigators that the rest were itinerant workers, too. That might explain why no one had reported them missing. Soon, the news media had a name for the killer: "The Machete Murderer." Little was known about Corona except that he was married, lived in a house in the area, and had four young daughters. He was a heavyset Mexican-American who spoke broken English and had been in the United States for about twelve years. The Sutter County sheriff, Roy D. Whitaker, told reporters that Corona was the prime suspect and that investigators were not looking for anyone else. He did not want to elaborate.

While examining the third grave, investigators found receipts from a local butcher shop. One was for $78.35 and the other for $35.63. Each had a recent date and had been made out to Juan V. Corona. The investigators confirmed the receipts with the shop owner, and soon they had enough circumstantial evidence to request a search warrant. A local judge quickly approved it. In the middle of the night, officers descended on Corona's house, where he and his family were sleeping. They found a rusty crowbar, a wooden club, a meat cleaver, a machete, and other possible weapons. Some had what appeared to be bloodstains.

A second team went out to the Sullivan ranch, which had a mess hall and a bunkhouse area where workers sometimes slept. Corona had a desk there. In his filing cabinet, the officers found an automatic pistol and some rounds of ammunition, along with a list of names. They would soon realize that the list contained the names of some of the men whose bodies they were still unearthing. Eventually, twenty-one bodies were identified as local vagrants who had been recruited as farmhands from time to time. The bodies of four adult men—assumed to be vagrants—were never identified. The bodies of fourteen identified victims, all middle-aged white men, were never claimed by relatives or friends. How could such a thing happen in an idyllic and peaceful farming community in northern California?

The time when Corona's murders were uncovered was a tumultuous and rapidly changing era in the country's history. The increasingly unpopular Vietnam War had set off college campus demonstrations across the country and simmering family arguments at home. The My Lai massacre in 1968 was still a focus of nightly news broadcasts and the stories in newspapers dropped on doorsteps each morning. American troops, sent to the Southeast Asian country to fight emerging communism, had killed some 500 unarmed people—men, women and children—in the village of My Lai, considered a communist stronghold. After a lengthy and highly publicized court martial in 1971, William L. Calley Jr., the Army lieutenant who led the attack, was convicted of twenty-two murders and sentenced to life in prison.

The era had begun with the assassinations of President John F. Kennedy in 1963 and his brother, Senator Robert F. Kennedy, in 1968, the same year that Martin Luther King Jr., the civil rights leader, was shot to death. During the 1968 Democratic National Convention in Chicago, demonstrators in Grant Park were attacked by the police in what an official report would later describe as a "police riot." In 1970, Ohio National Guard troops opened fire on students protesting the Vietnam War on the campus of Kent State University in Ohio, killing four and wounding nine.

Unthinkable multiple murders also dominated the news. Richard Speck, a twenty-four-year-old drifter with "Born to Raise Hell" tattooed on his arm, was arrested in 1966 for killing eight student nurses in Chicago. He had raped, strangled, and stabbed the women to death while he held them hostage in their apartment over a summer weekend. After a highly publicized trial, he was convicted and sentenced to death in the electric chair. The murders became known—if only for a while—as "the crime of the century." Speck was reprieved in 1972 when the U.S. Supreme Court declared the death penalty unconstitutional. He spent the rest of his life in prison.

Charles Whitman, a twenty-five-year-old ex-Marine, killed his wife and mother with a knife one day in the summer of 1966; he then took a trunk filled with weapons to the clock tower at the University of Texas in Austin. He shot a receptionist and two visitors before climbing to the observation deck at the top of the tower. From there, he went on a ninety-minute shooting spree. His final toll was fourteen dead and thirty-one wounded. In the end, Whitman was shot and killed by a police officer. He became known as the Texas Tower Sniper, a seemingly ordinary man whose actions were inexplicable and therefore more frightening.

A decade already marked by social upheaval and terrifying crimes came to an unthinkable end with events that played out in the summer of 1969. The world would quickly learn about the Manson Family, the Tate–LaBianca murders, and the apocalyptic vision Manson called Helter Skelter. Charles Manson, along with a band of drifters who had become his followers, lived in a remote stretch of desert in southern California. On Manson's orders, four of the followers—Susan Atkins, Patricia Krenwinkel, Linda Kasabian, and Charles Watkins—drove to the Benedict Canyon area of Los Angeles, near Beverly Hills, to the home of Sharon Tate, a rising movie star, and her husband, Roman Polanski, a film director. On August 9, 1969, as Watkins stood guard outside, they forced their way inside. In a frenzy of beating, stabbing, and shooting, they killed Tate, who was eight months pregnant, and three visitors who happened to be there. A fourth victim was shot in his car outside the house. Polanski was out of the country at the time.

The following night, a group of Manson followers broke into a home in the Los Feliz area of Los Angeles and, with similar savagery, killed Leno LaBianca, the owner of a grocery store chain, and his wife, Bianca. At both homes, the attackers smeared the walls with bloody messages, including "Death To Pigs." Hoping to foment a race war and mislead the police, they left bloody Black Panther paw prints. Manson and his followers were eventually tracked down and arrested. A lengthy and, at times, chaotic trial mesmerized the country, if not the world. Manson was convicted in January of 1971 and sentenced to death. He was reprieved in 1972 after the death penalty was declared unconstitutional and died in prison in 2017 at the age of eighty-two.

In the spring of 1971, a nation bewildered and exhausted by the spectacle of the Manson trial began to hear the drip-drip of news about the bodies in the orchards near Sacramento. It was almost too much to process. What could prompt so many vicious murders in an agricultural region of California?

Records from the county courthouse, quickly reported on by news outlets, described Corona as having a history of mental illness. He had been committed to a state mental hospital in 1956, when he was twenty-two years old, at the request of his half-brother, Natividad, who said that Juan believed everyone in nearby Yuba City was dead. A year earlier, thirty-seven people in the town had died when the Feather River, at the edge of the orchards, overflowed. That was about the time that Juan had moved to the area. He was born and raised in Mexico but had a green card allowing him to work in the United States. Two doctors diagnosed Juan as schizophrenic. They found him "confused" and "disoriented" and said he was suffering from hallucinations. He needed "supervision, care and restraint" or he might be dangerous to himself and others. He was released three months later as "cured."

In the following years, Juan would marry, buy a house, and have four daughters. He became a regular at St. Isadore's Roman Catholic Church in Yuba City. He had a degree of success supplying workers for the orchards. Each day, he gathered them up—mostly homeless vagrants who were middle-aged and white—and transported them to the fields for brief stints of harvesting and other work. He also provided their meals. But the need for such workers was declining because of the development of machines that could do the jobs more cheaply and efficiently. In early 1971, following an unusually rainy season that kept workers out of the fields, Juan applied for benefits in Sutter County. He was turned down. There were reports that he flew into a rage, but he was nobody's idea of a murderer, much less a mass murderer.

In the early hours of May 26, 1971, days before the rest of the bodies in the orchards were discovered, Corona was arrested at his home and taken to a jail cell in Yuba City. With a brown bag over his head to shield him from reporters, he was escorted into a courtroom, where a public defender was appointed to represent him. A chaotic legal free-for-all followed, one that would go on for more than a decade. But in 1971, as the Corona case played out, a nation still reeling from the social upheaval and unspeakable crimes of the 1960s faced new and unanswerable questions. What kind of human being could have done such a thing? What could have been the motivation? And how could twenty-five people disappear without anyone noticing?

At the time, before cell phones, it was harder to track a person's whereabouts. Missing persons databases would not emerge until a decade later. Communication among police departments—over radios, desktop telephones, and fax machines—was spotty. The internet and personal computers were years away, as were instant messaging, Facebook, Twitter, and the like. Hitchhiking was understood to be a safe way to get around, and some people in what was known as the "counterculture" disappeared intentionally. Overall, it was a less tolerant time. Those on the fringes were likely to feel excluded and to be seen as an embarrassment by their families.

The three broadcast television networks set the tone. *Father Knows Best* provided a weekly view of a bland middle-class white family with two young boys and a stay-at-home mother. *Leave It To Beaver* and *The Brady Bunch* were much the same. *Gunsmoke* focused on a white male sheriff in the Wild West. *Marcus Welby, M.D.* was a middle-aged white doctor who dealt compassionately with his patients. But there were hints of the cultural changes on the horizon. *The Mary Tyler Moore Show* told the story of an unmarried—yet still happy—career woman. *The Mod Squad,* a counterculture police team, featured a white man, a white woman, and a black man. *All In The Family* focused on a cranky middle-aged white man who watched a lot of television and complained about the hippies.

Juan Corona was sitting in a jail cell on the morning of May 26, 1971—some hours after he was arrested—when the Sutter County public defender stopped by. For six years, Roy Van den Heuvel had held the job of representing defendants who could not afford a lawyer, and he expected that he might be appointed to handle the case. He asked Corona if he had a lawyer, and Corona, using his brother as an interpreter, said that his family was getting him one. Van den Heuvel told Corona not to speak to anyone before he talked to his lawyer. Later that morning, Corona's wife, Gloria, visited him in the jail cell. Juan told his tearful wife that he wanted to have his youngest brother, Pedro, try to find him a lawyer. They had some money in the bank, he said. A lawyer had stopped by earlier, Corona told Gloria, but he wasn't sure how much the man would charge.

To be on the safe side, Van den Heuvel went to Corona's court appearance later that day. Judge J. J. Hankins, who had been assigned the case, asked Corona if he could afford to hire a lawyer, and Corona said he thought that he could. A lawyer would cost anywhere from $5,000 to as much as $20,000, the judge said. Corona conceded that he did not have that kind of money, so Hankins appointed Van den Heuvel. Meanwhile, Pedro Corona had begun looking for a lawyer for his brother. He talked to Tony Diaz, a field-worker who had once been charged with attempted murder and assault with a deadly weapon in a case involving a police officer. During an eight-day trial, the lawyer persuaded the jury that the police officer was a liar. After two hours of deliberation, the jury found Diaz not guilty. The lawyer let Diaz pay him in small amounts over time. His name was Richard Hawk.

Hawk was a lawyer at a firm in a wealthy town on the San Francisco peninsula. But he had spent several years working on his own and had signed up to take some cases as a public defender. He had handled fifty felony cases and fifty misdemeanors by the time he got the call from Tony Diaz. Reports of the bodies in the orchards had been all over television and newspapers for weeks. A sensational case like this could make him famous, Hawk reasoned. If he took it on, he would be able to raise his fees and pick and choose his clients. He met with Corona in his jail cell on June 13 and suggested that Corona might sell his house to come up with some money. Meanwhile, Hawk could start a Juan Corona defense fund and appeal to Mexican Americans for contributions. He believed that Corona was innocent.

It was not long before Hawk agreed to take the case. The June 16, 1971 edition of the *New York Times* reported that Richard E. Hawk of Concord, a San Francisco suburb, had been retained to defend Corona, replacing the public defender. Hawk had frequently represented Mexican Americans, the story said. News media were already focusing on Corona's mental health through records that became available in the local courthouse. One report, from an unnamed informant, said that Corona "was known to have fits of temper that were so bad the family had to take ropes and tie him down until he became quiet again." Mental health would be a pivotal issue in the litigation over the coming years.

The searching and careful probing of possible burial sites continued in late May and early June of 1971. In mid-July, a grand jury returned an indictment charging Corona with twenty-five murders. Until that point, he had been charged with only ten. Twenty-four of the victims were white men and one was black. Four of the twenty-five bodies never were identified.

Each body had been given a number in the twenty-five count indictment. The numbers represented the order in which the bodies had been found and unearthed.

1. **Kenneth Whitacre.** Forty years old. A transient from the San Francisco Bay area, he had been arrested six times for being drunk in public and had a 1966 conviction for robbery on his record.

2. **Charles C. Fleming.** Sixty-seven years old. Originally from Louisiana, he wandered from place to place. No one claimed his body, and it eventually was buried in a pauper's grave.

3. **Melford Sample.** Fifty-nine years old. He had been separated from his wife twenty years earlier and had little contact with his sister, who lived in southern California, near San Diego, or with his son, a police officer in Sunnyvale, in the northern part of the state.

4. **John Doe.**

5. **Donald Dale Smith.** About sixty-one years old. A combat infantryman cited for action in North Africa and Sicily, he left his small Kansas town in 1928 and headed west. Over the years he was arrested repeatedly for drunkenness, vagrancy, loitering, petty theft, and other misdemeanors. His body was buried in a pauper's grave.

6. **John J. Haluka.** Fifty-two years old. He left his hometown of Perth Amboy, New Jersey, while in his early twenties and headed west to California. A drifter, he mostly stayed out of trouble with the law as he worked in orchards from the Mexican border to the fields of northern California. Investigators found an old letter from his sister, but she had died about a year earlier. His body was buried in a pauper's grave.

7. **John Doe.**

8. **Warren J. Kelley.** Sixty-two years old. He left Texas—and his wife—in the 1940s and drifted from place to place, usually spending the winter in Arizona. He had sometimes worked in the orchard where his decomposing body was found. He was identified by the tattoos on his arms and hands: T-R-U-E on the right and L-O-V-E on the left. His wife declined to claim his body.

9. **Sigurd E. Beierman, also known as Pete Peterson.** Sixty-three years old. He lived in Marysville for twenty years and worked odd jobs. His wife had died after a long illness. He lived mostly off a Social Security disability check, which he collected from a hostel in a sketchy area of Marysville. An acquaintance realized

he hadn't seen Beierman for a few weeks and reported his disappearance to the police. Two checks were waiting for him at the hostel. Beierman was the only victim of the twenty-five—it seemed—that anyone had ever reported missing.

10. **John Doe.**

11. **William Emery Kamp.** Sixty-four years old. He was born in Wisconsin and worked odd jobs in several states. Over the years, he was charged with drunkenness and public intoxication; he had been arrested fifty-eight times. He gave up drinking late in life and frequently read passages from a well-worn Bible. He did odd jobs on the farms around Marysville. He was the only victim shot by the killer, who fired a bullet through his brain. His head had been hacked four times.

12. **John Doe.**

13. **Clarence Hocking.** Fifty-three years old. He left LaSalle, Illinois, in 1940 and headed west, where he did odd jobs and sometimes worked in orchards in California and Oregon.

14. **James W. Howard.** Sixty-four years old. He was a quiet man and a dependable day laborer who had worked in Texas and several areas of California. Sometimes he stayed with his brother in Sacramento, where he did construction and farm work.

15. **Johan R. Smallwood.** Fifty-six years old. He had been arrested ten times for vagrancy. He had served in the Navy and left it in 1952.

16. **Elbert J. T. Riley.** Forty-five years old. He lived with his wife in rural Farmersville. He had been in the Army, and he'd worked as an electrician and a carpenter. He had disappeared from time to time and had one hundred and fourteen arrests over twenty-three years. He was last seen getting into a pickup truck with the name "Juan V. Corona" on the side.

17. **Paul B. Allen.** Fifty-nine years old. His body was claimed by his brother and buried in a military cemetery in Fort Smith, Arkansas.

18. **Edward M. Cupp.** Forty-three years old. He was an Army deserter and had been convicted of grand larceny. He had escaped from a prison farm.
19. **Albert L. Hayes.** Fifty-eight years old. He was originally from Pennsylvania.
20. **Raymond Muchache.** Forty-seven years old. He was a member of the Pit River Tribe in Northern California. He was arrested eighty-seven times by the Sacramento police on charges related to drunkenness. He occasionally went to Marysville but rarely stayed very long.
21. **John H. Jackson.** Sixty-four years old. Known as a loner, he was the only black man among the twenty-five victims. Born in New York, he had turned up in Marysville from time to time over the previous three decades. He had no known family ties.
22. **Lloyd W. Wenzel.** Sixty years old. He had lived in South Dakota.
23. **Mark Beverly Shields.** Fifty-six years old. He was originally from Santa Rosa.
24. **Sam Bonafide.** Fifty-five years old. An itinerant farm laborer, he had worked on various sites in California over the previous three decades.
25. **Joseph Maczak.** Fifty-four years old. He was originally from Illinois.

An unusual legal battle erupted within days of the indictment. Hawk, Corona's lawyer, wanted to make Corona available for interviews with the news media, but the sheriff, Roy D. Whitaker, and the district attorney, G. Dave Teja, objected. They argued that Corona, who had been suffering chest pains, should not be subjected to interviews for health reasons; they also insisted that security measures at the Yuba County Jail were inadequate. But Hawk won a court order after arguing that barring interviews was a violation of Corona's First Amendment rights.

In a tiny interview room at the county jail, Corona blinked into television lights and tried to explain his situation. "I like this country very much. Lots of things you can do. Lots of ways to live," he said, according to the *Los Angeles Times*. He said he knew that the charges were not true and stated that he did not recognize the names of any of the twenty-five victims. "Mr. Hawk says I'm going to get out of jail," he observed. Hawk, who attended the interview along with a doctor from the county hospital, had said, "They don't want the public to know what he is really like. They want Juan to remain the monster he has been painted in the eyes of potential jurors. I want people to know Juan is not fifteen feet tall and that he doesn't have two heads."

Legal maneuvering continued over the following months as Hawk tried to get the case moved out of Sutter County. In April of 1972, an appeals court granted the request and ordered that the case be moved to a more urban area where potential jurors "will be less vulnerable to claims of insensitivity toward migratory farmworkers." Three months later, Corona was transferred to Vacaville State Prison in Solano County. His trial was to begin in September in nearby Fairfield, a town between San Francisco and Sacramento. But unusual legal wrangling continued. The trial judge, Richard E. Patton—sometimes referred to as "The General"—ordered Corona to provide prosecutors with samples of his handwriting so that it could be compared to the writing on a ledger with a list of names found in Corona's home. The list included the names of seven of the twenty-five farmworkers he was accused of killing. Following Hawk's advice, Corona refused. The judge fined Corona $250 and sentenced Hawk to two days in jail for contempt of court. Hawk appealed but lost.

On July 31, Hawk walked into the Solano County Jail to begin his sentence, but he soon saw a bright side to the episode. Reporters had been waiting for him as he entered the building on that day and as he left two days later. He was a lawyer who was willing to go to jail for his client and had come out looking good in the newspapers. "Corona is innocent," he told the reporters. He said that he knew who had really killed all those men and that so did the prosecutor. "This will be apparent after the trial begins," Hawk said. Hawk refused to identify "the real killer."

Hawk was back in court on August 14, and he and Corona again refused the request for writing samples. The judge fined Corona another $300 and ordered Hawk to spend another three days in jail. With the trial scheduled to begin in early September, Hawk gave up the fight and allowed Corona to provide the handwriting samples. Meanwhile, the handwriting issue would be sent to the court of appeals.

The trial began in earnest on September 11, with jury selection that was expected to take at least several weeks. Corona's wife and other family members sat in the back of the courtroom and shouted, "Good luck, Juan!" A handful of supporters demonstrated outside the courthouse, and Corona's sister, Feliciana Dansie, was arrested after she lay down on the concrete and refused to move. Corona had had two minor heart attacks by then. Meanwhile, Hawk had filed a $350 million lawsuit on Corona's behalf alleging false arrest by Sutter County officials.

Hawk's battles with the judge continued in the courtroom. Patton called Hawk into his chambers twice on the third day to warn him against arguing his case before the jury had even been selected. Hawk responded that he would be "just as persistent as I have to be to get the truth before the jury." Hawk had asked a prospective juror whether he thought the prosecutor would have "jerked Ronald Reagan out of his bed at 4 a.m.," as had been done in the Corona case. By the end of day three, no jurors had been chosen.

By the end of September—with a jury of ten men and two women finally chosen—the courtroom drama began in earnest. Bartley Williams, a private attorney hired by Sutter County to assist District Attorney Teja as a special prosecutor, outlined the case against Corona, most of which had played out in the news media over the previous year. As he spoke, jurors were able to mull over an eight-foot by twelve-foot board that had been set up in the courtroom to show where the bodies had been unearthed. Each location was marked with a small electric light. One surprise on the first day was the prosecutor's disclosure that some of the bodies appeared to have been sexually molested.

When it was his turn to address the jury, Hawk declared that the murders had been committed by a homosexual. It was impossible that Corona had been the killer because he was "hopelessly heterosexual," Hawk said. He pointed out that some of the bodies were found with their trousers down or off completely. And the investigators, he said, had mismanaged the evidence, including the fingertips that had been cut off from some of the bodies in an effort to identify them.

Over the next four tumultuous months, the prosecution produced 900 pieces of evidence and called 116 witnesses to testify about Corona's behavior and sightings of Corona near the scenes of the crimes and the burial spots. Corona had often been seen washing the interior of his van. But it became clear that some of the physical evidence had been mishandled or lost. At one point, the judge called the investigation "inept."

After a break for the Christmas and New Year holidays, the trial resumed on January 3, 1973. When everyone was seated in the courtroom, the prosecution rested its case. Then it was Hawk's turn. It came as a complete surprise to almost everyone involved when he announced that he was resting his case without having called a single witness. Outside court, he told reporters that putting on a defense would be like a doctor prescribing medicine after examining a patient and finding that he was not ill. "As the dapper Hawk left the courtroom Wednesday, his cherubic face was aglow with good humor," a reporter for the *Los Angeles Times* observed.

A week later, after unusually rancorous closing arguments, the case went to the jury. It would be another week before the jurors would reach the required unanimous verdict. At the beginning, the vote had been eight to four in favor of conviction, but as the days went on, three of the four holdouts changed their votes to guilty. There was only one holdout left: Naomi Underwood, a sixty-three-year-old retired Navy shipyard worker. By January 18, the verdict was unanimous: guilty on all counts.

Later that day, Underwood told a reporter that she was conflicted about her final vote. "I don't think they had enough evidence," she said. "I still doubt I made the right decision." In another interview that day, she told reporters, "I was never completely satisfied with Corona's guilt. I just don't know. I was on the spot for so long since I was the holdout." Later, it came out that the night before Underwood changed her vote, she had talked with a sheriff's matron, Georgia Wallis, who was assigned to the jurors at a motel where they were sequestered during deliberations. Underwood told Wallis about her doubts. Why, for instance, had no bloodstains been found on Corona's clothes, she wondered. Wallis assured her that she would tell her things after the trial that would ease her conscience, Underwood said.

When Hawk heard about the conversation, he called it "jury tampering" and said he would use it as part of his effort to win a new trial. It was a difficult day for both the prosecution and the defense. Judge Patton, who had been irked by the behavior of both sides throughout the trial, sentenced Teja and Williams to seven days in jail for contempt of court. Patton was tougher on Hawk. His sentence was two and one-half months in jail, and he was fined $4,200. In February, Patton denied Hawk's motion for a new trial and sentenced Corona to twenty-five consecutive life terms in prison.

Perhaps unsurprisingly, litigation in the case would go on for more than a decade. On May 8, 1978, the court of appeals in San Francisco reversed Corona's conviction and ordered a new trial. The lengthy decision was a scorching denunciation of Hawk. No one knew it at the time of the trial, but Hawk had arranged for a book deal as a way for Corona to pay for his defense. Hawk had persuaded Corona to give him exclusive rights to his story. It was a clear conflict of interest, the court said. Hawk was "devoted to two masters" and "was forced to choose between his own pocketbook and the best interests of his client." (See Appendix 1.) Hawk had hired Ed Cray, a professional writer "who participated in the proceedings as Hawk's investigator and sat at the counsel table during the trial," the decision said. The book, *Burden of Proof: The Case of Juan Corona*, was published by the Macmillan Publishing Company and in print by the end of 1973. Elsewhere in the seventy-one-page opinion, the court said that Hawk had "failed to present any meaningful defense at all." Obvious defenses would have been mental incompetence, diminished capacity, or legal insanity, the court said.

Corona's retrial in 1982 lasted seven months and cost California taxpayers about $5 million. By then, Corona was forty-eight years old and his wife had divorced him. Judge Patton presided over the new trial, but there was a different defense team: two San Francisco lawyers and Roy Van den Heuvel, the Sutter County public defender who had met with Corona in his jail cell on the morning of the day he was arrested. This time, the defense team implicated Corona's older half brother, Natividad. They portrayed him as a violent homosexual who, at the time of the killings, had been in a state of rage caused by the late stages of syphilis. But the jury found Corona guilty again, and he was again given twenty-five life sentences.

Corona made several attempts to win parole over the decades but was turned down each time. At a hearing in December of 2011, he admitted the crimes, but it was unclear whether he understood what he was saying. Early in his prison stays, he had been attacked by inmates and stabbed thirty-two times. He lost his left eye. Over the years, he had had three heart attacks. He died on March 4, 2019, in a hospital near the state prison in Corcoran, north of Bakersfield in Central California. His obituaries contained no information about his survivors. At a parole hearing, he had said that all of his brothers and sisters were dead.

2.

DEAN ALLEN CORLL, ELMER WAYNE HENLEY, AND DAVID OWEN BROOKS

It was the summer of 1973, and the Corona case—with its record-setting twenty-five murders—had faded from the headlines. Then in August, what seemed to be some kind of macabre homicide competition popped up in Texas. Elmer Wayne Henley, a seventeen-year-old, had shot and killed Dean Allen Corll at Corll's home in Pasadena, a middle-class suburb of Houston. Corll, who was thirty-three, was known as a pleasant employee of a utility company. He had once run a popular candy shop with his mother in a Houston neighborhood. Henley called the police and soon began leading investigators to areas where bodies had been buried. As the death toll mounted, news media descended on Houston, and Corll was dubbed "The Candyman." In little more than a week, the death toll had reached twenty-seven. This was the largest multiple murder case in the nation's history thus far.

The bloody incidents of torture and murder that had begun three years earlier came to an end on August 8 after a grisly night of torture and death threats. Henley had brought two friends, Tim Kerley, a twenty-year-old, and Kerley's fifteen-year-old girlfriend, Rhonda Williams, to Corll's house for a night of fun. They drank beer and sniffed paint fumes from a bag, Henley told investigators. But Corll was angry that Henley had brought a female to his house. When the three friends passed out or fell asleep, Corll tied them up. Eventually, Corll freed Henley. "I started sweet-talking him," Henley told the police. "I told him I would kill them for him if he would un-handcuff me." Corll, who had tied the couple to a torture board, began to sexually assault Kerley. Henley watched for a while and then grabbed Corll's gun. "I can't go on any longer," he said. "I can't have you kill all my friends." He fired at Corll, hitting him five times. Then Henley called the police, and the three waited on the front porch of Corll's house.

The events of that day and the following weeks had the feel of an improbable horror movie. When the police showed up at the house, Henley told them that he had killed Corll while Corll was torturing Kerley and Williams. During the torture session, Henley said, Corll taunted the couple by boasting that he had killed other people and buried their bodies in a boatyard. On the evening of August 8, Henley led the investigators to a boat storage lot in southwest Houston. Corll did not own a boat, but he had been renting the shed there for years. Before the investigators were done for the evening, they had unearthed the bodies of eight boys buried in graves that were six feet deep. Most of the bodies had been coated with lime and wrapped in plastic. Lime, the investigators knew, could be used to mask the smell of decomposing bodies. Two of the dead were quickly identified as Cary Cobble and Marty Ray Jones, seventeen-year-olds who had last been seen alive two weeks earlier. A third was David Hilligeist, a thirteen-year-old who had been missing since 1971. Henley told police that he had not killed any of the boys but had helped Corll bury the bodies.

The next day, August 9, investigators found nine more bodies buried in the shed, bringing the death toll to seventeen. A police officer said it was all the work of a "perverted, sadistic clown" who had sexually molested the boys and killed them over the previous two years. "When you're dealing with a nut like this, that is a sex pervert, you can expect anything," he said. Investigators planned to dig up the backyard of Henley's house in Pasadena to see what they could find. They found no bodies there.

But as the day went on, the mystery became more complicated. Henley told the investigators that there were bodies at two more sites; the total could be as high as thirty. He admitted that he had been involved in some of the killings. By then, the Houston police were involved. "No one man could have done it," a lieutenant from the homicide squad told reporters who had begun converging on Houston. "In twenty-two years of police work, I have never seen anyone capable of doing such a thing." Meanwhile, David Owen Brooks, Henley's eighteen-year-old friend, came forward after talking with his father. He told investigators that he had witnessed some of the killings and that he, too, had helped to bury some of the bodies. Over the years, Henley and Brooks had recruited young boys for parties at Corll's home by offering them food and "goodies," sometimes including marijuana. At Corll's home, the boys would be bound to a torture board and forced to commit sexual acts. The boys were usually strangled, but at least one was shot. Henley and Brooks were paid as much as two hundred dollars for each recruit they brought to a party.

In a brief encounter with reporters, Henley denied that he had said there were thirty bodies; he only knew of twenty-four. Later, the police said that Henley might not have been aware of some of the murders. Henley's mother, Mary Henley, told reporters that she had spoken with her son and that he had said, "Mama, I told them everything. But be happy for me because now, at last I can live."

At that point, with help from Henley and Brooks, twenty-three bodies had been found: seventeen at the storage lot, four near Lake Sam Rayburn, about 120 miles northeast of Houston, and two on a beach on High Island, east of Galveston near the Gulf of Mexico. Investigators were looking for four more bodies they believed were buried in the area. The bodies already found near the beach had been there for more than a year and had deteriorated so badly that they would have to be identified by dental records. Meanwhile, the medical examiner in Houston began the daunting task of identifying the remains. "We have many bones and we don't know which go with which bodies," he said. Sometimes investigators referred to this task as a "skull count."

Despite pleas from the county prosecutor's office in Houston, information about the investigation kept leaking out. In a written statement, Brooks had told investigators that the first killing he remembered happened in a townhouse where Corll once lived. There had been two boys there, and Corll told him later that he had killed them. "I don't know where they were buried or what their names were," Brooks said. He also remembered a killing at Corll's house in Pasadena. "Dean kept this boy around the house for about four days before he killed him," Brooks said. "This was about two years ago. It really upset Dean to have to kill this boy because he really liked him." Brooks told police that he had witnessed some deaths but was not directly responsible for any of the killings. Nevertheless, he was charged in the strangulation-murder of a fifteen-year-old boy that had happened a month earlier.

Reporters, then still called "newsmen," reflected the thinking of the time. Their stories, printed and broadcast from coast to coast, used

WORKERS UNEARTHING THE BODIES OF DEAN CORLL'S MURDER VICTIMS BURIED IN A HOUSTON BOAT SHED. THE OBJECT IN THE WHEELBARROW WAS IDENTIFIED AS THE SKULL OF THE TENTH VICTIM.

terms that suggested an unusual level of deviance—"homosexual torture ring," "homosexual murder ring," and "homosexual mass murder." Had anyone ever used the term "heterosexual murder?"

Truman Capote was intrigued. He had gone to Kansas in 1959—along with his childhood friend, Harper Lee—to look into the murders of four family members in a small farming community. Lee's first book, *To Kill a Mockingbird,* was about to be published. Capote was already a celebrity. His *Breakfast at Tiffany's* and other writing projects had brought him critical acclaim and financial success. As the search for the killers in Kansas went on, Capote followed the investigators around the rural area, making detailed notes and delving deeply into the psychology of the two men who were ultimately arrested and convicted. His book about the case was published in 1966. *In Cold Blood* was an instant bestseller. The film version, released the following year, had been nominated for several Academy Awards.

In an attempt to rejuvenate his career, Capote decided to delve into the Texas case. Journalists from around the country—and the world—were already there, sending out updates as the baffling situation unfolded. Capote arrived in Houston with some fanfare in August of 1973, along with a team of assistants, to do some research on the case. Meanwhile, Capote's agent, John O'Shea, was working on a lucrative deal with the *Washington Post* to syndicate Capote's stories from the scene. It was to be called "Houston Diary." Twenty-two newspapers in North America and eight on other continents signed up to run the dispatches. A *Washington Post* story about the new project described the Texas case as a "homosexual blood orgy." Capote said he had never worked on deadline: "I just want to see if I can do it."

But the project ended before it had begun. When Henley was brought into a Houston courtroom for a pre-trial hearing in January of 1974, Capote observed, "I've seen this before." He stood up and quickly left the courthouse. He was hospitalized for what was described as a heart condition. He had not yet filed his first report. Years later, a trove of artifacts and documents from Capote's research on the case was discovered in a house in Santa Fe, New Mexico. Capote and O'Shea, lifelong friends, had rented the house for a time in 1976. Among the items were a scrapbook, holographic images, and correspondence with Ben Bradlee, the executive editor of the *Washington Post.* The materials would later end up in the special collections archives of the New York Public Library.

The uproar in Texas in 1973 grew more contentious as the tangled investigation moved on. People from across the country began contacting the police about their missing children. A Houston police lieutenant told the press that the rising number of missing young people was a sign of the times and of America's changing social structure. "Ten years ago a runaway boy or a runaway girl used to attract attention and people would take special note of it," he said. "Now it's different. People show very little interest. These hippies travel all over the United States hitchhiking. They leave home and it's a big lark to them to shack up in these communes until they get it out of their system or something happens to them."

Few people had seemed to miss the middle-aged and older men who had been killed by Juan Corona in California, but this was different. In the Houston area, disgruntled parents and siblings began to emerge, and police officials responded that there was little they could do. They could take a report, put the names on a list, and hope that an officer might encounter one of the missing during the course of daily business. A woman whose thirteen-year-old son had left home two years earlier to go swimming with a sixteen-year-old friend said that talking to the police had been "like talking to a blank wall." The bodies of the two teens were later found among the disintegrating corpses in the Houston-area graves. The Houston police chief, Herman Short, told reporters that the department had little authority over runaways but viewed handling such cases as "a public service." Other relatives in Texas complained that the police should have taken the missing persons reports from the area more seriously. It was a criticism that would grow louder and more insistent over the coming years.

Amid the chaos of the investigation's early days, parents had an additional grievance: the police did not notify them when the bodies of their children were found. One man said he learned that the body of his eighteen-year-old son had been unearthed when he read it in a newspaper. He phoned the police to complain, he said, and a detective told him that officers were so busy searching for bodies they didn't have time to call all the parents. Another father complained that he had sat on the Houston Police Department's doorstep for weeks trying to get information about his missing sons, but the officers showed little interest. Others asked why the police didn't get suspicious when several boys from The Heights neighborhood of Houston disappeared at around the same time. Now officials were saying that as many as fifteen of the recovered bodies might be those of boys who had lived in The Heights, a lower-middle-class neighborhood where Corll and his mother had operated their candy shop.

Meanwhile, Henley and Brooks, now under arrest, continued to help the police. They accompanied investigators to the remote sites and pointed out spots where they thought bodies might have been buried. The final two bodies were found on High Island on Saturday, August 11, bringing the total to twenty-seven, two more than Juan Corona's toll in California. At that point, neither Henley nor Brooks had hired a lawyer or had had one appointed by the court. It was an usual situation that would emerge later as a legal issue.

Both Henley and Brooks came from "broken homes," as their family situations were called at the time. Both were high school dropouts. Henley grew up in The Heights with his mother, grandmother, and three younger siblings. His parents were divorced, and his mother worked as a cashier at a parking lot. He had worked odd jobs and tried to enlist in the Navy but was turned down. Brooks had married recently and had moved into an apartment with his wife, who was pregnant. Before that, Brooks had lived with his father, and, more recently, with Corll.

Corll's parents had divorced when he was young. The young Corll lived for a time with his mother in small towns, where she ran a business making and selling pralines, a candy made of ground nuts, sugar, and butter. Investigators said Dean Corll had been born in Fort Wayne, Indiana, and had been drafted into the Army. He served for about a year before getting a hardship discharge to help his mother. In 1962, when Dean was twenty-two, he moved with his mother to The Heights area of Houston. When she opened her candy shop there, he became the manager. He was quiet, considerate, and popular with children who frequented the shop, called the Corll Candy Factory. In 1969, Corll met David Brooks. He met Henley in 1970, the year that Henley, then in the ninth grade, had dropped out of school. Investigators assumed that Corll met many of the victims when they were young children or teenagers who came into the shop. There was an elementary school nearby.

When Corll's mother remarried and moved to Colorado, Dean got a job at the Houston Lighting and Power Company. He kept a low profile, and co-workers never had anything negative to say about him. He moved for a time to an upscale apartment complex in Houston. Brooks had gone to the apartment one day unannounced and seen two naked boys tied to Corll's bed, where Dean was molesting them, Brooks said years later in his confession to the police. Brooks, who viewed Corll as a father figure, quickly left. Initially, Corll told Brooks that he had been paid by a pornography ring to send the boys to California. But he later changed his story. He told Brooks that he had killed the boys and buried their bodies in the boat storage shed.

Corll's father, Arnold, owned the small Pasadena home where his son was living on the night he was shot to death. He had remarried and, like his son, worked as an electrician in the Houston area. He was among a small group of people who turned up for Dean's funeral in the tumultuous week after he was killed. The mourners quickly scattered when the ceremony ended to avoid the journalists and television crews that had gathered near the site.

Henley and Brooks were in isolation cells at the Harris County Jail. They needed protection from other inmates, who had threatened to kill them. By then, Henley had changed his story; he told investigators that he had helped kill some of the victims. In mid-August, a grand jury began hearing evidence and returned murder indictments. Henley was charged with three murders and Brooks was charged with one. In separate interviews, they told the police that they had procured young boys for Corll, and they implicated each other. Billy Ridinger, whom Brooks had freed on that final night with Corll, was seen leaving the grand jury room with a large paper bag over his head and two holes cut out for his eyes. The grand jury met again in the coming days as police worked on identifying the decomposed bodies. Ultimately, Henley would be charged with six murders and Brooks with four.

The legal proceedings began in earnest in late August when a judge took the unusual step of ordering psychiatric examinations for Henley and Brooks. Their lawyers protested loudly. They hadn't even had time to interview their clients, they said, and they had no idea whether they would raise an insanity defense. The Harris County district attorney, Carol S. Vance, suspected that they would raise an insanity defense and wanted the psychiatric tests to protect the prosecution's case. "In any kind of unusual murder case, particularly one of extremely sadistic acts like this, you expect an insanity plea," he said. "It's best to get ready for it."

Henley was the first to go to trial. It was January 1974, and District Court Judge William Hatten laid down the rules. He expected that families of many of the victims would be among the members of the public packed into his courtroom in Houston, and he was worried that violence might erupt. The press was another matter. So many reporters wanted to be in the courtroom that Hatten had to arrange for an overflow room where journalists could watch the proceeding on closed-circuit television. Hatten had telephoned the judge who'd presided over the tumultuous Charles Manson trial in Los Angeles for advice. "Hell, some of the judges in the mass murder cases have ended up clowns, idiots, or damned fools, or wound up being called that," the judge said. "You're going to be a celebrity whether you want it or not. I'm not sure it's all worth it."

By then, Henley had been charged with six murders. The victims were Marty Jones, Billy Lawrence, Johnnie Delone, Frank Aguirre, Homer Garcia, and Charles Ray Cobble, all teenagers. Cobble was seventeen when he disappeared about two weeks before Corll was killed. Henley's lawyer, Charles Melder, planned an insanity defense. He had lost in his attempt to have Henley's confessions suppressed. Henley had not been read his rights, he argued, and had been denied access to a lawyer when he'd first told police about the murders and led them to the burial sites. Henley's written confession, which had been printed verbatim in the Houston newspapers, was also an issue. Mary Henley told the judge that she had spoken to her son at the time and that he was hallucinating: "He talked incoherent. He didn't know the time or how long he'd been there. He was shaking all over. He would stop and cry. He was all to pieces."

Eventually, the defense, the prosecution, and the judge agreed that it would be nearly impossible to find an unbiased jury in the Houston area. It was, of course, a time when most people got their news from the local newspapers and television station. The trial was moved to San Antonio, 190 miles to the west. The lawyers for the defense had argued that even San Antonio was too close. Reporters found they were less than welcome when the trial began there on July 1, 1974, and a new judge, Preston Dial, took over. He said the journalists were "like a bunch of locusts" and barred them from the courtroom during jury selection.

When the first witness took the stand a week later, the jury of six men and six women began to hear the gruesome details. The first witness was Officer J. B. Jamison, the first to arrive at Corll's house on the morning that Henley called the Pasadena police. Henley, he said, was sobbing on the curb while two friends were trying to comfort him. And he said that he had just shot and killed Corll for trying to molest his friends. Henley then "blurted out that he didn't care who knew, he had to get it off his chest," Jamison said, "and that he knew where there were some more bodies." Another officer read from Henley's written confession: he had tricked a hitchhiker into trying on handcuffs and then left him with Corll, who paid Henley two hundred dollars. It was only later that he learned that Corll had killed the boy after sexually abusing him. Later, he picked up other boys for Corll to abuse. "I killed several of them myself with Dean's gun and helped to strangle some," Henley admitted. The jurors were shown instruments of torture and photographs of dead bodies.

Prosecutors introduced a plywood torture board they had found at Corll's home. A detective testified that Henley had told him one victim was tied to the board for three days because Corll liked him. In 1972, when Henley was visiting Corll at his Houston apartment, a friend of Henley's dropped by. Henley tricked the friend into putting on a pair of handcuffs. "We took him down and killed him after Dean Corll had had his fun with him," Henley said. Henley's grandmother and three younger brothers were in the courtroom. His mother, a potential witness, was outside in the lobby.

After a week of grisly testimony that ended on a Friday, the prosecution rested its case. The defense lawyers called no witnesses. The following Monday, the jury of six men and six women deliberated for ninety minutes before reaching a verdict of guilty. As the verdict was read out to the courtroom, Henley's mother, grandmother, and brothers wept.

Next, the jury had to recommend a sentence. Edwin Pegelow, Henley's lawyer, described his client as a confused and terrified teenager who had fallen under the influence of an older man. He pointed out that by grabbing Corll's gun and killing him, Henley had saved two lives. "Through his actions, he stopped this monster forever." When it was his turn, the Harris County district attorney, Carol S. Vance, called Henley "a monster" and said it was "too bad" that he couldn't be removed from society permanently. "I apologize to this jury that the laws of the state of Texas do not permit the death penalty, which would be the only just punishment," he said. In less than an hour, the jury agreed to recommend a sentence of ninety-nine years for each death, the maximum allowed under Texas law. The judge agreed. He sentenced Henley to six terms of ninety-nine years, the maximum allowed under Texas law. The terms were to be served consecutively.

Four years later, an appeals court overturned the conviction on the grounds that the trial judge had not given enough consideration to the defense request for a second change of venue. The lawyers had argued that a San Antonio jury would be as prejudiced as a jury chosen in Houston. At a retrial in Corpus Christi the following year, Henley was convicted again, but the jurors were a bit more sympathetic: they recommended that his six life terms in prison be served concurrently. In 1975, Brooks was tried in Houston on one charge of murder, and he, too, was convicted. Like Henley, he was sentenced to life in prison.

In the decades that followed, the increasingly weary parents of many of the victims made dozens of trips to parole hearings held for Henley and Brooks. Each time, the parole board took note. It appeared likely that Henley and Brooks would die in prison.

3.

RODNEY ALCALA

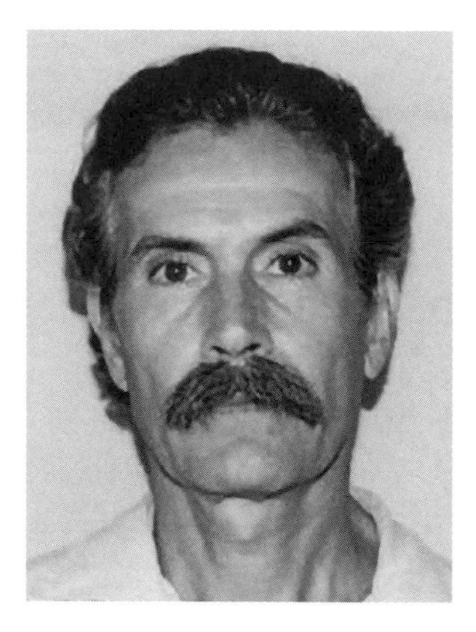

His face was clean-shaven and his broad smile showed off his glistening white teeth. A full head of long, wavy brown hair fell onto the shoulders of his brown suit jacket, and his starched white shirt was unbuttoned and opened wide to show off the hair on his chest. Rodney Alcala had somehow finagled himself a place on *The Dating Game,* a popular television show. He was "Bachelor Number One." The "bachelorette" on the other side of the curtain asked him to describe himself. "I'm called 'the banana,' and I look really good." Could he be more descriptive? "Peel me," he cooed.

Alcala won the competition that night in September 1978, beating out two other contestants. But the bachelorette never followed through on the prize: tennis lessons and a date at an amusement park. She said she found Alcala "really creepy." She didn't know it at the time, but Alcala was already a registered sex offender in California and had served more than two years in prison for the beating and rape of an eight-year-old girl in 1968. Investigators would later speculate about whether Alcala's *The Dating Game* rejection had given him a new hunger to kill.

It was nearly a year before the world began to learn the truth about Alcala. On July 24, 1979, Alcala, then thirty-five years old, was arrested at his mother's home in Monterey Park, a suburb of Los Angeles. Within a week, he was charged with murder. The victim was Robin Christine Samsoe, a twelve-year-old girl from Huntington Beach, a town about thirty miles to the south on the Pacific coast. The *Los Angeles Times* carried a photograph of Alcala looking very different than he had on his television debut. He was staring grimly into the camera, his hair thick and bushy and his face nearly covered by a mustache and beard. The police had described him as an unemployed part-time photographer. His last job, the *Times* story said, had been as a typist in the newspaper's composing plant.

The police in Huntington Beach had been looking for a man who had talked to Robin and a friend of hers on June 20, the day Robin disappeared. The man had asked the girls whether they wanted their picture taken while they were at the beach. Robin was last seen alive when she left her friend's house later that day on a bicycle to go to a ballet class. Her decomposed body was discovered two weeks later in the Sierra Madre foothills, about forty-five miles away. By then, investigators had come up with a composite sketch of the man who had approached the girls on the beach. They had also received tips from four informants. Everything pointed to Alcala. By the time he was brought into court on July 26, his background—or at least some of it—seemed to have come into focus.

Alcala graduated from the University of California at Los Angeles in 1968 with a degree in fine arts. He was hired by the *Los Angeles Times* in September of 1977 and resigned on May 12, 1979. He said that he intended to open his own photography business, the newspaper reported. He had been arrested in February of 1979 and charged with the rape and assault of a fifteen-year-old girl during a photography session in Riverside County. He was freed on bail a month later, and his trial was scheduled to begin in September. Much more would come out later.

Alcala's criminal history went back further—to 1968, shortly after he'd graduated from UCLA. One morning he spotted an eight-year-old girl walking to school on a sidewalk along Sunset Boulevard in Hollywood. He followed her and offered to drive her to school. She balked. He told her that he knew her parents. Eventually, she got into the car. Then he told her he would show her a psychedelic poster at his apartment before he dropped her off. Another driver, Donald Haines, had been watching and thought the situation looked suspicious, so he followed Alcala's car. He watched as Alcala and the girl entered an apartment. Then he decided—somewhat reluctantly—to call the police from a nearby pay phone.

When Los Angeles Police Officer Chris Camacho arrived and knocked on the door, the man inside told him to wait a minute—he was just getting out of the shower. Camacho thought he heard a faint moan, so he broke down the door. Alcala was nowhere to be seen, but the girl's nude body was on the floor of the kitchen. Her head had been bashed in and there was a dumbbell bar across her neck. She was hemorrhaging from between her legs. Camacho picked up the dumbbell, felt a faint pulse in the girl, and called an ambulance. The girl, who would be identified publicly only as Tali S., survived. But Alcala had made one crucial mistake. He'd left behind his UCLA student ID card with his photograph and the name "Rodney Alcala."

After Alcala escaped, he fled to the East Coast, where, using the name John Berger, he studied at New York University's School of the

Arts. He was finally arrested in New Hampshire three years later, when he was recognized on a poster in a post office. By then, he was on the FBI's Ten Most Wanted Fugitives list. He was working as a counselor at an arts and drama summer camp in New Hampshire under the name John Berger. Alcala was returned to California, where he faced charges of beating, raping, and kidnapping Tali. He was allowed to avoid a trial by pleading guilty to a charge of child molestation. In return, he got a sentence of one to ten years. He served twenty-seven months before he was paroled in 1974. Four months later, he was arrested on a marijuana charge—a violation of his parole—and was ultimately released in June of 1977.

On his job application at the *Los Angeles Times,* Alcala had lied about those years, claiming that he worked for Blue Shield in New York from 1969 to 1971, and at a company in Middlefield, Connecticut, from 1971 to 1977. Some years from his earlier adult life were missing altogether. Born in San Antonio, Texas, in 1943 as Rodrigo Jacques Alcala-Buguor, or Rodney, as he was called, he lived a middle-class life with a brother, two sisters, his parents, and his maternal grandmother. He attended Catholic schools there until the family moved for a time to Mexico.

After his grandmother died and his father left, the boy moved to Los Angeles with his mother and siblings. In 1961, he graduated from high school and joined the Army. But two years later, he went AWOL from his base in North Carolina and hitchhiked to his mother's home. At her urging, he turned himself in. He was hospitalized for a time but ultimately was dismissed from the Army in 1964 with a diagnosis of "anti-social personality disorder, chronic, severe."

By the time the Robin Samsoe murder case got to court in August of 1979, police departments around the country had taken notice. Investigators had hit dead ends on some troubling cases over the years, when records existed only on paper and were kept in locked filing cabinets. But now, having heard the news about Alcala, New York police investigators considered him the prime suspect in the murder of Ellen Hover, a twenty-four-year-old woman who had been with Alcala on the day she disappeared in July of 1977. Alcala had been paroled by then and had received permission from his probation officers to travel to New York. Hover had told friends that she was seeing a professional photographer named John Burger. Alcala had used the name Burger or Berger during the years when he was a fugitive. Still, it would be decades before the Hover case was resolved.

A key witness in the Samsoe murder trial in 1980 was Dana Crappa, who was working for the US Forestry Service in June of 1979. Crappa testified that on June 20 she had seen a man who looked like Alcala near the site in the foothills where the girl's body was found. But under intense cross-examination, Crappa conceded that she hadn't told the whole truth. She had also discovered the girl's body on the night of June 25, 1979, missing hands and feet and decapitated. But she did not report what she had seen. The body was found on July 2 by another forestry worker. (See Appendix 2.)

Earrings that looked like the ones Robin was wearing on the day she disappeared were later found among Alcala's belongings, but there was little other physical evidence. Prosecutors relied heavily on facts about Alcala's criminal past, including similar attacks. They also had testimony from inmates in the Orange County Jail, where Alcala was being held. Several said that Alcala had acknowledged luring the girl into his car and putting her bicycle in the back. When she realized he was not taking her to her dance lesson, she began to scream. He locked the door and hit her, they said. A similar yellow bicycle was later found behind a charity store about halfway between Alcala's home and the site where the girl's body was found. Alcala did not take the witness stand at his trial.

On April 30, 1980, after eleven and a half hours of deliberation, a jury of nine women and three men found Alcala guilty of first-degree murder. The judge ordered the jurors to return the following week to decide whether to recommend the death penalty. It took the jurors a little over four hours to decide that Alcala should be put to death. On June 20, 1980, the decision was up to Orange County Superior Court Judge Philip E. Schwab. The prosecutor, John Farnell, said, "The only appropriate sentence in a case like this is death. The only question is whether death is sufficient for this defendant." Schwab sentenced Alcala to die in the gas chamber.

Like the plot of some convoluted crime novel, the Rodney Alcala litigation—and body count—was escalating. The following month, Alcala was charged with murdering Jill M. Parenteau, a twenty-one-year-old woman who lived in Burbank. This, too, was a death penalty case. Parenteau was strangled in her apartment on June 14, 1979, six days before Alcala killed Robin Samsoe. Parenteau had told friends that she'd met Alcala in a bar but had rejected his advances. Investigators said Alcala broke into her first-floor apartment through a window. Two types of blood were found there: one matched Parenteau's, and the other was a subtype that matched Alcala's and eliminated ninety percent of other human beings. DNA comparisons were not available at the time.

Alcala had also been charged with the rape and beating of a fifteen-year-old girl, Monique Hoyt, on February 14, 1979, twelve weeks before Parenteau's death and thirteen weeks before Samsoe's. Monique was a runaway who was hitchhiking in Pasadena, northeast of Los Angeles, when Alcala offered her a ride. He told her his true name and drove her to his mother's house, where he was living at the time. Monique spent the night there, having agreed to pose for some photographs. The next morning, the two drove to a wooded area in the mountains. Alcala bashed Monique's head and then raped and sodomized her as she fell in and out of consciousness. Terrified, Monique played along with Alcala and asked if she could stay at his house for another night. He seemed to calm down, and as they drove back toward his mother's house, he stopped at a drive-through restaurant and she was able to jump out of the car and run to a nearby motel for help.

Police found Alcala at his mother's house and arrested him, but his mother posted the ten-thousand-dollar bond set by a judge, and he was released. In September of 1980, while he was already on death row, a jury convicted him of raping Hoyt. The jurors had been shown photographs Alcala had taken before and after the rape. He was sentenced to nine years in prison.

Meanwhile, in the spring of 1981, as Alcala sat on death row at the infamous San Quentin State Prison north of San Francisco, the Jill Parenteau murder case was foundering. The key witness, a convict who had served time with Alcala, had admitted committing perjury in another case and could no longer be seen as a credible witness. Without him, the case was too weak to go to trial, and it was dropped. But it was not forgotten.

For Alcala's prosecutors, there was worse news to come. On August 23, 1984, the California Supreme Court reversed Alcala's conviction for murdering Robin Samsoe and ordered a new trial. The judge in the Samsoe case should not have allowed testimony about Alcala's prior sex crimes because that could have improperly influenced the jury, the court said. It would be almost two years before the re-trial got underway. On May 28, 1986, a jury of six men and six women convicted Alcala once again of Robin Samsoe's murder. Robin's mother, Marianne Frazier, had sat through the trial, just as she had sat through the trial four years earlier. "I just thank God," she said. "Maybe now my daughter can go to sleep for the first time in seven years. Maybe the rest of my family can go back to life."

Three weeks later, the jurors had to decide whether to recommend the death penalty. Thomas Goethals, one of the prosecutors, summed up the situation for them. "The defendant is the epitome of malevolence. He is a sexual carnivore, and the meat he thrives on is our children." The jury voted for execution. Once again, Frazier was in the courtroom. She sobbed and cried out, "Oh, God." Later, she hugged the jury foreman and said, "Thank you. My daughter deserves this." The judge agreed with the jury's decision, and Alcala was again sentenced to die in the gas chamber. Appeals followed, and the California Supreme Court unanimously upheld the conviction and death sentence in a ruling on December 31, 1992.

Of course, it wasn't over. The legal maneuvering and new revelations about a man who had spent more than half his life on death row would continue for decades. Alcala was leading a quiet life at San Quentin. He worked in the prison's law library and sometimes gave advice to his fellow prisoners. But on March 30, 2001, he was squarely back in the limelight. A federal judge in Los Angeles ruled that there had been serious errors in the 1986 Robin Samsoe murder trial. The prosecutors had to either give Alcala a third trial for a murder that had happened twenty-two years earlier or release him. This time it was the prosecutors' turn to appeal—and to at least get a ruling that would keep Alcala in prison while the matter was pending. Alcala was kept in prison, but the appeal on the dismissal of the murder conviction dragged on for two more years. They turned out to be crucial years for the prosecution.

On June 27, 2003, a federal court of appeals finally granted Alcala's request for a third trial in the Samsoe case. But he also got some startling bad news that day. He would be charged with another long-ago murder. Law enforcement had begun regularly using DNA databases, and a new California law allowed prison officials to take samples from inmates. Investigators working on cold cases were reviewing the murder of Georgia Wixted, a twenty-seven-year-old nurse who had been beaten to death on December 16, 1977, in her apartment on the Pacific Coast Highway in Malibu. In the middle of the night, the killer broke in through a window, smashed her head with a claw hammer, and raped and sodomized her. Detectives had preserved a semen sample. Alcala was now charged with raping and murdering Wixted and with burglarizing her home. Murder perpetrated during the commission of another felony—rape and/or burglary—made this, too, a death penalty case.

And there was more commotion. By 2005, as legal wrangling about the upcoming Samsoe trial crept along, DNA and blood evidence had connected Alcala to the murders of three more women: Jill Barcomb, an eighteen-year-old whose body was found in the Hollywood Hills on November 10, 1977, shortly after she'd moved to California from her home in New York; Charlotte Lamb, a thirty-two-year-old legal secretary whose body was found on June 24, 1978, in the laundry room of an apartment complex in El Segundo, California, and Jill Parenteau, the twenty-one year old woman who was strangled in her Burbank apartment in 1979. Alcala had been charged with murder, but the case had been dropped in 1980 for lack of evidence and had been languishing ever since.

Prosecutors wanted to hold only one trial for all five cases—Samsoe, Wixted, Barcomb, Lamb, and Parenteau. But it was an usual demand, and it took another three years of arguments and appeals before the matter would be settled. In June of 2008, the California Supreme Court ruled that there would be one trial and that it would be held in Orange County. Prosecutors rejoiced. If they'd had to hold separate trials, it would have taken another ten years, they said.

Alcala was sixty-six years old and had been locked up for more than thirty years when the unusual trial got underway in January of 2010. It promised to be quite a show, orchestrated largely by the defendant himself. His request to be allowed to serve as his own lawyer had been approved, reluctantly, by the trial judge, Francisco Briseno. A reporter for the *Los Angeles Times* described it this way: "His performance at the trial might be classified as erratic, ranging from seemingly intimidated to absurd to, at times, knowledgeable." He was "well-spoken" and had developed a rapport with the judge, "who at times guides him through the legal process."

The jury took less than two days to reach five guilty verdicts on February 5, 2010. Families of the victims were pleased but apprehensive about the seemingly endless appeals process. Robert Samsoe was fourteen years old when his twelve-year-old sister, Robin, was killed. "It's not a victory yet," he said. "Until they inject him, or shoot him, or hang him, it's not over because of our appeals process."

A month later, the jurors had to vote on whether to recommend the death penalty. Alcala gave his own closing argument, in which he told the jurors that voting for the death penalty would make them "de facto killers" and "wannabe killers in waiting." Then, somewhat inexplicably, he played for the courtroom a recording of part of the Arlo Guthrie song "Alice's Restaurant," in which a draftee tries to persuade a psychiatrist to help him get out of military service by feigning an extreme desire to kill: "I wanna see blood and gore and guts and veins in my teeth. Eat dead burnt bodies. I mean: kill, kill, kill!"

It took the jury about an hour to agree that Alcala should be executed. He showed little reaction and returned to his life on death row.

But Alcala's days in the spotlight were far from over. In 2010, Manhattan District Attorney Cyrus R. Vance Jr. opened a cold case unit to re-evaluate thousands of unsolved murders. A year later, a grand jury in Manhattan indicted Alcala for the decades-old murders of two women that, Vance said, "have haunted New York since the 1970s." Before his final arrest in California, Alcala had rented a storage locker in Seattle, apparently intending to move there. Among the items authorities found in the locker were photographs of young women, some taken on the streets of Manhattan. Investigators learned that several women recalled being approached in New York by a photographer who said his name was John Berger.

Ellen Jane Hover was a twenty-three-year-old aspiring orchestra conductor when she disappeared in 1977. Her remains were found a year later on the Rockefeller estate in Westchester County, north of

New York City. Bruce Ditnes, who had dated Hover, told the *New York Times* that when she disappeared he put up posters with her picture near where she lived in Manhattan. He described Hover as having "gorgeous brown eyes" and said he was not surprised that Alcala had been attracted to her. "Ellen would literally cause traffic accidents," he said. "We would walk into restaurants, and people would spill things on themselves." Hover's father had once owned a nightclub in Hollywood, and the young woman's godfathers were Sammy Davis Jr. and Dean Martin, the newspaper said.

Cornelia Crilley was a twenty-three-year-old TWA flight attendant in 1971 when she was raped and strangled in her apartment in the Upper East Side of Manhattan. Some friends and relatives were relieved that they finally had answers, but Leon Borstein, Crilley's boyfriend at the time she was killed, told the *Times* he did not see the point of prosecuting a serial killer who was already on death row. "All it does is entertain him, and it doesn't do anything for us," he said. "He gets to fly out to New York, meet with his lawyers, sit in a courtroom for days on end. It certainly alleviates the boredom of sitting in a jail cell."

Alcala got his flight to New York on June 20, 2012—accompanied by a team of federal marshals—courtesy of the Manhattan District Attorney's Office. He was sixty-eight years old and had already spent more than half his life in prison, much of it on death row. The plane landed in Newburgh, and he was transported to Manhattan, where, for the umpteenth time in his life, he was fingerprinted.

What seemed likely to be his final courtroom performances played out with a minimum of drama. Alcala looked almost frail as he was escorted into a courtroom on December 14, 2012, wearing an orange jumpsuit and large brown-rimmed glasses. His hands were cuffed behind his back. His clean-shaven face was framed by curly, shoulder-length gray hair. He admitted that he had murdered Cornelia Crilley and Ellen Hover but had little else to say.

Alcala likewise had little to say when he returned to court for his sentencing on January 7, 2013. The judge, Bonnie G. Wittner, put Alcala's life in its wretched perspective. Like the tolling of a church bell, she read out the names of his many victims. At one point, Wittner's voice broke and she began to sob. When she regained her composure, she went on: "I just want to say I hope the families find some peace and solace." She sentenced Alcala, now sixty-nine years old, to twenty-five years to life. He was returned to California, where he spent his days and nights in the hospital wing of Corcoran State Prison in central California, about halfway between San Francisco and Los Angeles.

But there were still families around the country that had not found peace and solace. Christine Thornton was twenty-eight years old and pregnant when she disappeared in 1977. Her decomposed remains were found in a remote part of Wyoming in 1982. Decades later, science, zealous police work, and the enduring efforts of her grieving family brought another revelation. In November of 2016, Alcala was charged with Christine Thornton's murder.

Kathy Thornton was eleven years younger than Christine and had last seen her sister in the summer of 1977. Christine, twenty-eight years old and pregnant, had set off from their home in San Antonio, Texas, for an adventure panning for gold in Montana with her boyfriend. The family never heard from her again. Kathy never forgot about her sister. Her search, and a dogged investigation by a sheriff's deputy in Sweetwater County, Wyoming, brought the answer. Their work could be a template for others looking for lost women. The search for Christine's killer was chronicled in detail by the *Casper Star-Tribune* in Wyoming. Officials have long suspected that Alcala had many more victims.

The family had expected that Christine would return home after her summer trip, but that didn't happen. They remembered her as a happy, positive person. The San Antonio police were of no help, and they never heard from Christine's boyfriend again. In 1993, Kathy found his phone number, but he said they had had an argument during the trip and split up.

The first break came in 2013, when Kathy's son sent her an email about a serial killer named Rodney Alcala. *CBS News* had done a story about Alcala and had posted a gallery of photos online that had been found in his possession. Investigators thought some of the women and children in the pictures could have been his victims. Kathy found a photo that looked like a still-pregnant Christine on a motorcycle. She magnified it and realized that it was, indeed, her long-lost sister. Kathy called the police in Huntington Beach, California, and they took her information. Then she and her sister, Mary Ann, submitted their DNA to a database of missing people.

Meanwhile, Jeff Sheaman, a deputy sheriff in Sweetwater County, Wyoming, was delving into the mystery of a woman's body that had been found near the town of Granger in 1982. Over the decades, others had tried and failed to learn her identity. Sheaman, too, sent DNA samples for testing. The results came back with a name: Christine Ruth Thornton. Sheaman found the Facebook information Kathy had posted, in addition to the photo of Christine on the motorcycle. He also found information indicating that Alcala had been in the area at the time. Finally, they knew what had happened.

Sheaman, the county attorney, and another investigator flew to California to interview Alcala. Prison staff said he was feeble and possibly suffering from dementia. But the officials wanted to talk to him anyway. They showed Alcala a photograph of the place where the body was found, and he said, "It's part of my area." He acknowledged that he had taken the photo of Christine. But he never admitted to killing her. After two hours in the cell, the officials left and went back to Wyoming. Alcala was charged with first-degree murder, but the prosecutors decided it was not worth the trouble and expense of having him extradited to Wyoming for a trial. Kathy and her relatives had Christine's body removed from its unmarked grave and buried in a family plot in Michigan.

On March 13, 2019, Alcala got some unexpected good news, as did more than seven hundred condemned inmates on death row in California. Governor Gavin Newsom announced that he had signed an executive order imposing a moratorium on the death penalty in the state. "The intentional killing of another person is wrong and as governor, I will not oversee the execution of any individual," Newsom said in his order. "Our death penalty system has been, by all measures, a failure. It has discriminated against defendants who are mentally ill, black and brown, or can't afford expensive legal representation. It has provided no public safety benefit or value as a deterrent. It has wasted billions of taxpayer dollars. Most of all, the death penalty is absolute. It's irreversible and irreparable in the event of human error." Newsom, a former mayor of San Francisco and a former lieutenant governor, had taken office in January. He said the order would be effective for a long as he was governor.

RODNEY ALCALA'S VICTIMS

- **Tali S.** Eight years old. September 25, 1968. Alcala attacked and raped her in Los Angeles. He pleaded guilty to a charge of child molestation and was sentenced to one to ten years in prison.
- **Cornelia Crilley.** Twenty-three years old. 1971. Alcala raped and strangled her to death in her Manhattan apartment.
- **Jill Barcomb.** Eighteen years old. November 10, 1977. Her body was found in the Hollywood Hills. Alcala was convicted of her murder and sentenced to death.
- **Ellen Jane Hover.** Twenty-three years old. 1977. Alcala was convicted of her murder in New York and sentenced to life in prison.
- **Georgia Wixted.** Twenty-seven years old. 1977. Alcala was convicted of her murder and sentenced to death in California in 2010.

- **Charlotte Lamb.** Thirty-one years old. 1978. She was raped and murdered in El Segundo. Alcala was convicted and sentenced to death in California in 2010.
- **Monique Hoyt.** Fifteen years old. 1979. She was raped and beaten by Alcala in a remote area of Riverside County. He was convicted of rape in 1980 and sentenced to nine years in prison but was paroled after less than three years.
- **Jill Parenteau.** Twenty-one years old. 1979. She was raped and murdered in her apartment in Burbank. Alcala was convicted and sentenced to death in California in 2010.
- **Robin Christine Samsoe.** Twelve years old. 1979. Alcala sexually molested and murdered her in the Sierra Madre foothills on June 20. Alcala was convicted and sentenced to death in 2010.
- **Christine Thorton.** Twenty-eight years old. 1977. Alcala murdered her in Wyoming. He was charged with first-degree murder in 2016 but was deemed too medically frail to be moved to Wyoming for trial.

4.
EDMUND KEMPER

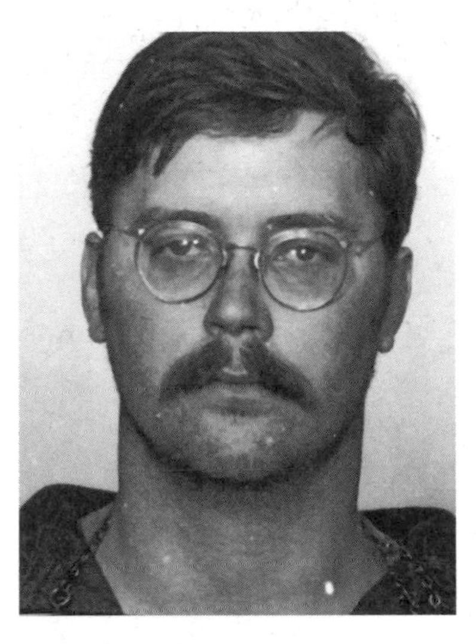

When Edmund Kemper was fifteen years old, he did not like living with his grandparents. They had a house on an isolated ranch in North Fork, a small town in the foothills of the Sierra Nevada Mountains in California's Central Valley. He was "mad at the world." So he called his mother in Helena, Montana, and told her what he had done about it: he had shot them both in the head, and they were dead. She called the police and he was arrested. Nine years later, Kemper, by then a tall, burly twenty-four-year-old, was living with his mother in a small town near Santa Cruz on the Pacific coast. He killed his mother and a friend of hers who was visiting and put their nude bodies in a closet. He had decapitated his mother and cut off her right hand. He placed her head on a bookshelf. He was then able to say all the things to her that he had never been able to say before without her interrupting, he later told a psychiatrist.

How was it possible that someone who had killed his grandparents in 1964 could be free nine years later? That was the obvious question, but there were many more. The authorities soon realized that they had finally caught the person who, in the vernacular of the time, was called the "Co-ed Killer." Six young women had been murdered in 1972 and '73 in the Santa Cruz area along the Pacific coast in Central California. Some had been decapitated. The local prosecutor had complained that Santa Cruz seemed to have become "the murder capital of the world." Now they had the killer in one of the most notorious cases. It was national news on a par with the Manson Family murders.

The media had taken little notice of fifteen-year-old Edmund E. Kemper III in 1964. It was, of course, a pre-internet time when people got their news from local papers and radio stations. When a deputy sheriff caught up with Kemper on the day he killed his grandparents, the teen said that he had shot his grandmother in the back of the head as she sat at her desk writing a children's story, according to a five-paragraph story in the far-off *Los Angeles Times*. Maude Kemper was sixty-eight years old. Twenty minutes later, the adolescent shot his grandfather in the back as he returned home from a shopping trip. Edmund Kemper, seventy-two years old, was a retired state employee. The couple's grandson had used a .22-caliber rifle on them.

Large and awkward as a child, Edmund III, sometimes known as Guy, weighed 280 pounds and was six feet, nine inches tall when he was brought into court in 1973. This time, the news media were paying attention. Early on April 24, Kemper had called the police in Santa Cruz from a pay phone in Pueblo, Colorado, about 1,300 miles to the east. He said he wanted to surrender. He had killed his mother and her friend three days earlier, and he was afraid that if someone didn't pick him up soon, he might go on a killing spree. Santa Cruz officers kept him on the phone while they sent officers to his apartment and contacted the police in Pueblo. Officers soon located him near a freeway exit and arrested him. They found two rifles, a shotgun, two pistols, and ammunition in his car. They also found something quite unexpected: a newspaper clipping that said he had become engaged a month earlier to a seventeen-year-old high school girl. The girl went into hiding soon after his arrest, and her parents begged that her name not be disclosed by the media.

In Colorado, Kemper surrendered to the police without a fight. Meanwhile, officers in California found the bloody mess and the decapitated body in Kemper's mother's apartment near Santa Cruz. They knew that five of the murdered "co-eds" had been decapitated. The body of one had never been found. Officials said Kemper soon admitted he had killed the six young women. Two had been students at the University of California campus in Santa Cruz. Kemper's mother, Clarenell Strandberg, who had remarried, worked at the university in an administrative job. Her friend, Sally Hallet, whose body was at the apartment, also worked at the university. Kemper also told the police about a human head he had buried near the apartment building. He said it belonged to Cynthia Ann Schall, a nineteen-year-old student at Cabrillo College. She had last been seen the previous January, and he had picked her up while she was hitchhiking. Parts of her body had washed up on beaches in the Santa Cruz area, but her head had not been found. Investigators soon found a putrefied human head where Kemper had said it would be.

In the fall of 1973, Kemper's case was ready to go to trial. He had pleaded both not guilty and not guilty by reason of insanity. He was charged with the murders of his mother, her friend, and the six young women: Mary Ann Pesce, nineteen years old, and Anita Luchessa, eighteen years old, both students at Fresno State College; Aiko Koo, fifteen years old, of Berkeley; Alice Liu, twenty years old, and Rosalind

Thorpe, twenty-three years old, both students at the University of California at Santa Cruz; and Cynthia Ann Schall, nineteen years old, a student at Cabrillo College in Aptos, not far from Kemper's apartment. Authorities believed that they had all been hitchhiking when Kemper offered them rides.

Soon it became clear what had happened in the years after he'd killed his grandparents. He was turned over to the California Youth Authority and committed to the Atascadero State Hospital for the criminally insane, a maximum-security institution. He was held there for four years, during which he received little psychiatric treatment. After another year in the custody of the California Youth Authority, the parole board discharged him as "cured." There were no psychiatrists or psychologists on the board. A prosecutor objected, but Kemper was turned over to his mother and got no additional psychiatric treatment. The board had given no consideration to Kemper's hostile feelings toward his mother. After he was released, he won a court order to have his record expunged.

Kemper took the witness stand at his trial in late 1973 and seemed in command of the courtroom as he testified for two days. He had already admitted—at a pre-trial hearing—that he had committed the eight murders. Now, he spoke "articulately" and "with cool detachment" as he recounted for the jury what he had done and what his motivation had been, a reporter for the *Los Angeles Times* wrote. "His recitation of the dismembering and abuse of his mother's corpse was given without an outward sign of emotion," the story said. The Santa Cruz County district attorney, Peter Chang, asked Kemper to describe his diagnosis of himself. "I believe very deeply there are two different people inside me," Kemper said. He spoke at length about his unhappy childhood, his cruelty to cats and dogs, and his difficulties with his mother.

A San Francisco psychiatrist appointed by the court to evaluate Kemper took a less sympathetic view of the self-analysis. Kemper was legally sane when he committed the eight murders, Dr. Joel Fort testified.

He said Kemper was "very intelligent" and had an IQ of 131. He pointed out that during Kemper's years in the psychiatric hospital, he had been given a job in which he administered psychological tests to thousands of patients. Kemper memorized the tests so that he would know how to answer the questions in the future. Given the chance, Fort said, Kemper would kill again.

On November 8, 1973, a jury of six men and six women rejected Kemper's insanity defense and found him guilty of first-degree murder in the deaths of his mother, his mother's friend, and the six hitchhikers. They found him legally sane at the time of the murders. In all, three psychiatrists had testified at the trial that Kemper had been sane, meaning that he knew the difference between right and wrong and understood the nature of his actions. Judge Harry F. Brauer, who had presided over the trial, addressed the jurors. "If I seem excited," he said, "it's because I feared you might arrive at a different verdict. I agree with your verdict." Kemper, dressed in an orange prison jumpsuit, remained calm and talked a bit with his lawyer. He had attempted suicide four times since his arrest.

The following day, the judge sentenced Kemper to life in prison. Brauer told Kemper that he would do everything in his power to see that he remained in prison for the rest of his life. Brauer pointed out that when Kemper had confessed to the crimes, he had also said that he would surely kill again if he were ever freed from prison. "I know you were not bragging. I know you were speaking in anguish and remorse," Brauer said. He ended by telling Kemper, standing before him in chains, "May God have mercy on your soul, Mr. Kemper. But you have to protect the rest of the people from people like you."

Several times over the following decades, Kemper went to court to get permission to have a surgeon alter what he believed was the portion of his brain that had made him kill women. He was turned down each time.

Donald T. Lunde, a psychiatrist on the faculty of Stanford University, did a case study of Kemper after his arrest in 1973. Lunde reported that Kemper was bitter about his childhood. He had lived in California with an older sister, a younger sister, his mother and his father until his parents separated when he was seven. His mother moved the family to Montana, and he rarely saw his father. When he was thirteen years old, he ran away from home to live with his father, but his father sent him back to his mother, who was about to remarry. Kemper was then sent—against his will—to live with his grandparents on their isolated ranch, where he eventually killed them.

Lunde described Kemper's early signs of "serious psychological disturbance" in *Murder and Madness,* his book about the mass murder surge of the late 1960s and early 1970s. He classified Kemper as a "sexual sadist," a category of mentally ill people who generally make a serious attempt to appear normal to others. Kemper had been fascinated by executions and would sometimes make one of his sisters blindfold him and lead him to a chair, where he would pretend he was dying in a gas chamber. "He recounted to me recurring fantasies of killing women, particularly his mother," Lunde wrote. In lengthy talks, Kemper told Lunde that he had frequently entered his mother's bedroom at night with a weapon and thought about killing her. As a teenager, he tortured and killed cats. After he killed the family cat, he decapitated it, cut it into pieces, and put the pieces in a garbage can. His mother later found the mess. He also fantasized about having sex with corpses. "If I killed them, you know, they couldn't reject me as a man. It was more or less making a doll out of a human being . . . and carrying out my fantasies with a doll, a living, human doll."

In 1972 and '73, when Kemper killed the eight women by shooting, stabbing, and strangulation, "he acted out his childhood fantasies by cutting off limbs of the victims, attempting sexual relations with the corpses, and committing acts of cannibalism," Lunde wrote. After he decapitated his mother in 1973, Kemper cut out her larynx and put it down the garbage disposal. "This seemed appropriate," Kemper explained, "as much as she'd bitched and screamed and yelled at me over the years."

Kemper has tried several times to win parole but has not succeeded. His most recent attempt was in 2017, at which time the parole board rejected his request and ruled that he could try again in 2024. More often, he has skipped his parole hearings, stipulating that he was unsuitable for release. He is being held at a California prison hospital in Vacaville, near Sacramento.

5.
DAVID BERKOWITZ

It was a low-key story at the bottom of page 3: "Chatting in a Car, Girl Met By Death." Fifteen sentences. Three hundred and sixty-five words. "A man crept up to a double-parked car in front of an apartment house in the Bronx early yesterday and fired four shots, killing an attractive teenager and wounding her girl friend," the *New York Daily News* article began. Over the coming months and years, the murder of eighteen-year-old Donna Lauria on July 29, 1976—and other shootings to follow—would evolve into an unparalleled episode of tabloid journalism intertwined with a frustrating police hunt for a taunting serial killer.

Lauria and her friend, Jodi Valenti, who was nineteen, had spent the evening at a discotheque. They were sitting in Valenti's car near the

Lauria's home in the Westchester Heights area at about 12:30 a.m. when Lauria's parents drove up and stopped to chat before parking their car. Her father said he would get the dog and return so that they could take it for a walk. While he was gone, a man fired four shots into the window on the passenger side, where Lauria was sitting. One bullet hit her in the temple. Valenti was hit in the leg, but she jumped out of the car, ran to the passenger side, and opened the door. Lauria's body fell onto the pavement. Valenti began to scream. The man with the gun fled into the darkness without saying a word. Moments later, Lauria's father walked outside with the dog and saw her body. He began to weep.

Valenti described the shooter as a white man in his late thirties. He was wearing a blue-and-white striped shirt. The police didn't have much to go on aside from the four bullets, which appeared to have been shot from a .45-caliber automatic weapon.

Things were quiet for the next four months. Then, at about 12:40 a.m. on November 27, two teenagers were shot in the Floral Park neighborhood of Queens. Joann Lomino and Donna DiMasi had gone to see a movie in Manhattan and were returning home. They took the subway and a bus, and then they walked a few blocks toward Joann's house. A man stopped them to ask for directions but soon pulled a gun from under his coat. The girls ran to the front porch of Joann's home but were struck by bullets. The gunman fled. Both girls were hospitalized with serious injuries, but they survived. The shots appeared to have been fired from a .44- or .45-caliber revolver, the police said. The story was on page 5 of the *Daily News.*

The third shooting came two months later, on January 30, 1977. "An attractive 26-year-old secretary who was sitting with her boy friend in his car in Forest Hills, Queens, was fatally wounded yesterday when an unknown assailant crept up and fired three shots through the window at close range," the *Daily News* reported. The *New York Times* took a different approach: "A young Wall Street worker from Queens was shot to death early yesterday, for no apparent reason, while sitting with her companion in a parked car on a quiet Forest Hills street waiting for the engine to warm up, the police said." The couple had gone to see the movie *Rocky* and then to dinner at a nearby restaurant. Two of the three bullets hit Christine Freund—one in her head and the other in her right shoulder. Then her head slumped onto the shoulder of her friend, John Diel, who was in the driver's seat. He shouted for help and drove to a nearby intersection, where he blocked traffic until the police arrived. Freund died several hours later at a hospital. The Queens District Attorney, John J. Santucci, said detectives were trying to determine whether there was any connection between the shooting and similar incidents over the previous year. He asked for the public's help.

The next shooting—the fourth—took place only five weeks later, on March 8, 1977, less than a block away from the spot where Christine Freund had been shot. Virginia Voskerichian, a nineteen-year-old student at Columbia University, was on her way home at about 7:30 p.m. when she was shot in the face at point-blank range. She had been carrying some books along with her purse, which had her student ID inside. Witnesses told the police that they saw a pudgy white man, about eighteen years old, running away after the shooting. He had pulled a stocking cap over his face and muttered, "Oh, Jesus," as he fled. Voskerichian died instantly. Now the toll was three dead and three wounded. The police put out a telephone number and asked for calls from anyone with information.

In mid-April, after the fifth shooting, things began to come into focus. Valentina Suriani, an eighteen-year-old college student, went to a movie with a longtime friend, Alexander Esau, a twenty-year-old tow-truck operator who lived in midtown Manhattan. At about 3 a.m. on April 17, they were sitting in a car about a block from Suriani's home in the Bronx. Suriani was in the driver's seat with the window closed. She was shot in the head and died at the scene. Esau died of bullet wounds the following day. Police announced that the bullets had come from the same .44-caliber revolver that had been used in the previous killings. And this time, the killer had left a note that was found near the car. It was addressed to one of the detectives working on the case. The police described it as "rambling and incoherent" and "ghoulish" in tone, the *New York Times* reported.

The *Daily News* was less restrained. The headline "KILLER TO COPS: 'I'LL DO IT AGAIN' Taunting Note Is 1st Solid Clue" took up most of the tabloid's front page along with two composite sketches of "possible witnesses" the police wanted for questioning. The note had been written by "the psychopathic .44-caliber killer," the story said. An "official source," whom the newspaper did not identify, "said the note confirmed suspicions that the killer is a homicidal maniac." It was written by a "real sicko" who was "taunting" the police, the source said. He was "probably an ugly man who has trouble with girls and had probably been rejected by a young woman with long brown hair." At that point, all the female victims had shoulder-length brown hair. And word had leaked out that the killer had referred to himself as the "Son of Sam."

On April 28, police officials finally held a press conference to address the rumors and the leaks—and to reply to the writer of the letter. "We have some feeling that he is reaching out," John L. Keenan, the chief of detectives, said. "He's suffering, he's had some serious pain or incident in his life. We want to reach him before something tragic happens. We are going on the assumption that he will kill again. He doesn't want to, but he is acting under a compulsion."

Keenan was a World War II veteran who had been involved in the invasion of Normandy and had worked in the Counter Intelligence Corps of the Fourth Infantry Division. The killer seemed to have a parent figure named "Sam" who had caused great suffering, Keenan said. "He may be symbolic, or he may be an hallucination." The killer, he added, had written that he was not a woman hater and didn't want to kill but felt compelled to do so. Keenan speculated that "Sam" might be a parent who had mistreated the killer.

Captain Joseph Borrelli, who was the supervisor of a task force working on the case, pleaded with the killer. "We wish to help you and it is not too late," Borrelli said. "Please let us help you." He gave a telephone number.

The envelope that contained the letter had been handled by so many people and had so many overlapping fingerprints that it was deemed useless as evidence of the writer's identity. But the envelope had not been opened by the time it reached police fingerprint experts. Inside, they found a nearly pristine document with no clear fingerprints. It appeared as if the writer had held the paper by the edges with the tips of his forefinger and thumb. Part of the letter was withheld—and hadn't been leaked by anyone thus far—so that only the true writer would be able to identify it. The full letter, addressed to Captain Borrelli, read:

I AM DEEPLY HURT BY YOUR CALLING
ME A WEMON HATER. I AM NOT.
BUT I AM A MONSTER.
I AM THE "SON OF SAM." I AM A LITTLE
"BRAT."
WHEN FATHER SAM GETS DRUNK
HE GETS MEAN. HE BEATS HIS
FAMILY. SOMETIMES HE TIES ME
UP TO THE BACK OF THE HOUSE.
OTHER TIMES HE LOCKS ME
IN THE GARAGE. SAM LOVES TO
DRINK BLOOD.
"GO OUT AND KILL" COMMANDS
FATHER SAM.

BEHIND OUR HOUSE SOME
REST. MOSTLY YOUNG—RAPED
AND SLAUGHTERED—THEIR
BLOOD DRAINED—JUST BONES
NOW
PAPA SAM KEEPS ME LOCKED
IN THE ATTIC, TOO. I CAN'T
GET OUT BUT I LOOK OUT THE
ATTIC WINDOW AND WATCH
THE WORLD GO BY.
I FEEL LIKE AN OUTSIDER.
I AM ON A DIFFERENT WAVE
LENGTH THEN EVERYBODY
ELSE—PROGRAMMED TOO
KILL.
HOWEVER, TO STOP ME YOU
MUST KILL ME. ATTENTION
ALL POLICE: SHOOT ME FIRST-
SHOOT TO KILL OR ELSE.
KEEP OUT OF MY WAY OR
YOU WILL DIE!

PAPA SAM IS OLD NOW.
HE NEEDS SOME BLOOD TO
PRESERVE HIS YOUTH.
HE HAS HAD TOO MANY
HEART ATTACKS. "UGH, ME
HOOT IT URTS, SONNY BOY."

I MISS MY PRETTY
PRINCESS MOST OF ALL.

SHE'S RESTING IN
OUR LADIES HOUSE
BUT I'LL SEE HER SOON.
I AM THE "MONSTER"—
"BEELZEBUB"—THE
"CHUBBY BEHEMOUTH."

I LOVE TO HUNT. PROWLING
THE STREETS LOOKING FOR
FAIR GAME—TASTY MEAT. THE
WEMON OF QUEENS ARE Z
PRETTYIST OF ALL. I MUST
BE THE WATER THEY DRINK.
I LIVE FOR THE HUNT—MY LIFE.
BLOOD FOR PAPA.

MR. BORELLI, SIR,
I DON'T WANT TO KILL ANYMORE,
NO SIR, NO MORE, BUT I
MUST, "HONOUR THY FATHER."

I WANT TO MAKE LOVE TO THE
WORLD. I LOVE PEOPLE –
I DON'T BELONG ON EARTH.
RETURN ME TO YAHOOS.

TO THE PEOPLE OF QUEENS.
I LOVE YOU. AND I
WANT TO WISH ALL OF
YOU A HAPPY EASTER.
MAY GOD BLESS YOU

IN THIS LIFE AND IN
THE NEXT AND FOR NOW
I SAY GOODBYE AND
GOODNIGHT.

POLICE—LET ME
HAUNT YOU WITH THESE WORDS:

I'LL BE BACK!
I'LL BE BACK!

TO BE INTERRPRETED
AS—BANG, BANG, BANG,
BANG, BANG—UGH!!

YOURS IN
MURDER

MR. MONSTER

The ".44-caliber killer" was about to morph into the more ominous-sounding "Son of Sam," who would terrorize the city during what would soon become known as the "Summer of Sam." It began in earnest when Jimmy Breslin, a highly popular columnist for the *Daily News,* received a letter in the mail signed by "Son of Sam." On Friday, June 3, the *Daily News* teased the letter with the front-page headline: "THE .44-CALIBER CASE NEW NOTE: CAN'T STOP KILLING." The story gave few details of the letter, but it said that the killer wished the detectives "luck." On Saturday, June 4, the *Daily News* offered another front-page tease: ".44 KILLER: I AM NOT ASLEEP." Again, little information was given about what the letter actually said.

On Sunday, June 5, half the front page was taken up by the headline: "Breslin to .44 Killer: GIVE UP! IT'S ONLY WAY OUT." The edition sold over a million copies. The story itself began on page 3, where Breslin recounted the opening paragraph of the letter: "Hello from the gutters of N.Y.C., which are filled with dog manure, vomit, stale wine, urine, and blood. Hello from the sewers of N.Y.C. which swallow up these delicacies when they are washed away by the sweeper trucks."

Most of the letter was revealed in the newspaper, but part of it was held back at the request of the police so that they would have something that only the writer would know. The published part read, "Don't think that because you haven't heard from me for a while that I went to sleep. No, rather, I am still here. Like a spirit roaming the night. Thirsty, hungry, seldom stopping to rest; anxious to please Sam . . . He won't let me stop killing until he gets his fill of blood." The writer warned that no one should forget Donna Lauria, and asked, "Tell me, Jim, what will you have for July 29?"

The letter ended:

"In their blood
and
From the Gutter.
'Sam's Creation' .44"

But then there were a couple of polite additions:

"P.S: J.B. please inform all the detectives working on the slayings to remain.
P.S: J.B., please inform all the detectives working on the case that I wish them the best of

luck. "Keep 'em digging, drive on think positive, get off your butts, knock on coffins, etc." Upon my capture I promise to buy all the guys working on the case a new pair of shoes if I can get up the money. Son of Sam"

Breslin responded in his column with offers of help. "I hope that the killer realizes that he is controlled by Sam, who not only forces him into acts of horror but will ultimately walk him to his death. The only way for

LETTER SENT TO JIMMY BRESLIN BY THE SON OF SAM

PS: J.B. PLEASE INFORM ALL THE
DETECTIVES WORKING THE
CASE THAT I WISH THEM THE
BEST OF LUCK. "KEEP EM
DIGGING, DRIVE ON, THINK
POSITIVE, GET OFF YOUR
BUTTS, KNOCK ON COFFINS, ETC.

UPON MY CAPTURE I PROMISE TO
BUY ALL THE GUYS WORKING
ON THE CASE A NEW PAIR OF
SHOES IF I CAN GET UP THE
MONEY.

SON OF SAM

the killer to leave this special torment is to give himself up to me, if he trusts me, or to the police, and receive both help and safety.

"If he wants any further contact, all he has to do is call or write me at the Daily News. It's simple to get me, the only people I don't answer are bill collectors.

"The time to do it however is now. We are too close to the July 29 that the killer mentions in his letter. It is the first anniversary of the death of Donna Lauria."

About three weeks later, on Sunday morning, June 26, there was another shooting. "The psychopathic killer who calls himself 'Son of Sam' struck again early yesterday when he shot at a couple, wounding them as they sat in a car parked on a street in Bayside, Queens," said the story on the front page of Monday's *New York Times.* Judy Placido, a seventeen-year-old from the Bronx, had driven to a discotheque in Queens on Saturday night with two friends. When her friends left, Placido stayed behind with Salvatore Lupo, a twenty-year-old from Maspeth, Queens. They were smoking cigarettes in a car about a block and a half from the discotheque when they were shot. Placido was hit in the right temple, the right shoulder, and the back of her neck. Rupo was hit in the right forearm. Placido ended up in intensive care, but she and Lupo survived. Police officials said the four bullets that were fired came from the same

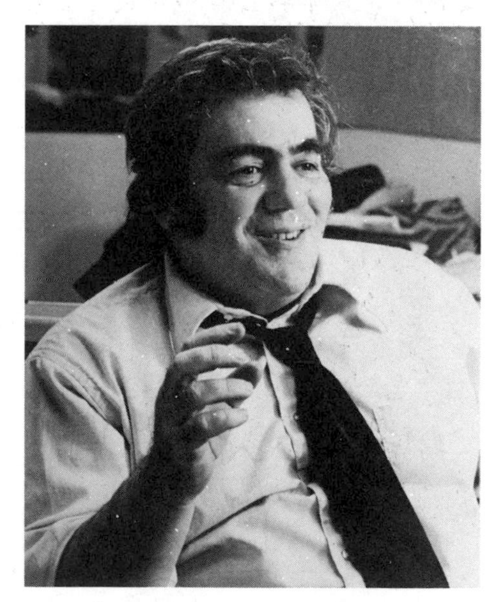

JIMMY BRESLIN OF THE *DAILY NEWS*

.44-caliber "bulldog" revolver that had been used in the six other "Son of Sam" attacks.

Pete Hamill, another columnist for the *Daily News,* wrote a plea published on July 1 with the headline "Dear Sam, Let Us Tame That Monster in You." He urged the killer to turn himself in to the police or to "walk into this newspaper and surrender." If he was afraid to do that, he could "call Jimmy Breslin or me." With the anniversary of Donna Lauria's death approaching, New York City seemed near hysteria.

What came next would have been far-fetched if it had been a plot for a movie. The blackout began at 9:34 p.m. on Wednesday, July 13. The lights went out across all of New York City, plunging nine million people into darkness. The shutdown, caused by lightning striking a power plant, lasted until 10:49 p.m. the next day. There were more than a thousand fires, and looting was widespread. Over three thousand people were arrested by an overwhelmed police department that was also trying to direct the snarled traffic and rescue people from stalled elevators and the crippled subway system. Some poorer neighborhoods, including East Harlem, were devastated.

The *New York Times* staff, working by candlelight on old-fashioned typewriters, was able to produce an edition on July 14 using the printing plant of a newspaper in New Jersey, where the lights were still on. The front page was all about the blackout: "Bellevue Patients Resuscitated With Hand-Squeezed Airbags"; "State Troopers Sent Into City As Crime Rises"; "Riders Safely Flee the Subway Though Some Swelter Hours."

The *Daily News,* too, was able to print an edition for July 14. "BLACKOUT! LIGHTNING HITS CON ED SYSTEM," the front page screamed.

But the *New York Post,* the city's third-ranking daily, was unable to produce its afternoon edition for July 14. The *Post* made up for it the following day with a "BLACKOUT SPECIAL" edition. The front page was all but consumed by the headline "24 HOURS OF

TERROR." It was a summer of rebirth for the *Post*, which had been purchased by Rupert Murdoch, the Australian publisher who had begun to produce supermarket tabloids full of celebrity gossip in Great Britain. He intended to pump up the *Post*'s circulation by competing with the *Daily News.*

On July 31, 1977, two days after the anniversary of Donna Lauria's death, Son of Sam struck again. This time the victims were a couple sitting in a parked car at 2:45 a.m. in what the *Daily News* called a "lover's lane" in Brooklyn. Twenty-year-old Stacy Moskowitz, who was shot in the head, died the next day in a hospital. Robert Violante, also twenty years old, was shot in the head and blinded, but he was out of danger. His left eye had been blown out by a bullet. The identity of the killer remained a mystery even though three hundred police offers had been assigned to search for him. Murdoch's *New York Post* seized the moment. In huge type, the entire front page on August 1 read:

'NO ONE IS SAFE'
FROM SON OF SAM

Killer outfoxes cops
1: MOVES OUTSIDE QUEENS
2: STRIKES AT SHORT HAIR
3: STRIKES AT BLONDES HAIR
4: SPOTTED BY FEW WITNESSES
DOWD: City in danger
12 suspects ruled out
Cops at square one
Task force is doubled
Girl clings to life

FULL COVERAGE OF THE DRAMA ON PAGES 2, 3 AND 4

The police renewed their appeal for witnesses to come forward and were deluged with hundreds of calls. "We have nothing more substantial than a general description [of] the killer and possibly a yellow Volkswagen," an official said. Seventy-five detectives had been assigned to the special task force in Queens responsible for investigating the mystery. They were pursuing a range of theories, including that the killer might be a laid-off policeman, a freelance journalist, a taxi driver, or a compulsive walker who roamed the city day and night, the *New York Times* reported on August 3. They had even "listened patiently to astrologers, seers, hypnotists and numerologists." On August 4, the police commissioner announced that 136 laid-off police officers would be rehired to work on the case. On August 6, Mayor Abraham Beame ordered police officers to chase away couples parked in cars in isolated areas of the city. On August 9, police began distributing fliers with new sketches of the killer.

On August 10, it was over. Late that Wednesday night, David Berkowitz walked out of his apartment building at 35 Pine Street in Yonkers, a city in Westchester County, just north of the Bronx. He was carrying a brown paper bag as he got into his gold-colored Ford Galaxie. When he started the car, Craig Glassman, an investigator for the Westchester County Sheriff's Department, put his gun through the open window and said, "Freeze. You're under arrest." A New York detective who had been among a contingent of officers staking out the area slapped handcuffs on Berkowitz. The killer smiled and said, "Well you got me. How come it took you such a long time?"

"Son of Sam," it turned out, had made one big mistake: he'd parked too close to a fire hydrant on July 31, the night he shot Stacy Moskowitz and Robert Violante in Brooklyn. Berkowitz's car had gotten a parking ticket there an hour or so before the shooting, and detectives tracked him down. The police found the .44-caliber revolver in the paper bag Berkowitz had been holding when he got into the car. They also found a loaded machine gun.

At 1:45 a.m. on August 11, Mayor Beame called a news conference at police headquarters in lower Manhattan. He said, "I am very pleased to announce that the people of New York can rest easy tonight, because police have captured a man they believe to be the Son of Sam."

Keenan, the chief of detectives, said Berkowitz had been traced after officers examined every ticket given to cars parked on July 21 in the area in Brooklyn where Stacey Moskowitz and Robert Violante were shot. A cream-colored Ford Galaxie had been cited for parking too close to a fire hydrant. Detectives went to the address where the car was registered, 35 Pine Street in Yonkers, and found the car parked on the street. They could see the butt of a machine gun sticking out of a sack inside the car. Police got a search warrant and surrounded the building, but Berkowitz walked out before they could attempt to serve him. He was quickly surrounded and arrested. A .44-caliber bulldog revolver was loaded and lying next to the driver's seat in his car.

FRONT PAGES OF THE AUGUST 11, 1977 ISSUE OF THE NEW YORK POST AND THE AUGUST 12, 1977 ISSUE OF THE DAILY NEWS

NEW YORK POST

METRO

TODAY'S RACING

CAUGHT!

Son of Sam was on way to kill again

'I wanted to go out in a blaze of glory'

By CARL J. PELLECK

The man police say is the Son of Sam was on his way to claim more victims when he walked into the arms of waiting detectives.

David Berkowitz, 24, had already written a letter—his third—addressed to Suffolk County and New York police and the press. He was going to leave it alongside his latest victim. It had no stamp on it.

'DID IT FOR SAM'

Continued on Page 3

FINAL

DAILY NEWS

SAM CHANGED AFTER LSD TRIPS

Took Drugs as Soldier in Korea

Exclusive

Hero Witness' Own Story

Breslin

Sam's Words Tumble Out

Eleven Pages Of Stories, Pictures

Finally, police had caught the mysterious and terrifying Son of Sam. He turned out to have a background that seemed quite ordinary—almost shockingly so. David Berkowitz was a twenty-four-year-old postal worker; he was quiet and calm under questioning at police headquarters in Manhattan. Some wondered whether they had caught the right man.

Berkowitz had been born Richard David Falco on June 1, 1953. He was adopted in 1954 by Nathan and Pearl Berkowitz, who changed his name and raised him in the Jewish faith. Pearl Berkowitz died when David was 14. Berkowitz graduated from Christopher Columbus High School in the Bronx, attended Bronx Community College for a semester, and then enlisted in the Army and served for three years. One of those years was spent in South Korea. In letters to friends, he sometimes wrote that he took LSD and other drugs. He converted to Christianity while he served at Fort Knox in Kentucky. When he returned from the Army, he lived with his father for a time. He stayed in New York when his father retired to Florida in 1975.

For half an hour on August 11, 1977, the police task force shot questions at Berkowitz. "Why did you kill them?" a detective asked. The response: "It was a command. I had a sign and I followed it. Sam told me what to do and I did it." Sam Carr was a neighbor in Yonkers "who really is a man who lived six thousand years ago. I got messages through his dog. He told me to kill. Sam is the devil." The police also asked Berkowitz about a letter that had been left at one murder scene, and he knew the answers.

Seven months of legal maneuvering followed. Then, on May 8, 1978, Berkowitz pleaded guilty to six murder charges and seven attempted murders. But the drama was not over. As Berkowitz was escorted into the courtroom for sentencing two weeks later, he started repeatedly saying, "Stacy was a whore." It was a reference to Stacy Moskowitz, his final victim. Her mother, Neysha, shouted out, "You're an animal!"

and ran from the courtroom. Berkowitz was quickly escorted from the courtroom, and the sentencing was postponed. On June 12, Berkowitz answered questions from the three judges involved in the cases and was sentenced to terms of 25 years to life in prison for each murder.

Berkowitz has been living a relatively quiet life in the New York prison system. He has spent most of his years at the Shawangunk Correctional Facility, about ninety miles south of Albany. He had surgery in Albany in 2018 after suffering a heart attack. At a parole hearing in 2016, he told the board that he has been a "wonderful" inmate and said, "I was constantly putting myself out there to help other individuals, with kindness and compassion." He said he was "deeply sorry" for what he had done. He said he has become a "caregiver" for other inmates and reaches out to those who have psychiatric problems. "I believe that's my calling," he said. He acknowledged that his hopes for parole were not "realistic."

6. TED BUNDY

Theodore Robert Bundy made a serious miscalculation on November 8, 1974. He drove his Volkswagen Beetle to a shopping mall in Murray, Utah, near Salt Lake City, on that rainy evening and watched people come and go in the parking lot. He liked the look of Carol DaRonch as she got out of her car, so he went into the mall and followed her around. As she browsed at a bookstore, he confronted her. Tall and handsome, he told her that someone had tried to break into her car, and he asked her to follow him. She assumed he was a security guard or a police officer. When she asked his name, he said, "Officer Roseland."

DaRonch had graduated from high school in the spring and gotten a job; she had a new Camaro. She followed Bundy and found that there was nothing missing from her car, but he persuaded her to head to the police station with him to file a report. When they got into his car, she smelled alcohol on his breath and quickly realized she had made a mistake. Eventually, he stopped the car and she opened the door. He pulled out a gun, grabbed a crowbar, and slapped handcuffs on her wrist. They struggled, and when she fell out, he sped away. A passing driver picked her up and took her to a police station, where officers removed the handcuffs and took a report. There was no "Officer Roseland." Ted Bundy had left a live victim.

Later that night, about twenty miles away in Bountiful, Utah, Debra Kent left a high school play to pick up her brother at a skating rink. She was seventeen years old. Her car was found in the high school parking lot, but she was never seen again. Police did find a handcuff key in the parking lot. They had heard about the incident in Murray, so they took the key there and tried it on the handcuffs that had been removed from Carol DaRonch. It worked, but handcuff keys can be interchangeable. Even so, it was a clue. It would be nine months before police investigators began to catch up with Bundy, the charming former law student and Republican campaign worker. And it would be years before the depth of his depravity would become clear.

On an August night in 1975, an officer from the Utah Highway Patrol pulled up in front of his home in a quiet suburb of Salt Lake City. He saw a Volkswagen passing by. It was after midnight, and he did not recognize the car as belonging to anyone in the neighborhood. He turned his headlights on to get a better look, and the car sped away, running through two stop signs. The officer chased the car, and the driver eventually stopped and got out. Bundy smiled and said he was lost. He gave the officer his driver's license, and soon, another highway patrol car pulled up. The front passenger seat in Bundy's car had been removed and put on its side in the back. The officer asked Bundy if it was okay to search his car. Bundy gave his permission, but later said he hadn't. Inside the car the officer found a crowbar, a ski mask, an ice pick, rope, some wire, a flashlight, gloves, and handcuffs.

Bundy was arrested on a charge of evading an officer and released on his own recognizance later that day. Despite his smiles and casual demeanor, he had been unable to charm his way out of the situation. Within a few days, a detective realized that the "Officer Roseland" who had picked up Carol DaRonch in his Volkswagen ten months earlier sounded a lot like Bundy. On August 21, he was arrested again and charged with possession of burglary tools, but he remained free on bail. Behind the scenes, though, much was happening. In early October, he was charged with aggravated kidnapping and attempted criminal assault in the Carol DaRonch incident. He sat in a jail cell in Salt Lake County until November 13, 1975, when his mother and stepfather finally came up with $15,000 to bail him out. Meanwhile, investigators in three states realized that they might finally have zeroed in on the mysterious person who was responsible for the deaths or disappearances of at least a dozen girls and young women in Washington, Utah, and Colorado.

To people who knew the twenty-eight-year-old Bundy, the charges and suspicions seemed absurd. The developments were especially troubling for Ann Rule, a former Seattle police officer who had met him in 1971 when they were working a late shift at the Seattle Crisis Clinic. He was a charming twenty-four-year-old work-study student who was a senior in psychology at the University of Washington. She was a middle-aged mother of four who volunteered once a week. They worked side by side answering calls from people with problems, some of whom threatened suicide. They became close friends. He planned to go to law school, and she was a correspondent for *True Detective* magazine. She hoped to expand her career as a true-crime writer so that she could support her family. (Eventually Rule got a contract to write a book about a series of unexplained murders of young women in the Northwest. Her research served as the foundation for her first book, *The Stranger Beside*

Me, her autobiographical account of Bundy and her discovery that he was a serial killer, published in 1980.)

During their nights at the crisis clinic, Bundy and Rule had confided in each other a bit about their personal lives. He told her that he had found out recently that he was "illegitimate" and had been born in a home for unwed mothers. That was in 1946, and given the sensibilities of the times, his grandparents agreed to say that he was their child—and that his mother, Louise, was his sister. But he had never believed the story. (In 1969, when he was twenty-two, he went to Vermont, where he'd been born, and obtained his birth certificate. His "sister" was indeed his mother.) When Ted was three, Louise decided to leave her parents' home in Philadelphia: she and Ted would start a new life in Tacoma, Washington. Louise married John Bundy, a cook at an Army hospital. They had four daughters and a son.

On March 1, 1976, Bundy was convicted of the attempted kidnapping and assault of Carol DaRonch, and in June he was sentenced to one to fifteen years in prison. By then, law enforcement officials in several states had coordinated their efforts and begun to suspect that Bundy was the so-called "Ted" murderer who drove a brown Volkswagen "Bug" and killed attractive young women or was seen somewhere nearby when they disappeared. Authorities had first been tipped off about "Ted" on July 14, 1974, when Janice Ott, a twenty-three-year-old probation caseworker, rode her bicycle from her home in Issaquah to Sammamish State Park near Seattle. The park was crowded on that warm Sunday afternoon. Witnesses told investigators that they had seen a man with a cast on his arm approach a young woman and ask for her help putting his sailboat onto his car. He told her his name was "Ted." Eventually, she walked off with him. A bit later, at least one witness saw "Ted" leaning against a brown Volkswagen, talking to Ott. She was never seen again. Two months later, her skeletal remains were found in a wooded area about two miles from the park, along with the remains of Denise Naslund, an eighteen-year-old from Seattle. She, too, had been at the park that day, and she had left her friends saying she was going to find a restroom. She was never seen alive again. At least four other young women had disappeared from the region within the last year.

In October, Bundy was charged with the rape and murder of Caryn Campbell, a twenty-four-year-old nurse from Michigan who had been vacationing near Aspen, Colorado. She had disappeared on January 12, 1975. Bundy had been in the area at the time. He was extradited to Colorado to stand trial, but he had other plans. On June 7, 1977, during a break in court proceedings, he was allowed to go to a second-floor law library in the Aspen courthouse. He jumped out a window and disappeared, setting off warnings across the area and a huge manhunt. Because he had been in the courtroom, he'd been allowed to wear ordinary clothes instead of a prison jumpsuit. That made it easier for him to blend in once he got outside. It was six days before he was caught. Police found him in a stolen car and returned him to jail.

TED BUNDY BEING ESCORTED OUT OF COURT IN PITKIN, COLORADO IN 1977.

His second attempt at escape was better planned. He had somehow obtained a small saw while in prison and, over several weeks, he carved out a twelve-inch square in the ceiling of his cell. No one noticed because a metal plate had been placed there temporarily so that a light fixture could be installed. Bundy was five feet, eleven inches tall and weighed 170 pounds, but he dieted down to 140. He was able to slip through the hole at night and move around in the ceiling, which enabled him to study the layout of the building.

On the evening of December 30, 1977, he climbed through the hole, let himself down through an office, and walked out of the jail. He found a car with the keys inside it and drove away into a snowy night. When the car broke down, a passing driver picked him up and dropped him off at a bus station in Vail. Bundy took a bus to Denver, got a cab to the airport, and landed in Chicago before anyone realized he was gone. In the coming days, he would make his way to Ann Arbor, Michigan, steal a car, and head to Florida with a new name—Chris Hagen.

His final destination was Tallahassee, the home of Florida State University. He arrived there on January 8, 1978, and rented a room with the small amount of cash he still had. He supported his quiet existence by grabbing wallets from purses in the shopping carts of unsuspecting women. "Chris Hagen" also had become adept at stealing cars.

In February, FBI officials announced that Theodore Robert Bundy had been placed on its Ten Most Wanted Fugitives list. The former University of Utah law student was suspected of the sexual slayings of thirty-six young women in California, Utah, and Colorado over the previous eight years. If convicted, Bundy would be "the most prolific mass murderer in American history," according to a brief item from United Press International, a widely used news service. Bundy had begun to get national attention.

In the early morning hours of February 15, 1978, a police officer in Pensacola noticed a car pulling out of an alley long after all the restaurants in the area had closed. Curious, he ran a check on the license plate. The car had been stolen. The officer turned on his lights and the car sped away, but eventually the driver pulled over and stopped. Bundy got out of the car, but as the officer tried to handcuff him, Bundy broke free. The officer fired his gun, and Bundy dropped to the ground. He was arrested. He said his name was Kenneth Misner. (The real Kenneth Misner, a star athlete at Florida State, was surprised the next day to hear on the radio that he had been arrested in Pensacola, about two hundred miles to the west of Tallahassee on the Florida panhandle.)

Within a few days, Bundy's identity became clear. More importantly to investigators in Tallahassee, they now had a suspect in the recent brutal attacks on five young female students at Florida State. In the early hours of January 15—a month before Bundy's arrest—a young sorority member returned home to the Chi Omega House and found the back door open. She heard a noise on an upper floor and then a pounding in the stairway. Concealed behind a door, she watched as a man with a knit cap pulled halfway down his face ran out the front door. He fled with a club in his right hand.

The young woman went upstairs, woke her roommate, and told her what she had seen. Then they saw another sorority sister stumble out of her room covered in blood. They called for an ambulance and for the police, who arrived to uncover a scene from a horror movie. Two sorority sisters were found dead in their beds. Margaret Bowman's brain could be seen through her shattered skull. A nylon stocking had been pulled tightly around her neck. Lisa Levy had been sexually assaulted either before or after she was beaten to death, apparently with some kind of a stick. One nipple had been all but bitten off. Two others, Karen Chandler and Kathy Kleiner, survived, but they'd been beaten so severely that they had no memory of what had happened to them.

A short time later, about eight blocks away, students heard pounding and thumping in the apartment next to theirs, where a friend lived. They called the police, who found Cheryl Thomas, a young dance major, moaning and bleeding in her bed. She had severe head wounds and her clothes had been ripped off. She lived, but she would never dance again.

Bundy's six weeks of freedom in early 1978 would be his last. He was no longer just a perplexing local news story in the West. He was now the focus of national media. Their stories tried to explain how it was possible that a person might carry out so many horrendous crimes over so many years without being caught. Who was Ted Bundy?

The "handsome, articulate and college-educated" thirty-one-year-old was being held in an armor-plated jail cell in Tallahassee, the *New York Times* reported. Police in several states suspected that he had killed at least thirty-six women. An investigator said that Bundy "was the kind of guy you'd want your daughter to bring home." Perhaps Bundy was just unlucky: the attacks seemed to happen when he was within miles of the murder scene. Even by the furthest stretch of the imagination, he was no one's idea of a mass murderer. Still, who could explain why Ted Bundy was always so close to horrible, bloody murders of similar-looking young women.

Bundy's résumé was impressive. He had graduated from the University of Washington in Seattle in 1972 with a degree in psychology. His time at the Seattle Crisis Clinic had been part of his undergraduate work there. He had also gotten involved in politics. In 1968, he'd worked in the Seattle campaign office of Nelson Rockefeller, the New York governor who was running for the Republican presidential nomination. Bundy also had worked as a precinct committeeman for the Republican Party and was hired in 1972 by the campaign of Dan Evans, the Washington State governor who was running for reelection. Bundy's assignment was to travel around the state to rallies and events held by Evans's Democratic opponent and blend in with the crowds so that he could monitor the speeches. Bundy reported directly to the governor and his top aides.

In December of 1972, he was appointed to Seattle's Crime Prevention Advisory Commission. He had been rejected by the University of Utah Law School in 1972, but he reapplied in 1973 with a letter of recommendation from Governor Evans. This time Bundy was accepted, but he decided instead to enroll at the law school at the University of Puget Sound in Tacoma. He went to work as an assistant to Ross Davis, the chairman of the Washington State Republican Party. But he dropped out of law school and moved to Salt Lake City in the fall of 1974 to start over at the University of Utah.

News reports in early 1978 were full of speculation about whether a person with such a background could be involved in what some officials said could be forty or more murders. There was one more surprise to come. In April, the body of a young girl was found in a wooded area near a state park in Florida. Kimberly Ann Leach, who was twelve years old, had been assaulted and murdered. Police had been looking for her since February 9, when she'd disappeared from her school in Lake City, Florida, in the middle of the day. Lake City is about ninety miles east of Tallahassee. In July, Bundy was charged with her murder.

The first case to go to trial centered on the five women attacked at the University of Florida. Bundy had a team of lawyers, but he sometimes questioned the witnesses himself and argued legal motions before the judge. Key evidence came from a dental expert, who testified that the bite marks around Lisa Levy's nipple matched Bundy's teeth. The jury deliberated for about six hours on July 23, 1979, before finding Bundy guilty on all charges—two first-degree murders, three attempted murders, and two burglaries. A week later, the jury recommended the death penalty. The trial judge agreed and sentenced Bundy to death in the electric chair. A year later, he was convicted of murdering Kimberly Leach, and again he was sentenced to death.

Nearly ten years of litigation would follow. When it became clear to Bundy that he had run out of appeals, he began to talk. In the days before he was to be executed on January 24, 1989, he offered to tell of additional murders in exchange for a stay of execution. Florida governor Bob Martinez refused, saying he would not "negotiate with a killer." In the end, Bundy confessed to at least sixteen other killings, including those of eight women in the state of Washington in 1974, a woman in Vail, Colorado, and others whose murders investigators had never connected to him.

Bundy, forty-two years old, was pronounced dead at 7:16 a.m. on January 24, 1989, about a minute after two thousand volts surged through his body in the electric chair at the Florida State Prison.

The precise number of murders committed by Bundy has never been clear. Estimates have ranged as high as one hundred. Shortly after Bundy's execution, Jerry Blair, the prosecutor in the death penalty case, said the toll might be about fifty. Blair told the Associated Press that after the final confessions, the FBI concluded that Bundy had confirmed suspicions about thirteen killings in Utah, Colorado, and the state of Washington. Additionally, Bundy had provided information about fourteen cases in Washington, Utah, Idaho, California, Vermont, and Pennsylvania. Bundy had also given information about twenty more cases around the country going back to 1969. "Those are the figures I've heard for many years," Bradford said. "I don't think we'll ever know exactly how many."

In a 1989 update of *The Stranger Beside Me,* Rule expressed the belief that Bundy had committed his first murder in 1961, when he was fifteen and living in Tacoma. Elementary school student Ann Marie Burr was living a few blocks away from him when she disappeared on August 31, 1961. Her parents found the front door and a first floor window open when they got up that morning. Burr was never seen again, and her body was never found. "Ted wanted to be noticed, to be recognized,"

Rule wrote. "He accomplished that. He left this earth a man almost as hated as the Nazis who intrigued him."

Rule kept in touch with Bundy over the years and visited him in prison, where they had long talks. In the early years after his arrest, she and others who had worked with Bundy at the crisis center did not believe that their charming friend could have committed the murders, she told the *Houston Chronicle* in 2003, adding, "We figured he was either guilty or he was the unluckiest guy there ever was, because every place he went the girls who fit the victim profile disappeared in the same sort of circumstances." In prison, Bundy "got a little cockier," she said. "I've always said that infamy became Ted Bundy. When he became infamous and the strobe lights were on him and the microphones were shoved in his face, he bloomed." In a 2009 update of her book, Rule described Bundy as "a sadistic sociopath who took pleasure from another human's pain and the control he had over his victims, to the point of death, and even after."

7.
VAUGHN GREENWOOD

As the multiple homicide cases played out in the Northwest in the '70s, Southern California had its own murder problems. In many ways, these were more baffling than even the Manson Family murders in the late 1960s. Someone was killing the inhabitants of the skid row area in downtown Los Angeles by slashing their necks. Inevitably, the mysterious attacker became known as the Skid Row Slasher. By the chilly Christmas season of 1974, four men had been slashed to death. The latest body had been found in a pool of blood in the shrubbery near the Los Angeles Public Library. The man's throat had been cut from ear to ear, the *Los Angeles Times* reported. A police lieutenant called the killing "another hobo-jungle type thing."

The first victim was forty-six-year-old Charles Jackson, whose body was found on the patio of the library on December 1. Originally from Louisiana, Jackson had recently spent some time in a Los Angeles jail on a charge related to drunkenness. On December 8, the body of Moses August Yakanak, a forty-seven-year-old Alaska Native, had been found in an alley nearby. The body of the third victim, Arthur Dahlstedt, was found on December 11 in an alley-side doorway of a vacant building. He was fifty-four years old, and police had identified him by his fingerprints but knew little else about him. The police also had little information on the fourth victim, whose body was found on December 22 in a pool of blood and litter.

By the end of January in 1975, the death toll had reached eight, and the Los Angeles Police Department had formed the "Slasher Squad," later expanded and renamed the "Slasher Task Force." It was to be deployed immediately to the scene of any new suspected slasher killings. The department issued a drawing of a white man with long, dark-blond hair, about six feet tall and 190 pounds, and probably "a homosexual." Within days, they had a suspect: Carl A. Eder, a thirty-two-year-old man who had escaped from a state prison the previous November. He had killed a family of five in El Cajon, a town near San Diego, ten years earlier. He had cut the throats of most of the victims. But Eder was quickly dismissed as a suspect. His slashing method had been different.

Police said the man they were looking for was a "sexually impotent coward, venting his own feeling of worthlessness on hapless derelicts and down-and-outers." Two of the dead, however, were clearly not derelicts, and the coroner's tests had shown that only one of the nine had been drinking near the time of his death. Amid the chaos, several men claimed to be the slasher, but they were quickly eliminated by police, who found that the "suspects" were unaware of key elements of the crimes that had been kept secret.

In mid-March, the task force announced that they had found the killer. It was not, in fact, a white man with blondish hair who was still roaming the streets. It was a black man, Vaughn Greenwood, who had been in custody for more than a month. He had been arrested in early February following a hatchet attack on two men sharing a home in the Hollywood Hills above Sunset Boulevard. They were awakened early on the morning of February 2 by a man carrying a hatchet and a knife. As they struggled with the intruder, one of the men fell through a plate glass window and ran to a home nearby that was owned by the actor Burt Reynolds. A caretaker at the house called the police. When officers arrived, they fired ten shots and the intruder fled into the foothills. Greenwood was arrested the next day at his home in South Central Los Angeles.

The killings stopped, but it would be nearly a year before the public learned precisely what was happening. Soon after Greenwood's arrest in February, a judge had imposed a gag order on all police and law enforcement officials. They had planned to make an announcement, but now they couldn't say anything about the Greenwood arrest. Edward M. Davis, the Los Angeles police chief, had said on March 16 that Greenwood would be charged with the murders; but the following day, Davis stuck a napkin in his mouth during a news conference to demonstrate the effect of the gag order. "I have great difficulty, as you know, saying no comment—so no comment," Davis said.

More than ten months later—ten months without another skid row murder—the case against Greenwood was made clear. On January 23, 1976, after five days of gruesome testimony, a Los Angeles County grand jury indicted Greenwood for eleven murders: two in 1964 and nine in the two-month spree on skid row that ended on January 31, 1975. The 1964 killings matched the pattern of the later "slasher" killings. The victims were David Russell, a sixty-four-year-old transient whose throat was cut near the public library in downtown Los Angeles, and Benjamin Hornberg, a retired sixty-seven-year-old who was stabbed to death in a downtown hotel.

Greenwood was to be returned to Los Angeles from Folsom Prison, where he was serving a thirty-two-year sentence for the 1975 attack on the two men in the Hollywood Hills house and for a burglary at the nearby home of Burt Reynolds. Investigators had found a dropped letter in Reynolds's driveway that was addressed to Greenwood and were able to track him down. The grand jury indictment on the slasher charges had been delayed by Greenwood's trial earlier in 1976 on charges stemming from the attack in the Hollywood Hills. The judge in that case had described Greenwood as a "phenomenal danger to society."

The trial on the eleven murder charges was expected to begin in the late fall of 1976, but much only-in-Hollywood drama would take place before then. Several top officials in the Los Angeles Police Department, including Assistant Chief George N. Beck, were brought up on disciplinary charges for surreptitiously having given files on the Skid Row Slasher case to a movie studio. The announcement by Police Chief Edward M. Davis came in October, but the investigation had begun in June. The *Los Angeles Times* reported, without disclosing its source, that Beck had received a loan of $42,500 "at a favorable interest rate" from Ralph Andrews Productions to develop a movie about the slasher case for Columbia Pictures. Beck had borrowed the money to build a home and had since paid it back.

The deal had been arranged by Sanford Lang, an official of Ralph Andrews Production who was also a friend of Beck's. Another police official under investigation was Lieutenant James F. Williams, who had dictated "voluminous" information about the slasher case into a tape recorder, the newspaper reported. The tapes were turned over to Lang. Columbia Pictures later fired Lang and abandoned the project. Beck was demoted one rank and suspended for ten days.

When the trial got underway in November of 1976, the testimony was grisly. Greenwood apparently had a ritual that involved drinking the blood of some of the victims. One of the most compelling witnesses was

Kenneth Ricker, who was dead. He had survived the attack by Greenwood at the house in the Hollywood Hills the day before Greenwood was finally caught. But a year later, he was shot to death at a store in Studio City. His testimony from the earlier Greenwood trial was read to the jury. Ricker told of being awakened to see Greenwood hitting his roommate, William Graham Jr., with a hatchet. Eventually, Greenwood and Graham crashed through a patio window and Ricker escaped.

Other evidence included a bloody footprint left by Greenwood near the body of one of the earlier slasher victims. All the victims had had their throats cut from ear to ear. In the end, the jury deliberated for nearly six days before convicting Greenwood of only nine of the eleven murders. They could not agree on verdicts in two of the deaths: one killing in 1964 and the first killing in the slasher series in the 1970s. Greenwood was found guilty of the first-degree murders of the following men:

- **Benjamin J. Hornberg,** 67 years old, retired. His body was found on November 14, 1964, in a restroom at the cheap downtown hotel where he lived.
- **Moses August Yakanak,** 47 years old, an Alaska Native from Anchorage. His body was found on December 8, 1974, in an alley behind a building on Broadway in downtown Los Angeles.
- **Arthur Dahlstedt,** 54 years old, a drifter. His body was found on December 11, 1974, in the doorway of a vacant building in downtown Los Angeles.
- **David Perez,** 42 years old, a drifter. His body was found on December 22, 1974, in the shrubbery near the downtown library.
- **Casimir Strawinski,** 58 years old. His body was found on January 9, 1975, by a maid where he lived at the Pickwick Apartment Hotel on Grand Avenue in Los Angeles.
- **Robert (Tex) Shannahan,** 46 years old, a truck driver. His body was found on January 15, 1975, in his room at the McDonald

Apartment Hotel on Valencia Street in Los Angeles. A wooden-handled butcher's knife was found in his left side, and his throat had been slashed. A bloody shoeprint matching that of Greenwood's shoe was found near Shannahan's body and was considered key evidence by prosecutors and, later, by the jurors in the trial.

- **Samuel Suarez,** 40 years old. His body was found on January 25, 1975, in his fifth-floor room at the Barclay Hotel on 6th Street in Los Angeles.
- **George Frias,** 45 years old, a catering clerk at the Los Angeles Hilton Hotel. His body was found, almost decapitated, on January 29, 1975, at his apartment in the Hollywood area of Los Angeles. A set of his cufflinks had been found among Greenwood's possessions.
- **Clyde C. Hay,** 34 years old, an employee of the National Cash Register Company. His body was found on January 31, 1975, in his apartment on Van Ness Avenue in Hollywood.

The jurors could not agree on a verdict in two of the deaths. The victims were:

- **David Russell,** 64, a transient. His body was found on November 13, 1964, on the steps of the Los Angeles Public Library in downtown Los Angeles.
- **Charles Jackson,** 46, from Louisiana. He had just been released from jail after serving a short sentence for drunkenness. His body was found on December 1, 1974, on the lawn of the Los Angeles Public Library.

In January of 1977, Superior Court Judge Earl C. Brody sentenced Greenwood to nine terms of life in prison and said that he hoped Greenwood "would never again be released into society." He bemoaned the fact that the law would not allow him to make the sentences consecutive. "I do not have the power to sentence him to life without parole," he said. But he noted that he was allowed to increase the minimum time that Greenwood must serve by invoking the habitual criminal statute, which took into account a defendant's history of criminal activity. That meant that Greenwood would have to wait fifteen years instead of ten before applying for parole. "His presence in any community would constitute a menace," Brody said.

Greenwood spent some years at the notorious Folsom Prison in Northern California and was denied parole repeatedly because of the brutal nature of his crimes. He was also deemed unsuitable for release because he refused to participate in any prison educational or vocational programs. He was eventually moved to the California Men's Colony in San Luis Obispo, along the Pacific coast, about halfway between Los Angeles and San Francisco. He has applied for parole frequently over the decades and has been turned down each time. The most recent hearing was on December 20, 2012, when he was sixty-eight years old. The parole board told him he could try again in fifteen years. He will be eighty-three years old in 2027.

8.
HERBERT MULLIN

As the case of Ed Kemper, the "Co-ed Killer," played out in Santa Cruz on California's Central Coast in 1973, another perplexing murder spree was coming into focus in the beleaguered city. The suspect was Herbert W. Mullin, a twenty-five-year-old who lived in a nearby town. He had been voted mostly likely to succeed by his high school classmates, but in the years after graduation in 1965, he began to change.

On January 25, 1973, Mullin drove to the home of Jim Gianera, who was twenty-five years old, and his wife, Joan, who was twenty-one, in the Santa Cruz Mountains. Jim had been a friend of Mullin's when they were in high school and later sold him illegal drugs. Mullin shot them both to death.

Earlier that same day, Mullin had driven to a cabin in the mountains where Gianera had lived previously but that was now occupied by Kathleen Francis, twenty-nine years old, and her sons, nine-year-old Michael and four-year-old Damion. Francis gave Mullin Gianera's new address. Mullin returned later in the day and killed Francis and her sons.

On February 10, 1973, Robert Spector, eighteen years old, Brian Card, nineteen years old, David Oliker, eighteen years old, and Mark Dreibelbis, fifteen years old, were staying in a makeshift cabin in a remote area of Santa Cruz. Mullin was hiking in the area when he came across the cabin. He shot each of the teens in the head fatally.

On February 13, 1973, Fred Perez, seventy-two years old, was working in his yard in Santa Cruz. Mullin, driving by in a station wagon with a load of firewood for his parents, saw Perez and shot him to death.

By the time investigators found the bodies of the four teenagers in the blood-spattered cabin in February of 1973, Mullin had already been arrested and charged with six murders. Within a month, he would be charged with four more, setting the stage for his eventual trial on ten murder charges.

He was also the clear suspect in three other deaths. On October 13, 1972, Mullin saw a man walking along a deserted stretch of highway. Mullin stopped and asked the man to help him, saying that he was having a problem with his car. The man took a look under the hood, and Mullin beat him to death with a baseball bat. He pulled the man's body off to the side of the road and left it there. Lawrence White, fifty-five years old, was considered the first of Mullin's thirteen victims.

On October 24, 1972, Mary Guilfoyle, a twenty-four-year-old student at a community college near Santa Cruz, was hitchhiking when Mullin offered her a ride. She got into his car and he stabbed her to death. He then dumped her body in the mountains. Her skeletal remains were found four months later. She was believed to be his second victim.

On November 2, 1972, Henri Tomei, a sixty-four-year-old Roman Catholic priest, was hearing confessions at St. Mary's Church in Los Gatos. Mullin stabbed him to death in the confessional, making him the third victim.

In May of 1973, a judge found Mullin sane and capable of standing trial on ten murders. Mullin had turned twenty-six by the time the legal wrangling over how to proceed with the case was worked out. In July of 1973, the California Court of Appeals ruled that, for the first time in the state's history, jury selection could be held in secret. Both the defense and the prosecution had made the request. The trial judge, Charles Franich, barred the public and news reporters from the sessions. He said this would allow some privacy for prospective jurors to answer questions about their views on homosexuality and mental illness.

Questions about their opinions on the subjects would quite likely come up during jury selection.

As he awaited trial, Mullin had spent much of his time composing a detailed autobiography in which he said he believed that his parents, as well as 95 percent of the population, were bisexual. He also wrote that he should have been given oral sex by a man when he was a child. He was drawn to men, but his first homosexual experience filled him with self-loathing. As a Catholic, he believed it was a sin, and he feared for his immortal soul.

"I may be wrong about this," Franich said, "but one has to take a few chances in life, and I'm hopeful this procedure will eliminate any evasiveness we see in courtrooms. We have too often worried about the comforts of the judge, defense, and prosecution, but seldom about the jurors. These people serve for five dollars a day plus travel expenses one way, and I think they deserve some consideration." Ultimately, the California Supreme Court upheld the closed questioning.

Like Edmund Kemper, Mullin had pleaded both not guilty and not guilty by reason of insanity. He took the witness stand in his own defense and admitted that he had killed thirteen people, although at the time of the trial he was charged with killing only ten. It was all his father's fault, he told the jury. His father, he said, "drove me kill crazy." He said he received telepathic messages that made him kill. One of those messages came to him when he was at a Roman Catholic church in the area. He had gone there "for reflection to get enough strength never to kill again." He saw a light in a confessional, he said, and got a telepathic message from himself. "I suddenly realized I could think," he said. "Well if you're in here, I guess I should kill you."

When the priest, Reverend Tomei, walked out of the confessional, "I thrust the knife through his chest," Mullin said. Then he kicked the priest in the head and stabbed him two more times. Asked whether the priest said anything, Mullin responded, "Bonjour." He also blamed the murders on "the killjoy sadism" of his family and friends. The murder of the priest, he said, was intended to prevent an earthquake from destroying California. Prompted by his defense attorney to describe the other killings, he offered similarly incoherent accounts.

When it was time for closing arguments, Mullin's lawyer, James Jackson, a public defender, described his client as "utterly mad." He had been diagnosed as a paranoid schizophrenic. Chris Cottle, the prosecutor, argued that Mullin's efforts to avoid detection showed that he knew right from wrong and was therefore legally sane. The real question before the jury was whether Mullin was legally insane or just mentally ill. And what was the difference? Two days later, the jury rejected the "legally insane" argument and found Mullin guilty of ten murders in a three-week spree.

Jackson said the verdict was "as insane as Mullin is." When Mullin was sentenced in September, the judge gave him the maximum: life in prison for two of the murders and five years to life for the other eight. Jackson said his client was "stark raving mad" and filed a notice of appeal. In December of 1973, Mullin withdrew his insanity plea in the case of the Catholic priest and was convicted of that murder too. The White and Guilfoyle cases never went to trial.

A particularly unusual aspect of Mullin's case was that all the experts for the defense and for the prosecution agreed on the diagnosis: paranoid schizophrenia. One of the defense experts was Donald T. Lunde, the Stanford University psychiatrist who had also worked on the Kemper case (see Chapter 4). Lunde spent many hours interviewing Mullin's family; he also interviewed Mullin himself in his jail cell. Mullin had a fundamental belief that throughout history, human beings had protected the continents from "cataclysmic earthquakes" by killing people, Lunde wrote in his book *Murder and Madness.* Murder was a way of demonstrating to the "great Creator" that humans were willing to die if it meant that "He" would keep the continents intact. Mullin explained that "murder decreases the number of natural disasters and the extent of the devastation of these disasters; therefore, we will always murder." According to Lunde, Mullin believed that "he had no more control over his actions than a falling rock does over gravity."

Mullin had killed thirteen people between October of 1972 and February of 1973 in an attempt to avert the great earthquake. He believed, therefore, that he had saved thousands of lives. During the trial, Mullin explained his theory to the jury. "You read in the Bible about Jonah. . . . Jonah stood up and said, 'If somebody doesn't die, you know, all thirteen of us are going to die.' And he jumped overboard . . . and he was drowned. . . . And the sea . . . in about a half hour or so it calmed down. . . . And so they get to town and they go to a bar and they tell the people in the bar about Jonah, and they say, 'We think Jonah saved our life by committing suicide,' and the people at the bar say, 'Well, maybe that will help us,' so they go out and kill somebody. So the story goes."

Mullin's parents said he had been a normal child who was born on April 18, 1947, after his father returned from World War II. Mullin's father had been a company commander in an automatic weapons battalion. In later years, Mullin attached great significance to his birthdate, according to Dr. Lunde. The great San Francisco earthquake occurred on April 18, 1906, and Albert Einstein died on April 19, 1955. Einstein's death, Mullin believed, had somehow prevented him from being killed in Vietnam. (Lunde said he was never able to make sense of Mullin's rambling explanation of how the two events might be connected.) After completing a two-year engineering program at a community college, Mullin began to change significantly. He decided to study comparative religions and began experimenting with LSD. He also got himself declared a conscientious objector to avoid being drafted, and he began working at Goodwill Industries.

Mullin quit the Goodwill job in early 1969 and announced that he was moving to India to study religion. But his parents, worried about his mental health, persuaded him to move north to work on the Christmas tree farm owned by his sister and her husband. A month later, the family gathered at the farm for a dinner. The family was shocked by Herbert's behavior. Whenever his brother-in-law, Al, picked up a fork or spoke, Herbert picked up a fork or repeated exactly what Al had said. It took a day, but the family persuaded Herbert to admit himself to the nearest

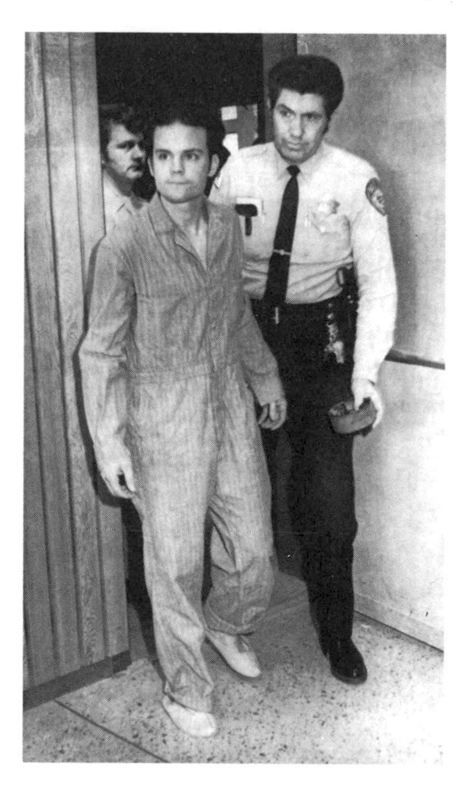

HERBERT MULLIN SHOWN LEAVING COURT AFTER BEING ARRAIGNED IN 1973 ON CHARGES OF MURDERING SIX PERSONS.

mental hospital. That was March 30, 1969. But Mullin did not like being there and did little to cooperate with the staff. Against recommendations, he discharged himself on May 9, 1969. His prognosis was poor.

He drifted around for a while, staying here and there. He began hearing voices. One instructed him to shave his head. He obeyed. Another told him to burn his penis. He obeyed, with a lighted cigarette. By the end of October, he was forcibly committed to a mental hospital. He was discharged a month later. His prognosis was "grave." He was in and out of mental hospitals over the following year and eventually moved to San Francisco. Evicted from his hotel room in 1972, he returned to his parents' home. But with state mental hospitals being phased out under Governor Ronald Reagan's administration, his parents were unable to find a place to have their son committed.

After the guilty verdict in Mullin's trial for ten of the murders was read in court on August 20, 1973, the jury foreman, Ken Springer, wrote an open letter to Governor Reagan and the California legislature. It said, in part: "I hold the state executive and state legislative offices as responsible for these ten lives as I do the defendant himself—none of this need ever have happened.

"We had the awesome task of convicting one of our young valley residents of a crime that only an individual with a mental discrepancy could have committed. Five times prior to young Mr. Mullin's arrest he was entered into mental facilities. At least twice it was determined that his illness could cause danger to lives of human beings. Yet, in January and February of this year he was free to take the lives of Santa Cruz County residents. . . .

"In recent years, mental hospitals all over this state have been closed down in an economy move by the Reagan administration. Where do you think these mental institution patients who were in these hospitals went after their release? Do you suppose they went to private, costly mental hospitals? Or do you suppose they went to the ghettos of our large cities and to the remote hills of Santa Cruz County? We know where Edmund Kemper went when he was released from a state mental institution!

"I freely admit that I write this at a time when my emotions are not as clearly controlled as perhaps I would like them to be, but I cannot wait longer to impart to anyone who may read this that my convictions that the laws surrounding mental illness in the State of California are wrong, wrong, wrong.

"Don't let another person in our country lose his life because our governor needs a balanced budget. Please, please write."

Mullin was sent to San Quentin Prison. Because he was found legally sane, he was receiving no meaningful treatment or therapy, Lunde wrote in his 1980 book, *The Die Song: A Journey into the Mind of a Mass Murderer.* Mullin was eventually sent first to Vacaville and later to Mule Creek State Prison, in Ione, California, near Sacramento. He has applied for parole seven times since his conviction and has been turned down each time. The last rejection came in 2011. Mullin has been told he can try again in 2021.

9.
THE ZEBRA KILLERS

California residents were jolted by a baffling crime threat in early 1974. At the end of January, seemingly out of the blue, police announced that "black gunmen" cruising around San Francisco in cars at night had killed four white people and wounded another, apparently at random. Precisely what had happened was unclear. Witnesses had given differing descriptions of the gunmen. At least two were involved, and they had taken turns as driver and shooter. It was possible that they had used two different cars.

The details were especially chilling. The shootings—four separate incidents—happened between about 8 p.m. and 10 p.m. in residential neighborhoods near the downtown area. Each time, a gunman had approached a lone person and, usually without saying a word, fired his gun before fleeing in a Cadillac waiting nearby. The victims were a thirty-year-old woman, a sixty-nine-year-old man, an eighty-year-old man, and a forty-five-year-old woman. Three had been shot twice in the back. A fifth victim, a twenty-three-year-old woman, was shot twice but survived. An official said the police were beginning what would be the biggest manhunt in the city's history.

Police officers and investigators began to keep a close watch around the city. They stayed in constant touch with each other on their shortwave radio systems. The bands on the systems were named for the letters of the alphabet. They chose band Z—as in zebra—for their secret communications about what they began calling "Operation Zebra." Some black residents were suspicious of the "Zebra" designation and speculated about a possible racial insult suggested by the name. But the news media quickly picked up on the jargon and began referring to the investigation as the "Zebra Murders." Television stations soon got to work and sent crews out at night to record the empty streets. Rumors began to circulate that an unnamed black sect was to blame, and people feared that it was the beginning of a race war.

By mid-April, the toll had reached eleven dead and six wounded. Officials revised their thinking to include two shootings that occurred the previous November. That did little to calm the nerves of an increasingly anxious city. At a news conference, Chief of Inspectors Charles Barca called the killings "senseless and vicious" and said the unknown shooters were "sick" and "mentally disturbed." Investigators had "no idea" about the motive for the shootings, he said, adding, "We're not any closer to nailing a suspect than last November." The latest shooting had occurred at 9:20 p.m. on April 14. Two white teenagers were hitchhiking near a bus stop when they were shot and wounded for no apparent reason. The shooter was described as a black man, about thirty years old, with a distinctive gold tooth, a beard, and a mustache. Zebra case investigators patrolling the area had noticed the teenagers shortly before they were shot. Both of the victims survived.

Two days later, the death toll reached twelve. Nelson T. Shields IV, the twenty-three-year-old son of a DuPont Company executive, went to a quiet neighborhood in San Francisco to help a friend pick up a rug. When the friend went into the house to get it, Shields stayed outside near the station wagon they were to use to transport the rug. Then there were three gunshots. "I ran outside and I heard Nick moan," the friend said. "But he was dead when I reached him." A neighbor told the police she had seen a black man running up the street.

That shooting was a turning point. The next day, San Francisco's mayor, Joseph Alioto, held a press conference and said, "Extraordinary situations like this call for extraordinary measures." He announced that the police planned to stop and frisk any black people fitting the descriptions of the suspects. "In the very nature of things," he said, "we are going to be stopping a lot of innocent people." He appealed for calm. Paul Halvonik, a lawyer for the American Civil Liberties Union, said the searches were "clearly indefensible" and vowed to take the matter to court. Amital Schwartz, the head of a group studying police practices for the ACLU and the National Association for the Advancement of Colored People (the NAACP), protested saying, "What is essentially happening is that individual policemen, with their inevitable racist tendencies, are out on the streets with a carte blanche to stop any black man and treat him as they see fit in their own discretion." Bobby Seale, the head of the Black Panthers, called Alioto's order "vicious and racist."

SAN FRANCISCO MAYOR JOSEPH ALIOTO ANNOUNCING ARRESTS IN THE ZEBRA KILLERS CASE.

The following day there was another attack. A man claiming to be the Zebra killer entered a two-story home at about midnight and, using a hammer and a chair, beat to death the twenty-five-year-old man he found in the first-floor living room. Then he went upstairs and beat and raped the man's twenty-four-year-old wife. She was able to stagger onto a balcony and call for help.

The legal wrangling began in earnest about a week later. A federal judge in San Francisco ordered the police to immediately halt their practice of stopping black men who resembled the profiles they had drawn up of the Zebra killers. He said that he believed the police had acted in good faith but that the searches violated the constitutional rights of the people the police stopped. A few days later, Mayor Alioto upped the ante. He announced that new information had linked the Zebra killers to eighty or more murders all over California since 1970. An informant, whom he would not identify, had given investigators information about killings in Long Beach, Oakland, and Sacramento, Alioto said. Alioto was running for the Democratic nomination for governor of California at the time, and his words were met with some skepticism by police departments in other parts of California.

The mysterious murder spree had pushed the residents of the San Francisco Bay Area into a state of bewilderment and helplessness by the spring of 1974. Robert Kistler, a writer for the *Los Angeles Times,* summed things up: "It has reduced tough, craggy veterans of law enforcement to helpless sputterers of, 'We don't know. We just don't know!' when pressed to explain the mayhem. It has driven steely, nameless fear into the over-the-shoulder glances of even daytime pedestrians in this city, a densely populated metropolis which has traditionally proclaimed itself the most 'sophisticated' in the land."

Things came into clearer and more frightening focus on May 1. In the early hours, more than one hundred San Francisco officers had broken down the doors at an undisclosed location and arrested seven black men who were then charged with suspicion of conspiracy to murder, Alioto announced at a packed press conference in his office. "I am satisfied that we have the men," Alioto said. "The ringleaders who perpetrated the wave of terror in San Francisco are now behind bars." These were the Zebra killers. They were part of a statewide group called Death Angels that was "kind of a reversal of the Ku Klux Klan," according to Alioto. And some of the members were "fanatical believers in black separatism." They reported to a leader in a Midwestern city Alioto would not name. The killers, he said, preyed on hitchhikers and got special credit from their leader for decapitation and other particularly gruesome acts.

On Thursday, May 2, the situation turned chaotic. Four of the men who had been arrested were abruptly released from custody for lack of evidence. That left three: Manuel Moore, who was twenty-nine years old, and J. C. Simon, who was twenty-eight, were charged with the murder of an eighty-one-year-old man who was shot as he was crossing a street in Berkeley the previous December and with the murder of a woman who was shot to death in a Berkeley laundromat in January. Larry C. Green, who was twenty-two, was charged with murder, robbery, and kidnapping in the decapitation killing of a woman and the attack on her husband, who survived. On an evening in the previous October, the couple had been walking near their apartment in the Telegraph Hill area of San Francisco when they were ordered into a white van and driven away.

On Friday, when Moore, Simon, and Green made their first appearance in court, Judge Agnes O'Brien Smith issued a gag order barring police and any other officials connected with the case from making public statements about the matter. She included Mayor Alioto. A week later, she extended the order to include the news media. An appeals court quickly overturned the media ban.

Alioto lost the Democratic primary race for governor that spring. He had been roundly criticized by his opponents for ordering the broad stop-and-search of black men.

In June, it became clear that an informant, Anthony C. Harris, had testified to a grand jury that members of the "black militant" group called Death Angels took pictures of each other murdering white people so that they could win promotions. He said that he went along on ten of the murder missions but did not take part. He told the grand jury that the Death Angels had more than two thousand members across the country. They got special credit for mutilations, he said. His testimony had led to the indictment of four black men: Larry C. Green, J. C. Simon, Manuel Moore, and Jessie Cooks, twenty-eight years old.

It was nearly a year before the trial began in March of 1975. All four defendants, black men, were now charged with three murders and four assaults. All the victims were white. The defendants also faced the broader charge of conspiracy in the deaths of thirteen white people and the wounding of seven others during the Zebra killing spree. Cooks was already serving a life sentence in San Quentin for a murder in San Francisco. All four defendants were members of the Nation of Islam, a religious group commonly called the Black Muslims.

The victims were:

- **Quita Hague,** twenty-nine years old, was walking with her husband Richard near their home on Telegraph Hill on October 20, 1973, when she was kidnapped in a van and nearly decapitated with a machete. Her body was found near railroad tracks.
- **Richard Hague,** thirty years old, was kidnapped along with his wife, but he was thrown out of the van after being attacked with the machete. He was seriously injured, but survived.
- **Linda Lou Enger,** a twenty-seven-year-old college student, was walking to her apartment on Waller Street at about 8:30 p.m. on

October 23, 1973, when she was followed by a man who grabbed her, put a gun to her neck, and forced her to walk to a park. He threatened to kill her, but she was able to persuade him to let her go.

- **Frances Rose,** twenty-eight years old, was shot to death in her car at about 9 p.m on October 30, 1973, near the University of California Extension on Laguna Street.
- **Saleem Erakat,** fifty-three years old; owned Erakat's Grocery and Delicatessen near City Hall. He was shot in the head on November 25, 1973. His body was found in a back room at the store.
- **Paul Roman Dancik,** twenty-six years old, was walking with a friend on a sidewalk about fourteen blocks from City Hall on the evening of December 11, 1973, when a man fired four shots before jumping into a waiting car and being driven away. Dancik died of a chest wound.
- **Arthur C. Agnos,** thirty-six years old, was hit by two of three shots fired at him on December 13, 1973, on a sidewalk in the Potrero district on the east side of the city. He was seriously wounded, but he survived.
- **Marietta Di Girolamo,** thirty-one years old, was shot to death about ninety minutes later near her apartment, about fourteen blocks from Erakat's grocery store. A man had walked up to her, fired three shots into her abdomen, and walked away.
- **Ilario Bertuccio,** eighty-one years old, was crossing a street in the Bay View area on December 20, 1973, when he was shot four times. He died at the scene. A witness saw a man run to a car and jump in. The driver, who had been waiting there, sped off.
- **Theresa DeMartini,** twenty years old, was shot two hours later in the Fillmore area. She was hit three times but survived. The shooter jumped into a waiting car, and the driver sped off.
- **Neal Moynihan,** nineteen years old, was walking in the City Hall area on the evening of December 22, 1973, when he was shot and killed.

- **Mildred Hosler,** fifty years old, was shot and killed a few minutes later, not far from where Moynihan had been shot.
- **Tana Smith,** thirty-two years old, was walking in her neighborhood on the evening of January 28, 1974, not far from the Zion Hospital campus, when she was shot twice in the abdomen and killed.
- **Vincent R. Wollin,** sixty-nine years old, was walking on the evening of January 28 near the rest home where he lived. He was about eight blocks away from where Smith had been shot ten minutes earlier. It was his birthday, and other residents were waiting inside for a celebration. He was near the front door when he was shot twice in the back at close range. The residents heard the shots. Wollin died four hours later at a hospital.
- **John Bambic,** eighty-four years old, was near Ninth Street and Howard Street about an hour later on January 28. He was about ten minutes away from where Wollin and Smith had been shot. He was shot twice in the back and died instantly.
- **Jane Holly,** forty-five years old, was taking her clothes out of a washing machine at a laundromat on January 28 when she was shot twice in the back. She died later in a hospital. The shooting happened about three miles south of the site of the Bambic shooting. Witnesses at the laundromat, all of them black, told the police that she had been the only white person there.
- **Roxanne McMillan,** twenty-three years old, was taking some things out of the family car, which was parked in front of their home about twenty blocks away from where Jane Holly had just been shot. As she walked toward the house, a man walked up to her. She said "hello," and he shot her twice—once in the chest and once in the back. She survived.
- **Thomas Rainwater,** nineteen years old, was walking to a market on Geary Street at about 9 p.m on April 1, 1974, when he was shot twice in the back. He died instantly.

- **Linda Story,** twenty-one years old, was walking with Rainwater on April 1, 1974. She, too, was shot twice in the back, but she survived.
- **Ward Anderson,** eighteen years old, was waiting for a bus at Hayes and Fillmore Streets at about 9 p.m. on April 14, 1974. He was shot twice, but survived.
- **Terry White,** fifteen years old, was waiting at the bus stop with Anderson on April 14, 1974. He, too, was shot twice and survived.
- **Nelson Shields,** twenty-three years old, was helping a friend drop off a carpet on Vernon Street at about 9:30 p.m. on April 16, 1974, when he was shot in the back three times. He died instantly.

It promised to be a complex trial. Some defendants were also charged with kidnapping and robbery, and each had his own attorney, meaning that each prosecution witness could be cross-examined four times. The Nation of Islam paid the fees for three of the four defense attorneys. A key witness for the prosecution was Anthony Cornelius Harris, who testified that while he was serving time in San Quentin in 1970, Cooks had told him about the Death Angels, a cult that had two thousand members and was planning to "start a race war" and to kill "white devils." On the witness stand for twelve days, Harris testified that after he got out of prison he had met with other members of the Death Angels, including J. C. Simon, who told him that a black person would

ARTHUR C. AGNOS WHO WAS WOUNDED BY THE ZEBRA KILLERS ON DECEMBER 13, 1973. HE WAS ELECTED MAYOR OF SAN FRANCISCO IN 1988.

have to kill four white children or as many as six whites in order to become a member. Harris said that he had accompanied the defendants as they killed white people, but he denied that he had killed anyone. In return for his testimony, Harris was granted immunity; he also received some of the reward money, along with new identities for himself, his girlfriend, and her child.

The trial went on for more than a year. Finally, testimony and closing arguments ended, and the jury began its deliberations. The jurors had heard the testimony of 181 witnesses and viewed 348 exhibits. During that year, the trial had been put on hold for a week so that one juror, a black woman, could deliver her baby. There was one black man on the jury, and the rest were Asian or white. The jury reached its verdicts on March 13, 1976, on their fourth day of deliberation. All four men were found guilty of at least one murder and of conspiracy to commit murder. They were later sentenced to life in prison, bringing to an end what was then, at just over one year, the longest criminal trial in California history.

But it was not necessarily the most infamous trial of the time. In an odd coincidence, the Zebra case jurors were housed each night during their deliberations at a local motel where the jurors in the Patricia Hearst trial were staying. Patty Hearst, as she was known, was a nineteen-year-old sophomore at the University of California's Berkeley campus when she was kidnapped from her apartment on February 4, 1974. This, too, was a sign of the tumultuous political times. Her dramatic saga played out over the next three years like a Netflix series, long before anyone had dreamed up Netflix.

Hearst was the daughter of the ultra-wealthy publishing tycoon William Randolph Hearst, whose life had been the inspiration for Orson Welles' character in the movie *Citizen Kane*. Patty, screaming and half-naked, had been taken off into the night by the Symbionese Liberation Army, a little-known radical group. Soon, her captors demanded that her father put up $230 million worth of food to feed the poor. In a tape recording sent to her father, Patty called herself a "prisoner of war."

Over nineteen months, Patty Hearst was repeatedly raped and brutalized by her captors. Eventually, she became radicalized, joined the SLA, and changed her name to "Tania." During that time, she accompanied members of the group as they robbed a bank in San Francisco. The action was caught on a closed-circuit camera, which caught images of her wielding an automatic rifle. After another violent incident at a sporting goods store, Hearst and some of the SLA members went into hiding. They were finally captured by the FBI in San Francisco on September 18, 1975. Hearst was ultimately convicted of bank robbery and sentenced to seven years in prison. She was freed on bond for a time as her conviction was appealed. In 1979, President Jimmy Carter commuted her sentence, and she was released after having served twenty-three months. President Bill Clinton made it a full pardon in 2001.

10.

KENNETH BIANCHI AND ANGELO BUONO

The bodies started turning up in the middle of October in 1977. Before the end of the year, the killer had a nickname: the Hillside Strangler. Someone had been murdering girls and young women in the Los Angeles area, and the toll had reached eleven. Police were unsure whether several other murders were connected. Most of the victims had been found naked, not far from the edges of highways in the suburbs just north of the city. The youngest was twelve, and the oldest was twenty-eight. The "Summer of Sam" had just ended on the East Coast, and now a similar wave of terror was erupting three thousand miles to the west.

Officials quickly formed the Hillside Strangler Task Force using investigators from local police departments as well as from the Los Angeles County Sheriff's Office. More than forty officers were working on the baffling cases as 1978 began. Rewards totaling $125,000 were being offered for any useful information.

The eleventh victim was Kimberly Diane Martin, a seventeen-year-old who worked for a massage parlor that ran an outcall prostitution business. She was heard screaming at a Hollywood apartment building on the evening of December 13. Her nude body was found the next day about fifteen feet down a slope in the Silver Lake area of Los Angeles. Like the others, she had been strangled. Detectives traced the telephone call that had led her to the apartment building and found that it had come from a pay phone at the Hollywood branch of the Los Angeles Public Library.

In Los Angeles, there was no media frenzy like the tabloid newspaper battle that had besieged New York City months earlier, but there was a simmering fear. In the neighborhoods where most of the bodies were found, "almost every woman you meet says she is afraid for her life," the *Los Angeles Times* reported. Women needed to know how to defend themselves, a personal defense teacher said. "No woman can pull a man's hands off her throat," the teacher said, but a woman could do "simple things, like eye gouges, groin pulls and simple kicks." She planned to hold a special Saturday class for the general public at the California State University campus in Los Angeles. Sixty-five women of all ages showed up—a second class had to be planned for the overflow. A special Strangler hotline set up at the Los Angeles police headquarters was flooded with calls.

One call came from Ned York, a thirty-seven-year-old television actor. He confessed that he was the Hillside Strangler. Investigators didn't take him seriously until he mentioned a friend who knew one of the victims. York was arrested at his home on February 8 and brought into police headquarters wearing only blue bathing trunks. He fell asleep while police were questioning him. When he was released two days later, he told the more than thirty reporters and photographers waiting outside that he had been using angel dust. Angel dust is the street name for phencyclidine, also known as PCP, which causes hallucinations. The Hillside Strangler Task Force was frustrated. "If we had a real good suspect, we'd be having the Goodyear Blimp going by with his name splashed all over the side," Dan Cooke, a lieutenant on the case, said. "We'd be shooting off rockets."

Within a week, the killer had struck again. On February 15, the nude body of twenty-year-old Cindy Lee Hudspeth was found in the trunk of her car at the bottom of an embankment near a road north of Los Angeles. She appeared to have been strangled. Police were saying little about the case, but Hudspeth's neighbors in the Silver Lake area described her as an aspiring actress who was working as a waitress while attending classes at Glendale Community College. And she loved the disco dancing that was highly popular at the time.

Suspects emerged in the following months, but investigators seemed to hit only dead ends. In May, the Strangler Task Force was reduced from thirty-five investigators to twenty-four. At its peak, the task force had 134 investigators.

Eight months later, things changed. On January 12, 1979, Kenneth Bianchi, a twenty-seven-year-old security guard, was arrested on a burglary charge in Bellingham, Washington, not far from the Canadian border. He was also a suspect in the strangulation murders of two young women in the area. Hillside Strangler investigators quickly flew to Washington to interview Bianchi, who had lived in the Los Angeles area when all thirteen of the Strangler murders were committed. In fact, Bianchi had moved several times in the Los Angeles area and had rented apartments near where three of the victims lived when they were murdered. He had also worked for a real estate title firm where the sister of the fourth victim worked. Bianchi's forty-four-year-old cousin, Angelo Buono, who owned an upholstery shop in Glendale, was also being investigated by the Strangler team.

Bianchi had grown up in a suburb of Rochester, New York, and had only a minor run-in with the police there. When he was sixteen, he married a high school classmate—over his mother's objections. The marriage was annulled, but an argument between Bianchi and his mother two years later turned violent, and police were called to their home. Kenneth was not arrested. He got a gun permit in 1972 and bought a pistol that he sometimes carried in his back pocket. He applied for a police training program but was rejected. In 1975, he moved to California and stayed with Buono for a while, eventually getting the job with the real estate title company. He dated many women, including a coworker at the title company, Kerri Kaye Boyd, who became pregnant with their child. Boyd moved back to her hometown of Bellingham, and Bianchi later moved there too.

Two weeks after his arrest in Bellingham, Bianchi was charged with the murders of twenty-two-year-old Karen Mandic and twenty-seven-year-old Diane Wilder, both students at Western Washington University in Bellingham. Their bodies had been found on January 12, stuffed into the back of a car. At the end of March, Bianchi, wearing a bulletproof vest, was brought to court in Bellingham. He pleaded not guilty by reason of insanity to the two murder charges. By then, he was clearly a suspect in the Hillside Strangler murders, but Los Angeles investigators had decided to let the case in Bellingham play out before proceeding with charges.

Bianchi's insanity plea was based partly on an examination by Dr. Donald Lunde, the Stanford University professor who had been involved in the cases of other California serial killers earlier in the 1970s. Lunde had testified as an expert witness for the defense in the case of Herbert W. Mullin (see Chapter 8) and had examined Edmund Kemper (see Chapter 4). Soon after Bianchi's arrest in 1979, his lawyer contacted Lunde to ask for his help, and in July, Lunde traveled to Bellingham to interview Bianchi.

Lunde and Bianchi covered many topics, and Bianchi's memory "worked like a charm," Lunde later wrote in his book *Hearst to Hughes: Memoir of a Forensic Psychiatrist.* Lunde asked Bianchi to describe his feelings at the times of the murders. Bianchi replied, "I've always felt a great anger—I mean a really intense, horrifying, just cut-loose anger. I've put the reasons for the killings, my motivation prior to and during the killings, in three categories. One category is meanness, the second one is sexual arousal—having sex knowing that the end product is going to be the killing itself—that being a source of arousal also, and third is because—this is terrible—this is in no way disrespect for the girls—but dead people tell no tales. No witnesses."

Lunde noted that Bianchi's behavior did not include delusions, hallucinations, or other signs of severe mental illness. "His behavior was despicable and abnormal, but it wasn't clear whether he was mad or bad," Lunde wrote. In that interview and a series of others that followed, Bianchi provided "a tremendous amount of information" about how he and his cousin, Angelo Buono, "went about their gruesome activities." The information was useful to the police, and it was also a good bargaining tool for Bianchi, Lunde noted. Bianchi began to negotiate a plea bargain that would implicate Buono in exchange for lenience in his own sentencing, with prosecutors agreeing to drop any death penalty request for Bianchi.

On April 21, the Hillside Strangler Task Force descended on Buono's home and the adjoining upholstery shop in Glendale. Investigators told reporters who showed up outside that Buono was not a suspect. Two days later, Daryl F. Gates, the Los Angeles police chief, announced that the department was seeking murder charges against Bianchi for ten of the thirteen Hillside Strangler killings. The victims are listed below.

- **Yolanda Washington,** nineteen years old. Her body was found in the afternoon on October 18, 1977, in the Griffith Park area.
- **Judith Lynn Miller,** fifteen years old. Her body was found nude and strangled on October 31, 1977, in La Crescenta.
- **Elissa Teresa Kastin,** twenty-one years old. Her body was found nude and strangled on November 6, 1977, in Glendale.

- **Kristina Weckler,** twenty years old. Her body was found on November 20, 1977, strangled and nude, in Highland Park.
- **Sonja Johnson,** fourteen years old. Her body was found on November 20, 1977, near Elysian Park, strangled and nude.
- **Dolores Cepeda,** twelve years old. Her body was found on November 20, 1977, near Sonja Johnson's in Elysian Park.
- **Evelyn Jane King,** twenty-eight years old. Her body was found on November 23, 1977, in Griffith Park, strangled and nude.
- **Lauren Rae Wagner,** eighteen years old. Her body was found on November 29, 1977, near Mt. Washington, strangled and nude.
- **Kimberly Diane Martin,** seventeen years old. Her body was found on December 14, 1977, near Silver Lake.
- **Cindy Lee Hudspeth,** twenty years old. Her body was found on February 17, 1978, near La Canada.

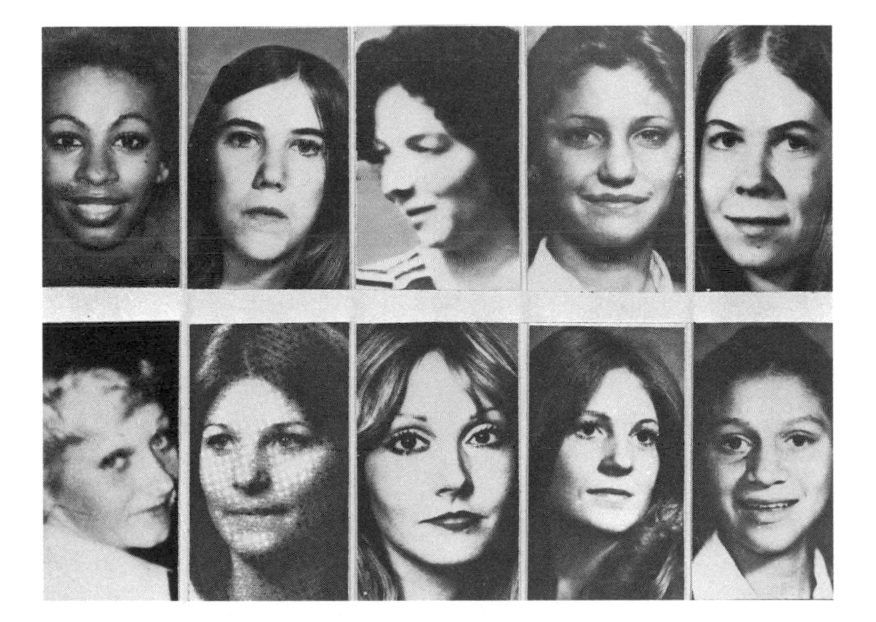

THE TEN CONFIRMED VICTIMS OF THE HILLSIDE STRANGLER. TOP ROW, FROM LEFT: YOLANDA WASHINGTON, JUDITH LYNN MILLER, ELISSA TERESA KASTIN, KRISTINA WECKLER, SONJA JOHNSON. BOTTOM ROW, FROM LEFT: KIMBERLY DIANE MARTIN, CINDY LEE HUDSPETH, EVELYN JANE KING, LAUREN RAE WAGNER, DOLORES CEPEDA.

With Bianchi a thousand miles away in northern Washington, Los Angeles investigators and news media focused on Buono. At a news conference on May 9, 1979, the Los Angeles County district attorney, John Van de Kamp, said Buono was a "central" and "very important" suspect in the case. When Buono heard about the press conference, he decided to break his silence and defend himself. "The only thing I have to say is I haven't did nothing," he told the *Los Angeles Times*. "They [investigators] can do anything they want, but they won't find nothing 'cause I ain't did nothing." The *Times* story described Buono as a "ruggedly handsome" forty-four-year-old who considered himself "something of a lady's man." He had been married three times and had six children. Buono complained that the untrue statements made about him by the Hillside Strangler investigators had destroyed his automotive upholstery business. "The phone don't ring anymore. Nobody comes in. As a businessman, I'm dead."

Five months later, at 9:45 a.m. on October 19, Bianchi agreed to drop his insanity defense in Washington and plead guilty to the murders of Karen Mandic and Diane Wilder, the two young victims in Bellingham, and to the murders of five of the Hillside Strangler victims. In return, the Washington prosecutors agreed not to pursue the death penalty. Instead, Bianchi was sentenced to two consecutive life terms in prison. "I can't find the words to express the sorrow for what I have done," he told the judge. "In no way can I take away the pain I have given to others, and in no way can I expect forgiveness." He wept during the brief courtroom appearance.

Thirty minutes later, Buono was arrested at his upholstery shop in Glendale and charged with ten of the Hillside Strangler murders. Bianchi had indeed gotten his plea bargain in Washington by flipping on his cousin. The following week, Bianchi was brought before a judge in Los Angeles and pleaded guilty to five of the Hillside Strangler murders, a conspiracy charge, and a sodomy charge. He was sentenced to six life terms in prison, but under California law, the sentences would be served concurrently, and parole would be possible after seven years. Bianchi remained in Los Angeles for a time to help prosecutors and detectives retrace the murders in preparation for Buono's trial. On nighttime trips, Bianchi pointed out the locations of the murders and the sites where the victims' bodies were taken. Nearly all had been murdered at Buono's house, he told the investigators.

One potential victim had been given a pass. In the fall of 1977, Bianchi and Buono were looking for a potential victim when they saw a young woman walking along a street in Hollywood. Posing as undercover police officers, they confronted the woman, flashed phony police badges, and demanded that she show them some identification. As the woman searched through her wallet, they noticed a photograph of the woman with her father. They realized that her father was Peter Lorre, the famous movie actor who often played murderous villains. Bianchi and Buono had intended to order her into their car, but they changed their minds and let her go. After hearing the story from Buono in late 1979, investigators tracked down Catherine Lorre and she confirmed the incident but said she had no idea who the two were or what they had planned.

Somewhat arcane legal proceedings went on behind closed doors well into 1980, but bits of information leaked out. The *Los Angeles Times* learned that Warren Schmuki, an aide to one of the county supervisors, had given Bianchi the official county police sticker that he'd put on the windshield of his Cadillac and used to persuade victims to get into the car. Schmuki told detectives that he had had work done on one of his cars at Buono's auto upholstery shop in 1977 and was introduced to Bianchi there. They chatted, and Bianchi admired the official seal on the windshield of Schmuki's car. Bianchi asked how he could get such a shield, and Schmuki later sent him one through the mail. Detectives called the car the "murdermobile."

The legal proceedings dragged on into 1981, with the news media barred from the courtroom and the participants silenced by a gag order. Word got out that Bianchi had suddenly reversed himself and denied that he had taken part in the killings. If he stuck to that story, prosecutors would have little evidence to present against Buono. By the end of 1980, Bianchi had reversed himself again and testified against Buono, thereby living up to the plea bargain that would keep him from dying in a California gas chamber. He spent eight weeks on the witness stand before the preliminary hearing—the longest in California history—ended in March of 1981.

The trial was set to begin in September, but in July prosecutors announced that they were going to drop the charges. Bianchi's story had been shifting; he recanted his confessions and then changed his mind and confessed again. The case, prosecutors said, was unwinnable. In an extraordinary ruling, Superior Court Judge Ronald M. George refused to let the county prosecutors drop the case. Some quick maneuvering followed, and California's attorney general, George Deukmejian, agreed to have prosecutors in his office take over the case. Jury selection for the trial was extraordinary, too. About 360 potential jurors were called to court, and it took three months to complete the selection. The trial itself began on March 1, 1982, and was expected to take up to a year.

Bianchi had turned thirty-one by the time he took the witness stand in the summer of 1982 to testify against his cousin. He said he didn't remember the killings and didn't know whether the confessions he had given to psychiatrists in Washington were accurate. The jurors had been shown videotapes of those sessions. Bianchi spent more than five months on the witness stand and gave graphic testimony implicating Buono. Psychiatrists said that Bianchi had been seized by a murderous rage against women. He testified that he and Buono had lured women into their cars by posing as police officers and would sometimes flip a coin to decide who would be the first to rape them.

The longest trial in the nation's history went to the jury on October 20, 1983, nearly two years after it had begun. Close to 800 witnesses had been called to testify, and more than 1,800 exhibits had been presented. The defense had presented twelve days of closing arguments. More than three weeks of jury deliberation followed. On November 14, the jury found Buono guilty of nine of the ten murders. Next, the jurors had to decide whether to recommend the death penalty. Buono spoke briefly before the jury. He said his "moral and constitutional right" had been "broken." He added, "I ain't taking any procedure in this trial. I stand mute." The jury voted to spare Buono the gas chamber and recommended life in prison without parole.

In January of 1984, more than four years after Buono's arrest, both he and Bianchi were sentenced to life in prison by Judge Roger M. George of the Los Angeles County Superior Court. "It is my express hope that Mr. Buono and Mr. Bianchi should never be seen outside of prison walls," the judge noted. He said he would not go beyond the jury's recommendation but added, "I would not have the slightest reluctance to impose the death penalty. If there ever was a case for which the death penalty was appropriate, it is this case." He sentenced Bianchi to seven concurrent terms of life without parole for the Los Angeles and Washington cases and ordered that he return to Washington to serve his time. Bianchi's last request for parole in 2010 was denied; he will be eligible to apply again in 2025.

Buono died on September 22, 2002, at Calipatria State Prison in Southern California. He was sixty-seven years old and had heart problems.

He had married for a fourth time in 1986. His new wife was Christine Kizuka, a thirty-five-year-old mother of three who was a supervisor at the Los Angeles office of the state Employment Development Department. Kizuka met Buono through her first husband, who had spent five months in a cell next to Buono's while serving a term for assault with a deadly weapon. The ceremony at Folsom Prison "was just a routine marriage," said Richard Wipf, the corrections official who presided over the wedding. "They were both happy." Bob Gore, a Department of Corrections spokesman, was more direct: "I want to emphasize that Buono has never had a conjugal visit. He is not recommended to ever have a conjugal visit . . . due to the nature of his crimes against women."

11.

PATRICK WAYNE KEARNEY

In the middle of a summer day in 1977, two men walked into the Riverside County Sheriff's Office, about fifty miles east of Los Angeles, and pointed to "WANTED" posters on the wall. "That's us," they said. Patrick Wayne Kearney and David Douglas Hill had brought the baffling era of the "Trashbag Killer" to an unexpectedly peaceful end. Over the previous two years, at least eight bodies had been found along roadsides and highways in Southern California. Nearly all the victims had been shot once in the head, and many of their bodies had been placed in plastic bags. One body was found in a trash barrel. All the bodies were nude.

Four days later, after the long Fourth of July weekend, Kearney and Hill were brought before a judge. They had each been charged with two murders. The Riverside County sheriff, Bernard Clark, said they might be responsible for thirteen more. All the victims were male, and their bodies had been found in five counties around the area. Some news reports described Kearney and Hill as "self-admitted homosexuals." Others called them "acknowledged homosexuals."

If there is such a thing as a typical serial killer, neither Kearney nor Hill would have been an obvious suspect. Kearney was thirty-seven years old, and Hill was thirty-four. Neither seemed to have had previous arrest records. Hill was born in Lubbock, Texas, and was one of nine children in a family that was described as devoutly religious. He dropped out of high school and joined the Army but was discharged for medical reasons that were unclear. He went back home to Texas and married his high school girlfriend, but they divorced after a short time. He moved to California in the early 1960s and held several temporary jobs. He sometimes worked as an attendant in bathhouses.

Kearney was born in California in 1939 and lived with his parents in South Central Los Angeles. His father was a salesman for a travel bureau. The family moved to Texas when he was in his teens, but he eventually returned to California and attended El Camino College. He did not graduate. Instead, he enlisted in the Air Force and was stationed in Texas, where he met Hill. The two eventually move to the Los Angeles area, and Kearney took a job as an electrical engineer with the Hughes Aircraft Corporation, a major defense contractor.

In 1968, Kearney and Hill moved into an apartment in Culver City, a town known for its major television and movie production companies. At the time, Metro-Goldwyn-Mayer studios had its headquarters there. The couple lived what seemed to be a quiet life in Culver City for two years and then moved to Redondo Beach, a suburb along the Pacific coast south of Los Angeles. There, too, they were known as quiet neighbors.

Kearney had a government security clearance and a good reputation at Hughes, and he was still working there until about a month before his arrest. A Hughes official told a reporter at the time that Kearney was "an extremely diligent worker" who kept to himself. An acquaintance familiar with his work called him " a real electronics whiz." He was also a licensed pilot who occasionally rented planes for weekend trips to Las Vegas and other destinations. One source told a reporter at the time that Kearney was humorless, colorless, and wore dark suits with narrow lapels and thin ties. Kearney displayed little remorse and talked about the murders in matter-of-fact terms, the source said.

They didn't realize it at the time, but the trouble for them began one morning in March of 1977, when Patricia LaMay began searching for her seventeen-year-old son, John. The LaMays lived in El Segundo, a suburb near Los Angeles International Airport. John hadn't come home the night before, and he hadn't called. That was unlike him. His mother called one of John's friends for help. He mentioned someone named Dave. It took two months, but police figured out who "Dave" was: David Hill, who lived with Patrick Kearney in a small house on Robinson Street in Redondo Beach.

The investigators had connected Hill and Kearney to a number of boys and men who had been reported missing over the previous two years. John LaMay, whose remains were found on March 18, seemed to be the last victim. His hands, feet, and head had been sawed off, but the rest of his body was found in a plastic bag in a trash barrel near a highway in Riverside County. In early June, a warrant was issued for the arrest of Kearney and Hill. They had left their home about a week earlier and were missing. Kearney had quit his job, and he, along with Hill, had written a letter to Kearney's grandmother instructing her to sell the house. They were being harassed by the police, they said, and planned to move to Canada. But they had actually gone to Hill's family home in Texas, where relatives tried to persuade them to return to California and surrender to the police. A week later, they turned themselves in.

Shortly after Kearney and Hill were taken into custody on July 1, 1977, investigators found the skeletal remains of another body in the ground near a garage behind their old Culver City apartment. Kearney and Hill were cooperating with the police and had led them there. This, they said, was the first victim. He had been shot in the head. Kearney said he remembered only that the victim's name was George. By mid-July, Kearney had given officials information about victims and burial sites in a wide area of Southern California. Investigators estimated that twenty-eight deaths might be connected to Kearney and Hill. At that point, they were charged with only two murders—those of Arturo Marquez, a twenty-four-year-old from Oxnard, and John Otis LaMay.

Much was happening behind closed doors during the days when Kearney and Hill were in custody. On July 14, the reason for what had seemed like unusual secrecy became clear. A Riverside County grand jury had indicted Kearney on three murder charges, and officials had dropped all charges against Hill. They arranged for Hill to leave the jail in Riverside County out of sight of the news media gathered nearby. Byron Hill, the Riverside County prosecutor, told reporters that the evidence against David Hill was "weak," and that much of it tended to exonerate him. No further charges were ever brought against Hill. He died in 1991, fourteen years after the two men

DAVID HILL

had turned themselves in, and his body was buried in a cemetery in his hometown of Lubbock.

His partner, however, was not released. Kearney appeared before a judge and was charged with killing Marquez, LaMay, and Albert Rivera, a twenty-one-year-old from Los Angeles. The investigation had begun two years earlier, in April of 1975, when Rivera's nude body was found along a highway east of San Juan Capistrano. He had been shot in the head before his body was stuffed into a heavy-duty trash bag.

Kearney had been talking to investigators about an astounding number of murders, as many as twenty-eight, according to some reports. Most of the victims had been killed by a single gunshot to the head, and police began to link bullets and casings to a gun found in Kearney and Hill's home. Before Kearney found a lawyer to represent him, he had given investigators incriminating details about twenty-five murders. He said he had committed a murder every four to six weeks over a period of more than two years and had been killing people since the 1960s. Soon, Kearney got a lawyer, and then he stopped talking to the police.

The identified victims were young and single, and many lived alone or were drifters who made easy prey. Most were believed to have been homosexuals. The news came at a time when debates about homosexuality were emerging across the country. In Florida, Anita Bryant, a beauty contest winner and popular singer with some Top 40 hits, had begun the "Save Our Children" campaign in response to an emerging push for homosexual rights. The campaign purchased a full-page ad in the *Miami Herald* that said homosexuals used to be stoned to death but that now "an attitude of tolerance" had developed "based on the understanding that homosexuals will keep their deviant activity to themselves, will not flaunt their lifestyles, will not be allowed to preach their sexual standards to, or otherwise influence, impressionable young people." On a television show, Bryant said, "We're not going after their jobs, as long as they do their jobs and do not want to come out of the closet." In California, a campaign was underway to ban homosexuals from teaching positions. Many homosexuals hid their orientation.

In September of 1977, Kearney pleaded guilty to the three murders he was charged with in Riverside County. But in December, the judge, John Hughes, told him to take a week to reconsider. The guilty plea in Riverside County would bring him a sentence of life in prison. But he could still be charged with murder in other counties where bodies had been found and could be eligible for the death penalty in those cases. Kearney went ahead with the plea and eventually was charged in Los Angeles with eighteen more murders. The youngest victim was five, and the oldest was twenty-eight.

After working out another plea bargain, Kearney was convicted of those murders, too. His lawyer, Jay Grossman, said he had advised Kearney to plead not guilty by reason of insanity because he could make a strong case, but Kearney had refused. In February of 1978, he pleaded guilty in a Los Angeles courtroom. Municipal Judge Dickran Tevrizian asked him a question. "I feel I have some obligation to the eighteen people whom you have silenced. The families of those victims want to know why. Can you tell us why?" Kearney replied, "I prefer not to." He was then escorted to another courtroom. Superior Court Judge Paul G. Breckinridge Jr. called Kearney "an insult to humanity" and sentenced him to life in prison. He said Kearney should never be released.

Kearney is housed at Mule Creek State Prison in Ione, California, south of Sacramento. He has been denied parole six times over the decades since his conviction. The last denial came in January of 2012. He was told that he could try again in January of 2027, when he would be eighty-seven years old.

12.
CORAL EUGENE WATTS

A week before he died in 2007, Coral Eugene Watts got an unusual piece of bad news. He had just been sentenced to life in prison for killing a college student in Michigan in 1974. His life until that sentencing had been marked by some perversely good luck. In 1982, he had made a very favorable deal with prosecutors in Texas. He would confess to the murders of twelve young women and, in return, he would be allowed to plead guilty to a single charge of robbery with intent to commit murder. He would be sentenced to sixty years in prison, but he could, at some point, apply for parole.

It had been a difficult decision for the prosecutors and the judge in the case. They believed that Watts was, in fact, the mysterious "Sunday

Morning Slasher" who had committed his first murder in 1974. Over the years, he had become a suspect in the murders of dozens of women. But no one had been able to prove it. Even so, they assumed he would never be free again.

On the afternoon of October 30, 1974, the body of nineteen-year-old Gloria Steele was found in her apartment near Western Michigan University in Kalamazoo. She had been stabbed thirty-three times. Watts had been attending school there at the time. Later he moved to Ann Arbor, the home of the University of Michigan. On Sunday, April 20, 1980, seventeen-year-old Shirley Small was killed outside her home near the university. On Sunday, July 13, 1980, twenty-three-year-old Glenda Richmond was killed outside her home near the campus. On Sunday, September 14, 1980, thirty-year-old Rebecca Greer Huff was killed outside her home in western Ann Arbor. All three had been stabbed to death, and their bodies were found early on those Sundays. The killer was the terrifying and mysterious new "Sunday Morning Slasher."

It would be nearly two years before Watts was arrested, and by then he had moved to Houston, where he was working as a bus mechanic. Investigators from Ann Arbor had been highly suspicious of Watts, who was their prime suspect in the murders. They warned Houston police about him when Watts moved there in early 1981. Sergeant Paul Bunton, an Ann Arbor homicide detective, sent Houston police a package of information that included photographs of Watts and descriptions of how he cruised around at night in his car, apparently looking for women. Bunton suggested that Houston should warn nearby communities about Watts. Houston police made spot-checks on Watts and even attached a tracking device to his car for a time.

Houston police remained suspicious, but it wasn't until the spring of 1982 that they had enough reason to arrest Watts. Someone abducted Lori Lister from the parking lot of her apartment building in Houston at about 6:30 a.m. on Sunday, May 23. He used coat hangers to tie up

Lister and her roommate, Melinda Aguilar, both in their twenties. As the man tried to drown Lister in the bathtub, Aguilar escaped and called the police. Lister was rescued, but Watts escaped. He was eventually arrested and charged with attempted capital murder, attempted murder, burglary, and kidnapping.

By August of 1982, Watts had worked out a highly unusual deal with the prosecutors in Houston. He would plead guilty to a much less serious charge of burglary with intent to commit murder. But there was an extraordinary catch. He also had to admit to nine killings in the Houston area. He would not be charged with those murders if he kept his promise to lead investigators to victims' gravesites in the states of Texas and Michigan and in Windsor, Ontario. During questioning, Watts had implicated himself in more than twenty unsolved murders. On August 9, Watts led investigators to a shallow grave along a freeway in Houston, where they found the decomposed body of Suzanne Searles, a twenty-five-year-old woman who had been reported missing in April. A few days later, he led them to the body of a young woman buried near a bayou in the Houston area.

"We didn't have a stich of evidence to go on in the killings," John B. Holmes Jr., the Harris County (Texas) district attorney, told reporters. "We figured that at least this way we'd get the bodies and the life sentence."

Doug Shaver, the Texas judge in the case, said he had qualms about the plea bargain. "It feels bad, but practically, it amounts to the same thing as a life sentence," he said. Prosecutors had agreed to the deal, Shaver said, because "we couldn't ever prove anything on him. No one could ever prove anything on him. But at least it will let us get those victims out of the shallow graves he's put them in and give them back to their families, where they can be properly buried."

Watts continued to lead investigators to burial sites around the area. His motive for the killings remained a mystery. "There is no reason,"

Judge Shaver told reporters after the hearing. "He does not rape, he does not rob. He just thinks women are evil and he kills them."

A state psychiatrist had certified that Watts was legally sane, but the defense hired a psychologist, Jerome M. Sherman, who said that Watts was a "schizophrenic paranoid" who was "very sensitive to the existence of evil." Watts "goes out looking for people to stamp out evil, and the evil always to him appears within women." Watts was twenty-eight years old at the time and had spent most of his life in the Detroit area. When he was fourteen years old, he was arrested after attacking a woman while he was delivering newspapers one morning. He was admitted to a psychiatric clinic for treatment, but after five months he was released.

The Watts case did lead to one reversed ruling that August. Howard Ware Mosley, a twenty-five-year-old man who had been convicted of stabbing a nineteen-year-old woman in Galveston, was released from prison, where he was serving a life sentence. The charges were dropped because Watts admitted that he had killed her.

Watts also admitted that he had killed a reporter for the *Detroit News* in 1979. Jeanne Clyne, a forty-four-year-old who had been a food writer, was stabbed to death on the evening of Halloween that year as she returned home to the suburb of Grosse Point Farms after a doctor's appointment. Watts told the investigators in Houston that he was "just driving around" when he saw her. He used a sharpened fourteen-inch screwdriver to stab her in the chest and throat. Watts was considered a suspect in about twenty murder cases in Wayne County, which includes Detroit. Wayne County officials had not agreed to give Watts immunity from prosecution as part of the agreement worked out in Houston. That would become a problem for Watts later.

Things came to what looked like a conclusion on September 3, 1982. Judge Shaver, who had been threatened and was wearing a bulletproof vest for protection, sentenced Watts to sixty years in prison "because the death penalty is not available to me." Under the terms of the long-negotiated agreement, Watts pleaded guilty to burglary with intent to commit murder. The names of thirteen women he had admitted to killing were read into the record. Then Judge Shaver gave Watts a lecture. "I want you to understand that the sentence I am imposing is not what I believe is an appropriate sentence for you," he said, "but it is simply the equivalent maximum sentence under the evidence the state has against you." Shaver said he never wanted to see Watts paroled. "If you do not act well in prison," he said, "it is my hope that they will put you so deep into prison that they'll have to pipe in light to you."

By 2002, Watts had behaved well enough in prison that he had accumulated credits for good behavior. A mandatory release program had been approved by the state legislature in 1977, and although it was rescinded in 1996, Watts remained eligible for parole because he had been sentenced while the law was in effect. Classified as a first-time offender, Watts was entitled to time off for good behavior. That meant three days would be deducted from his sentence for every day he served without getting into trouble. Barring any new developments, he would be released in May of 2006, when he would be fifty-two years old—and before he had served even half his sentence. Alarmed by the possibility, officials in Michigan, Texas, and Canada went back to work on the case.

Michigan law enforcement officials had assumed that Watts would die in prison. They quickly formed a task force at the end of 2002 to uncover other murders Watts might have committed to make sure he wouldn't be freed. Donna Pendergast, a Wayne County prosecutor, told reporters that the task force members planned to "go over every piece of evidence again with a fine-tooth comb." Andy Kahan, a Houston deputy mayor, began a national campaign to keep Watts behind bars. "We may not be able to prevent his release, but we can Hannibal Lechterize [*sic*] him and set him up to fail so that if he does anything at all, he'll be back in prison," Kahan said. "I expect him to flee the first chance he gets. He's got to know the eyes of the country will be on him."

Authorities in Texas, Michigan, and southern Canada began scouring their files for any unsolved killings that could be connected to Watts so that they might be able to charge him with another murder and keep him locked up. They quickly got a lead. Joseph Foy, a forty-seven-year-old resident of the Detroit area, called to report that he had seen Watts at a murder scene in 1979. He hadn't seen the actual murder, but he did get a look at the killer's face for a moment near the body of a woman in an alley in Ferndale, a suburb of Detroit. The victim was Helen Dutcher, a thirty-six-year-old who lived in Ferndale. Investigators quickly found records showing that Foy had in fact called the police in 1979 to report what he had seen. He had also helped a sketch artist produce a drawing of the man he'd spotted. Texas governor Rick Perry signed an order in 2004 to have Watts extradited to Michigan to stand trial for the murder of Helen Dutcher. If Watts was convicted of first-degree murder in that case, he could be sentenced to life without the possibility of parole.

Foy was the key witness at the trial in late 2004. He testified that on December 1, 1979, he was at home with his wife and children at about 9:30 p.m. Foy said that when his dog began barking, he looked out a window into the alley adjacent to his house and saw a gold- or tan-colored Pontiac driving away. (That was the kind of car Watts drove at the time.) Soon the dog began barking again, and Foy saw that the car had returned. He saw a man and a woman in the alley. The woman's back was against a wall. When Foy stepped onto his back porch, he saw the man make a slashing motion and the woman fell to the ground. Foy yelled for his wife to call the police. The man then turned and began to walk toward Foy's porch. "He had what I thought was a knife," Foy told the jury. "This man was in no hurry. It was like he had just dropped off his laundry."

Before Watts made it to his car, the two "locked glances" and the other man had an "evil" look in his eye, Foy testified. The prosecutor asked whether Watts, who was sitting in a chair in the courtroom, looked the same as he had when Foy had seen him that night. "His eyes do," Foy said. A few years later, Foy saw a television news report about Watts being arrested in Texas. He recognized the man's face instantly, he said, and called the police in Ferndale again, but nothing happened.

On November 17, 2004, as the jury was deliberating in the Dutcher case, prosecutors in Kalamazoo announced that Watts was being charged with the murder of Gloria Steele, the Western Michigan University student who had been stabbed to death in 1974. The city's cold-case team had reopened the case in 2003. By the end of the day, the jury had convicted Watts of murdering Dutcher. At his sentencing three weeks later, Watts denied that he had committed the murder. "I never seen her before in my life," he told the judge. "It's one murder in my life I did not do." Beth Mrozinski, the victim's niece, read a list of Watts's victims. "You have taken away and butchered our loved ones," she said. "You have made sure we are tortured every day."

Watts got the mandatory sentence of life in prison with no possibility of parole. He said he planned to appeal the conviction. Meanwhile, he had to stand trial for the Gloria Steele murder. The jury heard testimony that she had been stabbed in the chest thirty-three times at her apartment in Kalamazoo. Again, Watts was convicted of first-degree murder and sentenced to life in prison without hope of parole. Appeals were to follow.

But a little over a week later, on September 21, 2007, Coral Watts died of prostate cancer. He was fifty-three years old. His appeals were still pending.

13.
WILLIAM BONIN

Vernon Butts attached a towel to a bar in his jail cell late one night in January of 1981 and quietly hanged himself. He was in a high-security area of the Men's Central Jail in Los Angeles, and a guard had checked on him just after midnight. The guard checked again about forty minutes later, and Butts was dead. Jail officials said they were certain it was suicide—all the other inmates were locked down at that time of night and no one else was in the area.

Butts, a twenty-three-year-old who hoped to become a magician, had plenty of reason to be depressed. He had confessed to police that he was involved in the "Freeway Killer" murders, another of the nightmarish episodes that terrorized Californians during the 1970s. Media speculation had put the number of Freeway Killer victims—boys and young men—as high as forty going back to 1972, when the bodies of young men and teenage boys began turning up near freeways and major highways in Southern California. By the end of 1980, the real focus of the investigation into that long string of murders was William G. Bonin, a thirty-four-year-old truck driver from a suburb of Los Angeles. In the weeks before his suicide, Butts, more of a sidekick, had described for investigators—in gruesome detail—Bonin's attacks on some of the victims.

By early 1980, law enforcement officials in Los Angeles and four nearby counties had determined that twenty-nine murders in Southern California, dating back to April of 1978, were quite similar and were probably connected. But they stopped short of blaming them on one killer. The nude or nearly nude bodies of twenty-nine white males, all either teenagers or in their twenties, had been found along heavily traveled roadways in the area.

Bonin was in jail on the night of Butts's suicide at the end of 1981 and had been for more than a year. Police were suspicious of Bonin in 1980. They got a tip from a juvenile informant suggesting that Bonin might be involved in a string of murders, and on June 2, they put him under surveillance. Just before midnight on June 13, 1980, investigators tracked Bonin to a parking lot in Los Angeles and found him in the back of a van where, they said, he was having sex with a teenage boy. Bonin was arrested that night and charged with sodomy and oral copulation with an underage victim—a seventeen-year-old. More importantly, Bonin was also a suspect in the murder of Charles Miranda, a fifteen-year-old whose nude body had been found in February of 1980 in an alley in downtown Los Angeles. Miranda had been strangled to death. His face and other parts of his body had been beaten, and there were ligature marks on his neck, wrists, and ankles. To the public, it looked very much like the work of the Freeway Killer.

Prosecutors weren't quite ready to charge Bonin with Miranda's murder in June of 1980, but they did persuade a judge to set an unusually high bond of $250,000 in the case where he had been caught having sex with an underage victim. Bonin had a particularly disturbing criminal past. He was twenty-one years old when he was discharged from the Army in 1968 after serving a tour in Vietnam. He returned to California, and it wasn't long before he found himself in serious trouble. In late 1968 and early 1969, he sexually attacked four boys or young men and was arrested. He was convicted of molesting and forcibly orally copulating with a twelve-year-old, kidnapping and sodomizing a fourteen-year-old, sodomizing a seventeen-year-old, and forcibly orally copulating with an eighteen-year-old.

Bonin was declared a mentally disordered sex offender and sent to Atascadero State Hospital for treatment. But in 1971, officials decided that the treatment wasn't working, so he was sent to prison. He was released in June of 1974, but he was arrested again in 1975 and later convicted of a sexual attack on a fourteen-year-old boy. Again he was sent to prison. He was paroled in late 1978. That meant that he was still in prison when the first five of the twenty-nine murders connected by the police were committed. When Bonin was arrested in June of 1980, he was living at his mother's home in Downey, a suburb southeast of Los Angeles. As a truck driver, he was on the road much of the time.

Throughout the country, school officials, law enforcement authorities, and parents had been warning people—especially young people—about the increasing danger of hitchhiking. Young women seemed to have taken heed, fearing sexual attacks, but young males seemed less concerned, possibly assuming that, at the worst, their wallets might be stolen. It was also a time when homosexuality was not openly discussed in most places and was commonly viewed as wrong, or at least deviant. The *New York Times* reported that in 1980, detectives in the Hollywood division of the Los Angeles Police Department found that sexual preference was a factor in ten of forty-two murders that had occurred in their jurisdiction, which covered nineteen square miles. They found that the victims were frequently runaways from the "less tolerant" Midwest. Some ended up making their livings as homosexual prostitutes, and many were hitchhikers.

Bonin sat in a jail cell for weeks after his arrest in June of 1980. In July, he was hit with a surprise. He would not be charged with the murder of Charles Miranda, as police had hinted. Instead, prosecutors charged him with the murder of Marcus Grabs, a seventeen-year-old student from Germany. Grabs's nude body had been found in the Malibu Canyon area in August of 1979. He had been hitchhiking around the country as a tourist and had been seen near Newport Beach, about seventy-five miles south on the Pacific coast, on the day before his murder.

By the end of July, the full picture had emerged. The Los Angeles County Sheriff's Department announced that Bonin and Butts were believed to be responsible for the kidnapping, torture, and murder of at least twenty-one young males between May of 1979 and June of 1980. Bonin was charged with fourteen murders in Los Angeles County and was expected to be charged later with seven more in other areas around Southern California. He also faced a charge of "mayhem" for mutilating the genitalia of one of the victims. Butts was charged with six of the same murders.

Butts had worked as a sales clerk in the magic shop at Knott's Berry Farm for about seven months in 1978 and 1979, but he'd been

VERNON BUTTS WHO WAS CHARGED WITH WILLIAM BONIN IN SIX OF THE "FREEWAY KILLER" MURDERS.

fired for poor performance. Butts had met Bonin through a mutual friend in 1978. They began to spend time together, talking and going out to see movies, and when Butts was evicted from his apartment in Norwalk for failure to pay rent, he moved into Bonin's house in Downey. Butts, too, had a troubled past. He was charged with burglary and arson in 1976 after breaking into a neighbor's home and setting it on fire. He spent a year in the custody of the California Youth Authority. Butts became a suspect in mid-July of 1980 when investigators were interviewing Bonin's friends and acquaintances. One of them reported that Bonin had said Butts had been present during one of the murders.

A third suspect in the killings was arrested at the end of July by the Michigan State Police. James M. Munro, a nineteen-year-old, had worked at the trucking company that employed Bonin. He had gone home to Michigan and would be extradited back to California, where he would be charged with playing a part in the murder of Steven Wells, whose body had been found behind a gas station in Huntington Beach on June 2, 1980.

In August, a fourth suspect was charged. Gregory Matthew Miley, a nineteen-year-old who had lived in the Los Angeles suburb of Bellflower, was arrested at the home of his stepfather in Houston, Texas. He was charged with participating in the murders of two hitchhikers: Charles Miranda, the fifteen-year-old from Bell Gardens, and James McCabe, a twelve-year-old from Garden Grove. Miley waived extradition proceedings and was brought back to California, where he pleaded not guilty.

It would be difficult to design a more complex criminal case than the one that faced authorities across several jurisdictions in Southern California in 1980. It looked as if there could be four defendants and at least two major trials—one in Orange County and the other in Los Angeles.

Miley had begun confessing shortly after he was arrested in Houston. He told a detective that he and Bonin had picked up a homosexual on a street in Hollywood and tied his feet and hands together. Bonin sodomized the victim and strangled him, he said. Then they drove to

Huntington Beach and picked up a boy who was ten or twelve years old. When Bonin got into the back of the van with the boy, Miley began to hear crying sounds. At some point, Miley held the boy down while Bonin strangled him. They drove a long distance and dumped his body next to a dumpster, Miley said.

In early 1981, it finally became clear how investigators had come to suspect Bonin in the first place. Sealed court documents were released that told the story of a teenager in juvenile detention who had decided to tell a counselor what he knew about the Freeway Killer. An investigator visited the boy in the spring of 1980, and he repeated what he knew. He had met Bonin at a party at the home of a friend, and Bonin had given him a ride home. He'd refused Bonin's requests to participate in sexual acts. When Bonin asked him to help him with some killings, he tried to jump out of the van, but Bonin grabbed him. Bonin told the boy that he liked to pick up teenagers and strangle them with their own T-shirts. In the end, Bonin let the boy go. He said he could not kill the boy because people had seen them together. Bonin was quickly put on twenty-four-hour observation.

It also became clear in early 1981 that Vernon Butts, who was by then under arrest, was telling authorities everything he knew about his codefendant Bonin. He had described in detail how he went out with Bonin one night and they'd picked up a young boy and had sex with him. Then Bonin beat him to death. Bonin, he said, was not worried about Butts turning on him and telling the police because Butts had participated in the attack. It was just a few days after a transcript of Bonin's testimony was unexpectedly released to the public that Butts hanged himself in his jail cell.

By the end of January, William Ray Pugh, the teenager who had first tipped off investigators to Bonin's activities, had been charged with murder, robbery, and sodomy. He had turned eighteen by then. Pugh was later convicted of voluntary manslaughter and got a reduced sentence of six years in prison in return for helping police with information about Bonin.

In April, James Munro, the teenager who had been charged with the murder of Steven Wells, agreed to a plea bargain deal that ensured he would not face the death penalty. He agreed to testify against Bonin and, in return, he would be allowed to plead guilty to second-degree murder.

In May, Gregory Miley agreed to plead guilty to a charge of first-degree murder and to testify against Bonin. In exchange, prosecutors would not seek the death penalty.

Then the trials started. Los Angeles was to go first, then Orange County would try Bonin for additional murders. In either case, Bonin could be sentenced to death.

The Los Angeles trial began in the fall of 1981 with the cases of twelve victims:

- **Marcus Grabs,** a seventeen-year-old from Germany who was killed on August 5, 1979. His nude body was found the following day in Malibu Canyon near Las Virgenes Canyon Road. Except for his backpack, there was no clothing or other identifying evidence at the scene. He had been stabbed to death, and his body showed signs of beating about the face and elsewhere. Ligature marks were visible on his neck and one ankle.
- **Charles Miranda,** a fifteen-year-old who was killed on February 3, 1980. His nude body was found in an alley in downtown Los Angeles. No clothing or other identifying evidence was found at the scene. He had been strangled to death with a ligature the same day. The body showed signs of beating about the face and elsewhere, exhibited ligature marks on at least one ankle and wrist as well as on the neck, and revealed indications of sexual activity before death.
- **James Macabe,** a twelve-year-old who was killed on February 3, 1980. His fully clothed body was found on February 6 near Walnut Drive in Walnut, in front of the Pomona Freeway. Other than his clothing, no identifying evidence was found at the scene. He had been strangled to death with a ligature. He had been beaten

about the face and elsewhere and had ligature marks on at least one ankle and wrist and on his neck. There were signs of sexual activity before death.

- **Donald Ray Hyden,** a fifteen-year-old who was killed on August 25 or 26 of 1979. His nude body was found on August 27 in the area of Liberty Canyon near the Ventura Freeway. No clothing or other identifying evidence was found at the scene. He had been strangled with a ligature. There were signs of beating on his face and elsewhere, along with ligature marks on at least one ankle and wrist as well as on his neck. There were indications of sexual activity before death.
- **David Murillo,** a seventeen-year-old who was killed on September 9, 1979. His nude body was found alongside the Ventura Freeway near the Lemon Grove overpass. No clothing or other identifying evidence was found at the scene. He had been strangled with a ligature. There were signs that he had been beaten on his face and elsewhere, and ligature marks were found on his wrists and neck. There were signs of sexual activity before death.
- **Darin Lee Kendrick,** a nineteen-year-old who was killed April 29 or 30, 1980. His nude body was found on April 30 on Avalon Street in Carson, about eighteen miles south of Los Angeles, near the Artesia Freeway. No clothing or other identifying evidence was found at the scene. He had been strangled by a ligature and stabbed in the upper cervical spinal cord. He had been beaten on the face and elsewhere, and had ligature marks on at least one ankle and wrist and on his neck.
- **Frank Dennis Fox,** a seventeen-year-old who was killed on November 30, 1979. His nude body was found on December 2 on the side of the Ortega Highway in Caspers Wilderness Park in Orange County. No clothing or other identifying evidence was found at the scene. He had been strangled to death with a ligature on about November 30. There were signs that he had been beaten on the face and elsewhere. Ligature marks were found on his ankles and wrists. There were signs of sexual activity before death.

- **Ronald Gatlin,** a nineteen-year-old who was killed on March 14 or 15 of 1980. His nude body was found on March 15 near Central Avenue in Duarte, about twenty miles northeast of Los Angeles. No clothing or other identifying evidence was found at the scene. He had been strangled to death with a ligature and beaten on the face and elsewhere. There were ligature marks on at least one ankle and wrist and on his neck. There were signs of sexual activity before death.
- **Harry Todd Turner,** a fifteen-year-old who was killed on or after March 20, 1980. His nude body was found on March 25 in an alley in Los Angeles. No clothing or other identifying evidence was found at the scene. He had been beaten on the face and elsewhere, and there were ligature marks on his neck. There were signs of sexual activity before death.
- **Steven Wood,** a sixteen-year-old who was killed on April 10 or 11 of 1980. His nude body was found in an alley in Long Beach near the Pacific Coast Highway. No clothing or other identifying evidence was found at the scene. He had been strangled to death. He had been beaten on the face and elsewhere, and there were ligature marks on at least one ankle and wrist, as well as on his neck.
- **Steven Wells,** an eighteen-year-old who was killed on June 2, 1980. His nude body was found on June 3 behind a gasoline station in Huntington Beach. No clothing or other identifying evidence was found at the scene. He had been strangled to death. He had been beaten on the face and elsewhere and had ligature marks on his neck, at least one ankle, and his wrist. There were signs of sexual activity before death.
- **Thomas Lundgren,** a thirteen-year-old who was killed on May 28, 1979. His body was found off Mulholland Highway in the Malibu Canyon area. He had severe slash wounds in his neck and deep stab wounds in his chest, and his skull had been fractured by something like a jack handle. His sexual organs had been cut off and left nearby.
- **Sean King,** a fourteen-year-old from South Gate in San Bernardino County who disappeared on May 19, 1980, while waiting for a bus or hitchhiking in Downey. The remains of his body were found in

December of 1980, scattered in the underbrush in Live Oak Canyon near the San Bernardino-Riverside County line. A dentist identified him by examining the jawbone.

In January of 1982, after a lengthy and emotional trial, the Los Angeles jury convicted Bonin of ten of the twelve murder charges. The jurors found him not guilty of the murders of Sean King and Thomas Lundgren. Bonin had confessed to a television news reporter that he had killed Sean King, but the jurors had not been allowed to hear about that interview. The jury recommended the death penalty, and Superior Court judge William Keene sentenced Bonin to die in California's gas chamber. He said the murders had been "sadistic, deliberate, and unbelievably cruel."

Next came the trial in Orange County, where Bonin was charged with four murders.

- **Russell Rugh,** a fifteen-year-old who was killed on March 21 or 22 of 1980. His nude body was found on March 22 off the Ortega Highway in the San Juan Campgrounds in Orange County. No clothing or other identifying evidence was found at the scene. He had been strangled to death with a ligature and beaten on the face and elsewhere. There were ligature marks on his ankles and wrists. There were signs of sexual activity before death.
- **Glen Barker,** a fourteen-year-old who was killed on March 21 or 22 of 1980. His nude body was found on the same day and in the same place as the body of Russell Rugh. No clothing or other identifying evidence was found at the scene. Like Rugh, Barker had been killed by ligature strangulation. He had been beaten on the face and elsewhere, and there were ligature marks on his ankles and wrists. There were signs of sexual activity before death.
- **Lawrence Sharp,** a seventeen-year-old who was killed on May 17 or 18 of 1979. His nude body was found on May 18 at a gasoline station on the corner of Westminster Boulevard and Bolsa Chica in Westminster, a city in northern Orange County. No clothing

or other identifying evidence was found at the scene. Sharp had been strangled to death with a ligature; he had been beaten on the face and elsewhere, and he had ligature marks on his ankles and wrists. There were signs of sexual activity before his death.

- **Frank Fox,** a seventeen-year-old whose nude body was found on December 2, 1979, along Ortega Highway about five miles north of the San Diego Freeway. He was hitchhiking when Bonin picked him up. Bonin bound his hands and feet, sodomized him, and strangled him to death.

The jury convicted Bonin of all the murders and recommended the death penalty. In August of 1983, the judge ordered Bonin's execution. More than a decade of appeals followed. During that time, California stopped executing people in the gas chamber. Bonin was to become the first person in California to be executed by lethal injection. On February 23, 1996, he spent his last day at San Quentin visiting with friends. He ordered a final meal of two large pepperoni-and-sausage pizzas, three pints of coffee ice cream, and three six-packs of regular Coca-Cola. Near midnight, he offered his last words to the warden: "That I feel the death penalty is not an answer to the problems at hand. That I feel it sends the wrong message to the youth of the country. Young people act as they see other people acting instead of as people tell them to act. And I would suggest that when a person has a thought of doing anything serious against the law, that before they did, that they should go to a quiet place and think about it seriously."

After Bonin's execution, the funeral director submitted some routine paperwork on his death, and this led to the startling disclosure that Bonin had been collecting Social Security disability checks for mental illness during the nearly fourteen years he had spent on death row. He'd had the money sent to his mother, who had received about $75,000 by the time of his death. She said she didn't know she had done anything wrong—she had used the money to pay her mortgage.

14.

JOHN WAYNE GACY

In almost every way, execution day was all that John Wayne Gacy could have hoped for. Gray-haired and still pudgy after fourteen years in prison, he took the stage for the final act with a spectacular entrance: the whoosh of a sleek white helicopter through a cloudless blue sky. He was ebullient throughout the two-hour flight from the Menard penitentiary in southern Illinois to death row at Stateville, not far from Chicago. It was his big day and his alone. Other than the part where the star of the show was supposed to die at the end, he had just one complaint: the flight staff had neglected to offer cocktails or those little bags of peanuts, and that irked him.

But Gacy was an optimist. As the flight descended toward the prison on that warm May morning in 1994, the scene on the ground was oddly festive. Television vans and satellite dishes were already in place, not far from the blue-and-white-striped press tents that suggested a Midwestern state fair or a tailgate party. TV crews in shorts and jeans sat idly in the sun on the outdoor furniture they had brought along in preparation for the long day and night to come. Gacy's lawyers, working on last-minute appeals, said their client was remarkably calm. He had reminded the lawyers that he was a very positive person, and he did not believe that he would be executed just after midnight.

With the bluff and bluster that had served him so well during his seven-year murder odyssey and its long legal aftermath, Gacy set up shop in Unit 1 of Building X. He had a sink, a toilet, a small table, a stool, and a thin mattress on a shelf. The other fifteen cells were empty. He had ordered a final meal of fried chicken and french fries; then he changed his mind and notified staff that he wanted fried shrimp or lobster instead. He was in charge.

After all, he had been a successful businessman and emerging politician back in 1978, when he finagled his way into a Polish Constitution Day celebration in Chicago and got himself photographed with First Lady_Rosalynn Carter. That photo was a testament to his skill: Mrs. Carter was smiling, and the "S" pin issued to him by the Secret Service was clearly visible on his lapel. By then, he had already strangled twenty-nine young men and boys and buried most of their bodies in the crawl space under his small suburban house. When he ran out of space down there, he had to dump some of the bodies in a nearby river. Obviously, the Secret Service could not have known about the bodies. But the agents should have known that Gacy had been sentenced to ten years in prison in 1968 for sodomizing a fifteen-year-old boy in Iowa. A model inmate, Gacy had gotten himself paroled after eighteen months. Then he'd moved to Chicago for a new start.

He had found over the years that he could just about always talk his way out of things. Even when investigators finally started sniffing around his property in Illinois in 1978—when the death toll had reached thirty-three—there was no need to panic. John Wayne Gacy, the popular and successful contractor, was innocent, and he knew how to work the system. After all, people assumed that he had been named after John Wayne, the tough-talking cowboy movie star who would surely have gone down fighting. The truth was less impressive. He had been named after his father, John, and an uncle, Wayne.

The real John Wayne Gacy began to come into focus just before Christmas in 1978. Gacy made his big mistake on December 11, 1978, at the Nisson Pharmacy in Des Plaines, a suburb not far from his house. He was talking to one of the owners about doing a renovation job when he noticed a young employee stocking the shelves. Gacy left the pharmacy but returned later that evening. The young employee, Robert Piest, was still there. A high school student, he was saving up to buy a Jeep when he turned sixteen in March. Just before his shift ended at 9 p.m., his mother, Elizabeth, stopped by to drive him home. It was her birthday, and the family was waiting to light the candles on the cake back home. Rob asked her to wait for a few minutes. A contractor wanted to talk to him out back about a construction job. She said she didn't mind. But she got impatient when he didn't return to the store and she couldn't find him outside. Her agitation soon turned to worry. She had been told that the contractor's name was John Gacy.

Elizabeth Piest went home and described the situation to her husband, Harold, and their two other children, who were waiting around the birthday cake. Before the night was over, they had gone to the police and made a missing person's report. The Piests got the telephone number of the man named Gacy from the pharmacy, but when they called his home, there was no answer. They stayed up all night, Elizabeth by the phone at home and the others searching the dark streets of the area for

Rob. His older brother and sister, Kenneth and Kerry, each took one of the family's dogs out in their cars to search for Rob along roadways and snowbanks. They never saw Rob alive again.

The investigators who had taken the report from the family found their story unusual and worrisome. Robert Piest was not the typical runaway. They looked into Gacy's background and eventually got a report from Waterloo, Iowa. They saw that in 1968, Gacy had been convicted of sodomy and sentenced to ten years at the Iowa Men's Reformatory in Anamosa. He was paroled to Chicago in 1970. In 1972, he had been charged with aggravated battery and reckless conduct in a northern suburb of Chicago. That charge was later dismissed. He was arrested again in 1978 on an aggravated battery charge in Chicago, but it wasn't clear how that case had ended.

Greg Bedoe was an investigator for the Cook County State's Attorney's Office when Rob Piest disappeared. He was assigned to a suburban branch, and he helped interview Gacy in the early days of the search. Gacy seemed oddly uninterested in helping and made excuses about having to go to a relative's funeral, Bedoe said in an interview later. "He didn't care. He didn't care about anything," Bedoe recalled. When the investigators saw Gacy's rap sheet, they decided to get a search warrant for his house. Late on December 13, a team went in to conduct the search, over Gacy's objections. They found a number of items of interest, including handcuffs, books about pederasty, a switchblade in a drawer next to the bed in the master bedroom, driver's licenses belonging to other men, police badges, and what appeared to be bloodstains on the carpeting and the walls. There was also a strange odor emanating from the crawl space under the house.

More significantly, they found a photo receipt from the Nisson Pharmacy dated and time-stamped on the evening that Rob had disappeared. A young woman working the cash register had borrowed Rob's jacket that night because the store was so cold. She returned the jacket to Rob just before he went outside to talk to Gacy. The receipt she put in the jacket pocket would become an important piece of evidence establishing Gacy's contact with Rob Piest.

By December 21, 1978, ten days after Piest's disappearance, investigators knew much more about Gacy's activities and the young men he had known in the Chicago area. By then Gacy had hired a lawyer, Sam Amirante, and had spent a long night talking in Amirante's suburban office while investigators sat outside in cars and watched. They had no clear reason to arrest Gacy, but they knew that they needed to get a search warrant for his crawl space. In the morning, Gacy left the lawyer's office and led the investigators on a wild car chase around the area, during which he seemed to be bidding farewell to friends. At one point, they saw tears in his eyes. Eventually they arrested him for possession of marijuana, which he had picked up from a friend along the way. Before the end of the day, a judge had approved a search warrant for the crawl space. The investigators went to work.

A suburban newspaper had noted the disappearance of Robert Piest and his family's attempts to find him, but the world had not yet heard about John Wayne Gacy. And no one had notified the upper ranks of the Cook County State's Attorney's Office in Chicago.

When the phone rang at the home of William J. Kunkle sometime after 1 a.m. on December 22, he was sound asleep. Kunkle was among the hundred or so prosecutors and guests who had spent the evening at Villa Marconi in one of Chicago's old West Side neighborhoods, not far from the fortress-like Criminal Courts Building. It was the annual Christmas party for the Felony Trial Division of the State's Attorney's Office. They were the elite of the office, and they shared a fierce determination never to lose a contest or a trial. Kunkle was their boss. Now, a prosecutor from a suburban district was on the phone. He was speaking very quickly and he sounded strange. Something about a "missing kid from Des Plaines . . . Robert Piest . . . suspect is a contractor named

John Gacy . . . digging in Gacy's crawl space . . . finding human bones . . . confessed to thirty murders."

The words "human bones" and "thirty murders" got Kunkle's attention. The medical examiner was on the scene and in control of the situation. The house, at 3218 West Summerdale Avenue, was in an unincorporated area not far from O'Hare International Airport. This meant that no local police department had jurisdiction over the crime scene, so Cook County was in charge. Kunkle made some calls and then set his alarm for 8 a.m. By morning, someone had alerted the media. The chaos had begun. Reporters, television crews, and curious onlookers had descended on the scene.

Gacy had told his lawyers, and then investigators, that he had killed thirty people and buried most of the bodies under the house. It was an outlandish claim, but there was a distinctive odor of rotting flesh wafting up from below. They had to check it out. Reddish worms squirmed around as a technician forced a small hand tool into the earth. It hit something. Within minutes, the man had unearthed a kneecap, a bone from an upper arm, and two leg bones. It was baffling, but it was time to stop digging and call in reinforcements from downtown. In the weeks and months that followed, it became clear that they were confronting one of the most prolific and proficient serial killers in the nation's history. Gacy, a thirty-six-year-old building contractor, had molested and killed thirty-three young men and boys over the previous seven years. He had buried most of the bodies in that space, and no one had noticed.

The chaos was escalating. The headline "Four bodies found; total climbs to 22" consumed a chunk of the *Chicago Tribune*'s front page on December 29, 1978. Much of the space was taken up by a leaked photograph of Gacy sitting upright in a bed at the Cook County Jail's hospital. His eyes were closed, and he was wearing a dotted, short-sleeved hospital gown. Leather restraints around his wrists kept him tethered to the armrests. He was a thirty-six-year-old "acknowledged homosexual."

What followed was one of the last great print newspaper wars, rivaling the one that chronicled New York's "Summer of Sam." This time it was the *Chicago Tribune* versus the *Chicago Sun-Times* in addition to dozens of local and national television crews suddenly camped out in the narrow street in front of a small suburban house nestled among a line of houses built in a postwar development. Neighbors could easily see out their windows into each other's homes, and they could certainly have heard anyone shouting nearby. But they hadn't really noticed anything especially unusual until then.

The excavation at Gacy's home would go on for days as officials carefully unearthed each body, took photographs, and gathered whatever physical evidence they could. Neighbors said that for a time some years earlier they had heard Gacy digging in his yard each night. Eventually he covered that area with blacktop. And he frequently seemed to have young boys working for him. At least three boys who had worked for him were missing. Police heard from two boys who said that in 1977 Gacy had hired them to dig trenches in his crawl space. He told them that the trenches would be lined with drainage tiles to fix a flooding problem. Investigators found bodies in the trenches, but no tiles.

As the digging went on, Gacy was being held in the psychiatric section of the Cook County Jail's hospital. He had claimed a variety of ailments, apparently out of fear of what the inmates in the jail cells might do to him. The hospital director, Robin Dean, said that Gacy might fear for his life. "The inmates have a strange code," he said. "One thing they do not tolerate is child molesting."

Gacy had told investigators that he had buried twenty-seven bodies on his property and had dumped five more in the nearby Des Plaines River. By the beginning of January, they had unearthed the twenty-seven on his property—nearly all from the crawl space—and the rest under the garage and in the backyard. Only two bodies were found in the river. Neither was the Piest boy's, which they assumed was in the river too.

Despite Gacy's on-and-off admissions about the murders, there was no sign that he had any intention of pleading guilty to anything. It seemed clear to everyone involved that he had only one option: to plead not guilty by reason of insanity. Gacy's lawyers filed motions to quash evidence, arguing, among other things, that the search warrants for his house had been illegal. Judge Louis B. Garippo, assigned to handle the case, rejected the requests.

Garippo had been selected to preside over the trial because of his even-tempered demeanor and his background with difficult cases. In a city accustomed to savage crimes, it was difficult to imagine a killer more monstrous than Richard Speck, who had stabbed or strangled to death eight student nurses in their Chicago apartment one night in the summer of 1966. Garippo, then a prosecutor, supervised the trial team in that grisly case. Speck was convicted and died in prison twenty-five years later. To his fellow judges, Garippo was the obvious choice to handle the Gacy case, which promised to be much more complex and troublesome.

Within minutes of getting the assignment on January 10, 1979, Garippo got a taste of the tense courtroom atmosphere that would emerge in the coming year. Amirante, Gacy's lawyer, asked Garippo to order a halt to the search on Gacy's property. Twenty-seven bodies had already been found there. "When will it end?" Amirante demanded. Kunkle, the head of the prosecution team, responded curtly: "The search will stop when we are satisfied with scientific certainty that there is not a twenty-eighth body buried there." Garippo ordered that the search continue. Prosecutors had already announced that they would seek the death penalty. Through it all, Gacy showed no sign of concern. He insisted on going to trial.

It would be a year before the trial got underway. By then, Gacy had been charged with thirty-three murders. The witness list contained more than two hundred people. Kunkle and the prosecution team cut their witness list by more than a half to keep the trial moving. In the end, at least half of the potential witnesses—including Rosalynn Carter—would never be called to the stand.

A trial in such a case presented daunting challenges, especially in 1979 and 1980. The prosecution set up what was basically a war room at the Criminal Courts building. Every desk held a typewriter, along with a box of carbon paper and a stack of index cards. There were, of course, no Macs or PCs or email or even document scanners to deal with the blizzard of reports that was surely on its way. The documents would hold significant clues and information about thirty-three victims, thirteen psychiatrists and psychologists, dozens of law enforcement officials, hundreds of interviews and test results, and endless bits of miscellany. It all had to be organized right away. Some kind of index was needed, and it had to be created by humans.

Victim witness advocates are commonplace today, but the concept was just emerging in 1979. One of Kunkle's secretaries, Ann Hensley, was given the task of acting as the liaison with the victims' families and other traumatized witnesses—and there were many.

The Chicago Police Department, too, saw that it was time to make some changes. Each year, it got nearly twenty thousand missing persons reports. Fourteen thousand of those missing were juveniles. Each report meant about four pages of paper stored in a filing cabinet. The police superintendent ordered that the information be fed into a new computer program. If such a program had existed a few years earlier, investigators might have seen a pattern, such as the disappearance of people who worked for the same employer. Eventually, they realized, law enforcement agencies might be able to use computers to share information across the country.

Views about homosexuality had begun to change in the 1970s and promised to be an issue at the trial. A police raid on a gay bar in Manhattan led to the Stonewall Uprising of 1969, viewed by historians as the start of a nationwide push for public acceptance of gay rights.

From the beginning of the Gacy case, it was clear that homosexuality was a factor in some of his victims' having disappeared unnoticed by their families. Some, perhaps, had cut themselves off from disapproving parents and moved to the Boystown area of Chicago. Greg Bedoe, the Cook County Sheriff's investigator involved in Gacy's arrest, spent much of the year before the trial working with prosecutors and, at times, visiting gay bars in Chicago, where frightened young men told of their encounters with Gacy. Meanwhile, Kunkle took a trip to Las Vegas to track down the truth about reports that Gacy had molested dead bodies while working for a funeral director there. He anticipated that the reports, if true, would become an element of Gacy's emerging insanity defense.

There was little hope of finding an unbiased jury in the Chicago area, where television and newspaper reporting had been relentless over the year since the first body was recovered. Normally, the solution would be a change of venue. But the idea of moving thousands of documents, dozens of police officers, investigators, and, possibly, hundreds of witnesses to another city for a trial that could take months was daunting.

Garippo came up with a novel solution. The jury would be selected in Rockford, a small city about ninety miles northwest of Chicago, near the Wisconsin border. The twelve jurors and four alternates would be moved to Chicago and sequestered in a hotel during the trial. To shorten their stay, the trial would be held six days a week, with Sundays off. The potential jurors were questioned separately and asked about their views on the death penalty, the insanity defense, and homosexuality. Jury selection took less than a week, and testimony began in Chicago in early February of 1980. By then, twenty-nine bodies had been unearthed on Gacy's property, and four more were found in Illinois rivers. Robert Piest's body was among them. Gacy was charged with thirty-three murders.

At the time of the trial, only twenty-two of the victims had been identified:

- **John Butkovich,** eighteen years old, from the North Side of Chicago. He disappeared on August 1, 1975. His body was found under Gacy's garage.
- **Darrell Sampson,** eighteen years old, from the North Side of Chicago. He disappeared on April 6, 1976. His body was found in the crawl space.
- **Randall Reffett,** fifteen years old, from the North Side of Chicago. He disappeared on May 14, 1976. His body was found in the crawl space.
- **Samuel Stapleton,** fourteen years old, from the North Side of Chicago. He disappeared on May 14, 1976. His body was found in the crawl space.
- **Michael L. Bonnin,** seventeen years old, from the North Side of Chicago. He disappeared on June 3, 1976. His body was found in the crawl space.
- **William Carroll Jr.,** sixteen years old, from the North Side of Chicago. He disappeared on June 10, 1976. His body was found in the crawl space.
- **Rick Johnston,** seventeen years old, from Bensenville, Illinois. He disappeared on August 6, 1976. His body was found in the crawl space.
- **Gregory Godzik,** seventeen years old, from the North Side of Chicago. He disappeared on December 12, 1976. His body was found in the crawl space.
- **John A. Szyc,** nineteen years old, from the North Side of Chicago. He disappeared on January 20, 1977. His body was found in the crawl space.
- **John S. Prestidge,** twenty years old, from Kalamazoo, Michigan. He had just moved to Chicago when he disappeared on March 15, 1977. His body was found in the crawl space.

- **Matthew Bowman,** eighteen years old, from Crystal Lake, Illinois. He disappeared on July 6, 1977. His body was found in the crawl space.
- **Robert E. Gilroy,** eighteen years old, from the North Side of Chicago. He disappeared on September 15, 1977. His body was found in the crawl space.
- **John Mowery,** nineteen years old, from the North Side of Chicago. He disappeared on September 25, 1977. His body was found in the crawl space.
- **Russell Nelson,** twenty-two years old, from Cloquet, Minnesota. He disappeared while visiting Chicago on October 19, 1977. His body was found in the crawl space.
- **Robert Winch,** sixteen years old, from Kalamazoo, Michigan. He disappeared on November 11, 1977. His body was found in the crawl space.
- **Tommy Boling,** twenty years old, from the Chicago area. He was married and had one child. He disappeared on November 18, 1977. His body was found in the crawl space.
- **David Talsma,** nineteen years old, in the Marine reserves, lived with his parents. He disappeared on December 9, 1977. His body was found in the crawl space.
- **William Kindred,** nineteen years old, from the North Side of Chicago. He disappeared on February 16, 1978. His body was found in the crawl space.
- **Timothy O'Rourke,** twenty years old, from the North Side of Chicago. His body was recovered from the Illinois River near Grundy County on January 6, 1979.
- **Frank Landingin,** nineteen years old, from the North Side of Chicago. He disappeared on November 4, 1976. His body was found in the Des Plaines River.
- **James Mazzara,** twenty years old, from Elmwood Park, Illinois. He disappeared on November 20, 1978. His body was found in the Des Plaines River.

- **Robert Piest,** fifteen years old, from Des Plaines, Illinois. He disappeared on December 11, 1978. His body was found in the Des Plaines River.

The issue of homosexuality came up in the first days of the trial. The prosecution had to demonstrate that each victim had, in fact, been alive and was now dead. The task fell to Robert Egan, an assistant state's attorney assigned to the case. A relative or friend of each identified victim had to take the witness stand for what turned into emotional and harrowing testimony. Quickly, the subject of homosexuality came up. Donita Ganzon, a thirty-three-year-old registered nurse, was called to testify about her friend, Timothy O'Rourke, who, she said, had lived with her for a few months, until the fall of 1977. He went out one night to buy cigarettes and never returned. "No further questions," Egan said.

Quickly, Gacy's lawyer, Sam Amirante, took over. Ganzon had taken the witness stand with a bit of a flourish, wearing a long red dress. "Miss Ganzon, is it Miss or Mrs.?" Amirante asked. "Miss Ganzon," she answered. "How long has your name been Donita?" he asked. "Objection," Egan said. "I don't see how that is relevant." The judge told Amirante he could proceed.

"Since March, 1977," Ganzon answered. "What was it before that?" Amirante asked. "Don Ganzon," she replied. Amirante went on with his questions until Ganzon was forced to reveal that she was transitioning to female and that she had met Timothy O'Rourke in 1977, when she was still a male. Amirante pushed on and asked her about the progress of her transition and whether she had had a sex reassignment surgery yet. She said she hadn't. Then he asked her to describe the gay bars in the area.

As the trial moved on, a basic problem for the prosecution was the obvious logic of the insanity defense: a person who kills thirty-three people and buries most of the bodies under his house has to be crazy.

For the defense, the problem was that it seemed highly unlikely that Gacy, who ran his own successful business and entertained children at children's parties as Pogo the Clown, would have killed anyone if a police officer had been standing nearby. Gacy did not testify at the trial, but thirteen psychiatric professionals were drawn into the case. Their reports and long hours of testimony showed that Gacy had, over the years, offered a range of explanations about his behavior, including a multiple personality disorder—"Jack" had done it. He had also said, at times, that he did not know who buried all those bodies. He had been out of town frequently, and lots of people had had access to his house.

At one point in the middle the trial, Gacy wrote Judge Garippo a letter saying he would no longer have anything to do with his lawyers. Garippo summoned him to the bench and asked him why. "Because I'm not running the case," Gacy said. Asked if he disagreed with his attorneys, Gacy said, "I was against the insanity defense from the start." After a recess for lunch, Gacy returned to the courtroom and called his lawyers "some of the finest in the country." He said his biggest problem was that he had not been able to help them because he "couldn't remember." He went on: "I have never denied any of it. It's just that I do not know if, when it happened, was I aware of what I was doing." Earlier in the day, Gacy had blurted out, "I did not commit the crimes."

For relatives of the victims, it was a harrowing time. Many were called to the witness stand to testify about the last time they had seen their brother or son alive. Elizabeth Piest told the jury about her son Rob and about her trip to the Nisson Pharmacy where he worked. He was a sophomore in high school and had been on the honor roll his first year. He was two merit badges away from becoming an Eagle Scout and was working on a community service project to clean up the Des Plaines River. He had a crush on a girl name Carrie, and they were dating. And she described how she had sat by the phone all night while her husband and two other children were out searching for Rob.

Two weeks later, the defense called Gacy's mother to testify. Marian Gacy was seventy-two years old, and she made her way into the courtroom slowly, leaning on a metal walker. "I love my son. I still don't believe any of it," she testified. "I can't believe it. I can't believe he'd do any of it. Not my son. I'd just like to erase everything." She wept quietly into a handkerchief. During nearly twelve hours on the witness stand, she recounted what she knew about his life. John had been a sickly child, and at the time of his birth in 1942, the doctors had not expected him to live. He'd had blackout spells and was in and out of hospitals for a while. One doctor thought he had epilepsy. When he was a teenager, a doctor thought he should get psychiatric care. "John pleaded with me: 'Mom, don't send me to the psychiatric ward. I'll be good,'" Marian testified. "So I went and signed him out, which I probably shouldn't have done."

Overall it was an unhappy childhood, during which Gacy's father, John S. Gacy, was "mean" to him, demanded perfection, and always called him "stupid." Marian said her husband was an alcoholic with a "Jekyll and Hyde personality." Her son, she said, loved his father—a Polish immigrant who worked in a factory—but could never seem to please him. After high school, her son had worked in a shoe store for a while and was eventually transferred to a branch in Springfield, in central Illinois. There he met and married Marlene Myers. They had a daughter and a son. In 1966, the family moved to Waterloo, Iowa, where Marlene's father offered Gacy a management job at one of his Kentucky Fried Chicken franchises. After Gacy was arrested on the sodomy charge in Iowa in 1968, he never saw his wife or children again.

Gacy's sister, Karen, also took the witness stand. "The brother I knew was always sweet, loving, and generous," she said. Their father, who died in 1969, used to hit him, she said, and once threatened to kill him. She recalled an incident when the family had to call the police to pull her father off of John. He had disliked one of John's friends, whom he called "a fairy or a queer," and said John would end up that way.

In 1970, when he was released from prison in Iowa, Gacy moved back to the Chicago area and lived with his mother, who bought the house on Summerdale Avenue in January of 1971. Within a month, Gacy was arrested. A young man told the police that Gacy had picked him up at a bus stop and tried to force him to have sex with him. The charges were dropped after the young man failed to appear in court.

Gacy committed his first murder in January of 1972, when he picked up Jack McCoy, a sixteen-year-old, at the Greyhound station in downtown Chicago. McCoy's body was found in the crawl space. At about the same time, Gacy's mother moved out of the house, and his girlfriend, Carole Hoff, moved in, along with her two children. Gacy and Hoff got married in July of 1972; they divorced in 1976. Hoff had remarried by the time she testified at the trial, and her surname was now Lofgren. She said she had complained to Gacy repeatedly about the smell emanating from the crawl space, but he dismissed it as a plumbing problem and sometimes spread lime in the area. He promised to cover the whole area with concrete, she said. Summing up their relationship, she said, "I think he was sane all the time I have known him." Her testimony brought one of the few times Gacy showed emotion during the trial. He had been a good husband and a good father to her two young daughters, she said. "I feel sorry for him. My heart goes out to him." As she left the witness stand, Gacy put his hand to his head and covered his eyes.

Few of the thirteen psychiatrists and psychologists who testified at the trial agreed on a diagnosis. Some said Gacy was sane at the time of the murders, some said he was insane, and some had no opinion. In the end, the jury reached its thirty-three guilty verdicts in one hour and fifty minutes. The following day, they voted, after a deliberation of two hours and fifteen minutes, to recommend the death penalty. (See Appendix 3.)

As they passed each other in the back of the courtroom, Gacy stopped for a moment and spoke to Kunkle. "I think it was God's will," Gacy said. "All the jury did was to do the same thing I have been trying to do to myself for the last ten years: destroy myself." Kunkle replied, "John, all you've got left is to try and make peace with yourself."

Judge Garippo approved the jury's decision in an emotional courtroom statement. "I don't know what this trial will cost. Whatever the cost, it was a small price. What we do for the John Gacys of the world, we will do for everyone." It was a difficult decision for Garippo, who opposed the death penalty. A low-key but charismatic figure in the legal community, he left the bench and went into private practice not long after the trial, weary of the high-profile cases that had marked his career.

Because of the uproar and media frenzy over Gacy, Garippo had cut himself off from friends and colleagues while the case was pending—more than 16 months. At times, while shopping or walking along Michigan Avenue, he was approached by autograph seekers. They knew that they had seen his face somewhere. Some thought he was John Cassavetes, the Hollywood actor. Several weeks before Garippo's death in 2016, he ended decades of public silence about the Gacy case and his own misgivings about the death penalty. "I see no moral prohibition; however, it's a political solution to problems that legislatures can't solve," he said during an interview at a retirement home. He considered overruling the jury, which had voted unanimously for death, but decided against it because of the "rumpus" it would cause. "I've never been a fan of the death penalty," he said. "It's a political remedy to a social problem, and it's inadequate." On the night of Gacy's execution, Garippo was at home with his family.

Gacy had spent fourteen years on death row by the time all the appeals ended and the date of his execution was set: May 10, 1994. There had been no serious argument that police had gotten the wrong guy.

CLOWN ART BY JOHN WAYNE GACY.

Over the years, Gacy granted interviews to journalists and others, frequently changing his story, sometimes in small ways and sometimes significantly. He produced oil paintings that he offered for sale and generally seemed content.

But life on death row had its problems. Gacy was wounded in 1983 by Henry Brisbon, a fellow inmate who had been sentenced to death for killing an inmate in 1979 with a knife made from a soup ladle. He slashed Gacy with a sharpened piece of heavy-gauge wire. Brisbon was serving a sentence of one thousand to three thousand years imposed by a judge who said, "I'm sorry I can't execute you." He had been convicted of the brutal murders of a couple he encountered along a highway. When he was sentenced to death, he boasted to his guards: "You'll never get me. I'll kill again. Then you'll have another long trial. And then I'll do it again." Brisbon and more than 150 other death row inmates had their sentences commuted to life in prison in 2003 when Illinois abolished the death penalty.

Relatives of Gacy's victims seethed as the years of appeals wore on. Meanwhile, his appellate lawyers never prevailed on any issue. On execution day, they tried a variety of last-ditch maneuvers, including a claim that he could not legally be executed because he denied the reality of the pending execution.

For opponents of the death penalty, it would have been difficult to conjure up a less sympathetic martyr to the cause than Gacy. Simply put, he had no remorse. He tortured, raped, and strangled his victims over seven years and then, each time, went on with his life. He did, however, have abundant empathy—but only for himself. He never explained. He never apologized. If he were allowed to escape capital punishment, how could an argument ever be made that anyone deserved to be put to death? Gacy was, in essence, the embodiment of incomprehensible evil—the poster boy for supporters of the death penalty.

Still, small contingents of death penalty opponents stood their ground in downtown Chicago on the morning before the execution, scheduled for 12:20 a.m. on May 10, 1994. They were far outnumbered and outshouted by boisterous groups cheering for Gacy's death. It was as if a carnival had sprouted up at Daley Plaza, a government office and court complex in the Loop. More than a thousand demonstrators gathered there with signs urging that Gacy be executed. "Death To Gacy," read one. "Stick It To Him," read another.

On the pavement, thirty-three white body bags—one for each victim—were laid out by the Guardian Angels, the volunteer crime patrol group. A man dressed in a puffy white costume and a bright orange wig popped up here and there, a reminder that Gacy had performed as Pogo the Clown at children's parties. Death penalty enthusiasts launched a raucous musical tribute to the tune of "Hello, Dolly!"—"Hello, Gacy! Well hello, Gacy! It's so nice to have you right where you belong. You're not so swell, Gacy. You belong in hell, Gacy. You were killing. You were willing. No respect for life."

At about 11 p.m., as the witnesses began to settle into the chairs that had been crowded into the viewing room, Gacy was offered a sedative to calm his nerves. He turned it down. The viewing room was separated from the execution chamber by a glass wall. A large hood on the ceiling of the chamber reminded the witnesses of earlier decades, when the electric chair was used.

The death process, which began shortly after midnight, was quite clinical. The blinds on the window were opened, revealing Gacy on a stretcher with an IV attached to his arm. A solution of sedative was sent through the IV from a machine in an adjoining room. A solution intended to stop his breathing came next. Then, abruptly, the blinds on the window were closed. The witnesses were left to wonder why the expected third injection had not been administered and why there had been no declaration of death. They sat still and quiet. After eighteen minutes, the blinds were reopened. Gacy got the third and final shot, and he was pronounced dead. Officials explained that the IV line had been kinked or the needle had clogged. Replacements were made and the line was flushed with saline; then the process was completed. From beginning to end, Kunkle recalled, Gacy was quite still and showed no sign of agitation. His breathing appeared to stop shortly after the second solution was injected.

For Bedoe, the investigator, the execution was unexpectedly chilling. Gacy never looked around, neither in general nor at anyone in particular. There was no look of fear. No emotion. The only movement was in Gacy's chest—where he was breathing—and maybe a thumb. "That was it," Bedoe reported. "Very peaceful." But the scene reminded him of standing in the courtroom in 1980, face-to-face with Gacy, as Garippo announced the death sentence. Gacy did not blink an eye, Bedoe recalled. "He scared me, though. That sentencing thing got me. When he didn't blink an eye." Still, he thought Gacy had been fortunate, in a way. He explained, "If they said, 'Greg, you're going to die next Wednesday. How do you want to go?'—that's the way."

When it was over, the witnesses were led back to the prison's gym, where they signed the death certificate. Those who were willing to face the media were escorted to the large press tent on the lawn near the prison's main entrance. Dozens of microphones jammed the podium, and TV cameras were everywhere. A set of bleachers was crammed with reporters eager to ask questions—thoughtful, loaded, or otherwise. Prison officials went first, fielding a barrage of questions about the eighteen-minute delay in Gacy's death.

THE FACE OF THIS DOCUMENT HAS A COLORED BACKGROUND ON WHITE PAPER

STATE OF ILLINOIS

MEDICAL EXAMINER'S – CORONER'S CERTIFICATE OF DEATH

XX PERMANENT CERTIFICATE — REGISTRATION DISTRICT NO. 99.0 — STATE FILE NUMBER 139771

TEMPORARY CERTIFICATE — REGISTERED NUMBER 001004

DECEASED

1. JOHN WAYNE GACY — 2. SEX: MALE — 3. DATE OF DEATH: MAY 10, 1994
4. COUNTY OF DEATH: WILL — 5a. AGE–LAST BIRTHDAY: 52 — 5d. DATE OF BIRTH: MARCH 17, 1942
6a. CITY, TOWN, TWP. OR ROAD DISTRICT NUMBER: LOCKPORT TOWNSHIP — 6b. HOSPITAL OR OTHER INSTITUTION: STATEVILLE CORRECTIONAL CENTER
7. BIRTHPLACE: CHICAGO, ILLINOIS — 8a. MARRIED, NEVER MARRIED, WIDOWED, DIVORCED: DIVORCED — 9. WAS DECEASED EVER IN U.S. ARMED FORCES? NO
10. SOCIAL SECURITY NUMBER: 344-34-3840 — 11a. USUAL OCCUPATION: CONTRACTOR — 11b. KIND OF BUSINESS OR INDUSTRY: OWN BUSINESS — 12. EDUCATION: 12 / 5+
13a. RESIDENCE: KASKASKIA STREET — 13b. CITY, TOWN, OR ROAD DISTRICT NO.: MENARD — 13c. INSIDE CITY: YES — 13d. COUNTY: RANDOLPH
13e. STATE: ILLINOIS — 13f. ZIP CODE: 62259 — 14a. RACE: WHITE — 14b. OF HISPANIC ORIGIN? XX NO ☐ YES

PARENTS

15. FATHER: JOHN STANLEY GACY — 16. MOTHER: MARION ROBERTSON SCOW
17a. INFORMANT'S NAME: JOHN GREENLEES — 17b. RELATIONSHIP: LAWYER — 17c. MAILING ADDRESS: 3039 W. IRVING PK. RD. CHICAGO, IL. 60618

CAUSE

18. PART I.
(a) ACUTE CONGESTIVE HEART FAILURE
DUE TO, OR AS A CONSEQUENCE OF
(b) LETHAL LEVELS OF POTASSIUM CHLORIDE
DUE TO, OR AS A CONSEQUENCE OF
(c) LETHAL INJECTION
PART II.
19a. AUTOPSY: YES — 19b. YES
20a. NATURAL, ACCIDENT, HOMICIDE, SUICIDE, UNDETERMINED: HOMICIDE — 20b. DATE OF INJURY: MAY 10, 1994 — 20c. HOUR: 12:17 A. M. — 20d. HOW INJURY OCCURRED: victim injected with lethal drugs per judicial order
20e. INJURY AT WORK: NO — 20f. PLACE OF INJURY: STATE PRISON — 20g. LOCATION: LOCKPORT TWP, WILL COUNTY, ILLINOIS — 20h. YES ☐ NO ☐

CERTIFIER

21a. I CERTIFY THAT IN MY OPINION BASED UPON MY INVESTIGATION AND/OR THE INQUISITION, THIS DEATH OCCURRED ON THE DATE, AT THE PLACE AND DUE TO THE CAUSE(S) STATED, AND THAT — 21b. THE DECEDENT WAS PRONOUNCED DEAD ON MAY 10, 1994 — 21c. AT 12:58 A. M.
22a. CORONER'S–MEDICAL EXAMINER'S SIGNATURE: PATRICK K. O'NEIL *Patrick K. O'Neil* — 22b. DATE SIGNED: JUNE 17, 1994
23a. CORONER'S PHYSICIAN'S SIGNATURE — 23b.

DISPOSITION

24a. CREMATION — 24b. RIVER HILLS CREMATORY — 24c. BATAVIA, ILLINOIS — 24d. MAY 14, 1994
25a. FUNERAL HOME: McKEOWN-DUNN FUNERAL HOME, LTD. 210 MADISON STREET OSWEGO, ILLINOIS 60543
25b. FUNERAL DIRECTOR'S SIGNATURE: WILLIAM F. DUNN — 25c. 034-010714
26a. LOCAL REGISTRAR — 26b. DATE FILED BY LOCAL REGISTRAR: JUN 24 1994

CERTIFICATION

STATE OF ILLINOIS
COUNTY OF WILL

DATE December 12, 1994

I, JAN GOULD, COUNTY CLERK, DO HEREBY CERTIFY THAT THIS DOCUMENT IS A TRUE AND CORRECT COPY OF THE ORIGINAL RECORD ON FILE IN THE WILL COUNTY CLERK'S OFFICE, JOLIET, ILLINOIS.

Jan Gould
COUNTY CLERK, WILL COUNTY, ILLINOIS

(COUNTY SEAL)

Shirley Chapman
DEPUTY

THE BACK OF THIS DOCUMENT CONTAINS AN ARTIFICIAL WATERMARK – HOLD AT AN ANGLE TO VIEW

JOHN WAYNE GACY'S DEATH CERTIFICATE, SIGNED ON JUNE 17, 1994 AFTER GACY'S EXECUTION BY LETHAL INJECTION ON MAY 10, 1994.

Kunkle stood by, a little impatient with the officials' increasingly defensive answers. When his turn came, he spoke on behalf of the victims, their families, and the people. It was a shame, he said, that it had taken fourteen years to get the full measure of justice, but he was very glad that the scales of justice had finally come to rest. Someone asked him about the eighteen-minute delay. In his layman's opinion, he said, based on the sequence of lights on the machines and the cessation of chest movement, indicating no further breathing, Gacy was indeed dead before the delay. If something had gone wrong, Kunkle said, and Gacy was still alive until the third solution was administered, "then he got eighteen minutes more than he was entitled to."

Walter Jacobson, a Chicago television news anchor, shouted out, "Oh, Bill! You don't really mean that!"

"As far as I'm concerned, they could have done it with a baseball bat," Kunkle replied.

Attorney Egan followed Kunkle to the podium and gave the press another ten-second sound bite: "He had it a lot better than his victims. He just went to sleep."

Six Gacy victims remained unidentified forty years after the bodies in the crawl space were found. Five have been identified in the years since the trial ended, some by the use of DNA technology. They are:

- **Kenneth Parker,** sixteen years old, from the Chicago area. He disappeared on October 24, 1976. His body was found in the crawl space and identified in 1980.
- **Michael Marino,** fourteen years old, from the Chicago area. In 2016, DNA testing cast doubt about whether he was a victim. He disappeared on October 24, 1976.
- **Timothy Jack McCoy,** sixteen years old, from Iowa and Nebraska. Picked up at the downtown Chicago Greyhound bus station in January of 1972. His body, found in the crawl space, was identified in May of 1986.
- **James Haakenson,** sixteen years old, from St. Paul, Minnesota. He disappeared on August 5, 1976. His body, found in the crawl space, was identified in July of 2017.

- **William George Bundy,** nineteen years old, from Chicago. He disappeared on October 26, 1976. His body was identified in November of 2011. He is believed to have been a construction worker for Gacy. His body was found in the crawl space.

EPILOGUE

Samuel Little was seventy-nine years old in October of 2019 when the FBI declared him the most prolific serial killer in American history. He had confessed to committing ninety-three murders from California to Florida, and investigators had been able to confirm his connection to fifty of those cases. Many more, they said, were still under review.

For four decades, Little had pretty much flown under the radar of the country's hundreds of overlapping law enforcement agencies. He served some time in jails and prisons for a range of crimes beginning in 1956, but his relative good fortune came to an end in 2012. He was arrested in a homeless shelter in Kentucky and extradited to Los Angeles, where he faced a narcotics charge. DNA testing had, by then, become a routine procedure, as had nationwide sharing of information. It wasn't long before the Los Angeles Police Department matched Little's DNA to the murders of three women in the 1980s. The women had been beaten and strangled; the body of one was found in an alley, another in a dumpster, and the third in a garage. The prosecution called other women to testify about surviving similar violent encounters with Little. He angrily denied the murders and allegations. Nonetheless, he was convicted in 2014 and sentenced to three terms of life in prison without parole.

In the years since his sentencing, he has been cooperating with investigators by offering detailed confessions about many of the murders. Investigators have noted that he has an unusual ability to recall details of the killings, which seemed to peak in the 1970s and '80s. He chose his victims carefully, focusing on the fringes of society to find women who were prostitutes, drug addicts, alcoholics, or homeless. He chose "marginalized and vulnerable women" whose bodies were never identified and whose deaths were never investigated, the FBI said. Because he did not use a gun or a knife, some of the deaths were attributed to drug overdoses, accidents, or natural causes. Little, whose health has been failing, spent many hours in 2018 and 2019 helping investigators create sketches of his victims, which are posted on the FBI's website along with a request for any information from the public about who they might be. The FBI has also posted video interviews conducted with Little about murders he says he committed over the decades in Kentucky, Florida, Louisiana, Nevada, and Arkansas.

Another prolific killer at work in the 1980s was Gary Leon Ridgway, perhaps better known as the "Green River Killer." He holds second place in the ranking of American serial killers. He had admitted to murdering forty-eight women, but law enforcement officials suspect he committed more. The mystery of the Green River Killer began in 1982, when the body of a sixteen-year-old prostitute was found under a bridge in the Green River in Kent, Washington, a town between Seattle and Tacoma. Ridgway, a truck painter, lived in Auburn, a small town near Kent. Ultimately, five bodies were found in the river. Ridgway picked up his victims—all female—in the Seattle area over a sixteen-year period. He disposed of most of their bodies in wooded areas around King County, which includes Seattle. Most of the victims had been strangled.

Like Samuel Little, Ridgway was caught after DNA technology emerged. He was arrested in 2001 after investigators matched his DNA to one of the victims. At first he denied the killings, but later he struck a deal to avoid the death penalty. He agreed to lead investigators to the killing sites and to help them identify victims. In return, Ridgway, who was fifty-four years old at the time, was sentenced to forty-eight consecutive terms of life in prison without the possibility of parole.

Women make up a small percentage of known serial killers, but the end of the 1980s brought national attention to two females who, at least on the surface, seemed quite different from one another. Dorothea

Montalvo Puente was fifty-nine years old in 1988 when investigators using backhoes began digging up bodies in the yard of the Victorian boarding house she operated as a care home in Sacramento, not far from the State Capitol building. Ultimately, the bodies of seven tenants were found on the property, and two were found elsewhere. Prosecutors charged Puente with committing nine murders from 1982 to 1986. The victims were marginalized people with mental illnesses or disabilities and few family connections. The youngest was fifty-two and the oldest was eighty. Puente continued to cash their Social Security checks for months or years after they died. In the end, a jury found her guilty of two first-degree murders and one second-degree murder but was unable to reach a verdict on six of the deaths. Puente died in prison in 2011 at the age of eighty-two.

Aileen Wuornos was thirty-three years old in 1989 when she killed a middle-aged man who had picked her up as she was hitchhiking along a highway. By the time she was arrested a little over a year later, she had killed at least five more men who'd stopped to pick her up along Interstate 4 or Interstate 75 in Florida. She was an instant media sensation as a "female drifter," a "prostitute," and, eventually, a "bisexual prostitute" who lured unsuspecting middle-aged men into secluded areas before robbing and shooting them. She was the "Damsel of Death."

A difficult childhood, during which her mother had abandoned her, led to questions about Wuornos's mental health and sanity. She claimed that she killed the men in self-defense because they attempted to rape her, but she eventually said that she had intended to kill them. She was convicted of one murder and pleaded no contest to five others. Wuornos was executed by the state of Florida in 2002. On the evening before her death, she told a friend that she was "looking forward to being home with God and getting off this earth." In 2004, actress Charlize Theron won an Oscar for her portrayal of Wuornos in the film *Monster*. The critic Roger Ebert called it "one of the best performances in the history of cinema."

Florida was equally tough on Bobby Joe Long, who was arrested near the end of 1984 after killing at least ten young women and raping many more over the previous eight months in the Tampa, Florida, area. Some of the victims were sex workers, but others were women selling furniture or other items through newspaper advertisements. Long became known as the "Classified Ad Rapist." He was caught after he released one of his victims in November of 1984. He had abducted the seventeen-year-old as she was riding her bicycle home after ending her shift at a Krispy Kreme shop. He raped her repeatedly over twenty-six hours and then let her go. She went to the police, who tracked him down and arrested him. Long confessed to having committed ten murders and was eventually convicted of eight. He was executed by lethal injection in Florida in May of 2019.

Jeffrey Dahmer was in his twenties during the 1980s when he began honing his skills as a murderer, necrophile, and cannibal. His story would have made an improbable Hitchcock movie, but it was real. He admitted that from 1978 to 1992 he had killed seventeen men and boys, nearly all in the Milwaukee, Wisconsin, area. He sometimes boiled decapitated heads, and he cooked and ate parts of the victims' bodies. He claimed that he was driven to kill because he had an irresistible compulsion to have sex with corpses. Dahmer was arrested in 1991 after one of his victims, who was partially handcuffed, flagged down Milwaukee police and led them to Dahmer's apartment, where they found parts of eleven bodies. After a trial, Dahmer was sentenced to fifteen consecutive life terms in prison. In 1994, Dahmer was beaten to death in a Wisconsin prison by another inmate. Dahmer's body was cremated in 1995, but his brain was preserved at the request of his mother, who wanted to have it examined to determine whether biological factors had contributed to her son's behavior. Dahmer's father objected, and a few months later a judge ordered the brain destroyed.

Much farther north, in the wilds of Alaska, Robert Christian Hansen was committing a long string of murders. Sometimes called the "Butcher

Baker," Hansen confessed in 1984 to abducting, raping, and killing seventeen women in the 1970s and '80s. Hansen, who owned a bakery in Anchorage, was forty-five years old when he confessed to the killings. Beginning in 1973, he said, he killed prostitutes and topless dancers around Anchorage, Alaska, and dumped their bodies in the frozen wilderness. In 1984 he was sentenced to 461 years plus life in prison for four of the murders. At the time, only four of the bodies had been found. Sometimes he raped the women, freed them into the wilderness, and then hunted them down and killed them with a rifle or a knife. He was portrayed by the actor John Cusack in the 2013 film *The Frozen Ground*, which also featured Nicolas Cage as a police officer investigating the murders. Hansen died in prison in 2014 at the age of seventy-five. By then, twelve of the seventeen bodies had been discovered.

Thousands of miles to the east in upstate New York, there were echoes of the Hansen case in the late 1980s. Arthur Shawcross, sometimes called the "Genesee River Killer" or the "Rochester Strangler," was arrested in early 1990 and charged with the murders of ten women—most of them prostitutes who worked in the Rochester area. At his trial in 1990, the jury rejected his insanity plea and convicted him of all ten murders. He died in prison in 2008.

The American West seemed to have the nation's largest share of brutal serial killings. Gerald and Charlene Gallego were suspected of having killed at least ten women and girls in Nevada and Northern California by the time they were arrested in November of 1980. Most of the victims were teenagers whom the Gallegos exploited as sex slaves. Gerald Gallego had been on death row in a Nevada prison for eighteen years when he died of cancer in 2002. His appeals were pending at the time. Charlene Gallego, who testified against her husband in return for a plea deal, was released from prison on parole in 1998.

Leonard Lake and Charles Ng were suspected of killing at least twelve people—and as many as nineteen—in 1984 and 1985 at a remote house in the foothills of the Sierra Madre, east of San Francisco. Ng escaped and went to Canada, but he was caught a month later while shoplifting a soda. After a long extradition fight, he was returned to California in 1991. Lake committed suicide at the scene by swallowing a cyanide capsule he carried with him. Investigators soon found pounds of charred and dismembered human remains on the property in the foothills and scattered in the surrounding area. Ng was eventually convicted of killing six men, three women, and two babies. At the end of 2019—thirty-four years after his arrest—Ng remained on death row at San Quentin Prison.

Another notorious resident of San Quentin's death row was Richard Ramirez, known as the "Night Stalker" for a series of killings in 1984 and '85. A Satan worshipper and serial rapist, he terrorized California from San Francisco to Los Angeles until he was caught in 1985. He broke into homes in the middle of the night and then shot, stabbed, or beat his victims, sometimes raping them. Some victims survived and were able to describe their attacker to police. He was ultimately tracked down and held by an angry mob until police arrived. He was convicted of thirteen murders and sentenced to death, but while appeals were still pending, he died of natural causes in 2013 at the age of fifty-three.

It took more than three decades for authorities to catch up with the mysterious "Golden State Killer." He left a trail of bodies and rape victims all over California from the mid-1970s to the mid-1980s. Through a genealogy website, Joseph James DeAngelo, a former police officer in Auburn, California, was tracked down in 2018 and arrested. He has since been charged with thirteen murders.

Some speculate that the 1970s and 1980s were the last workable decades for serial killers. The horrors of those years, particularly the 1970s, led to the formation of the FBI's Behavioral Science Unit in Quantico, Virginia. Donald T. Lunde, the Stanford University psychiatrist who was involved in some of the most notorious cases of the

1970s, recalled getting a call after his book *Murder and Madness* was published. Robert Ressler, who studied serial killers for the FBI, wanted Lunde to consider heading up the program. Lunde declined, but the unit grew into an important resource over the following decades. It was an era when forensic psychiatry and other forensic specialties began to come into their own.

APPENDIX 1

Excerpt from People v. Superior Court (Corona) , 30 Cal.3d 193

[S.F. No. 24282. Supreme Court of California. November 16, 1981.]

THE PEOPLE, Petitioner, v. THE SUPERIOR COURT OF ALAMEDA COUNTY, Respondent; JUAN VALLEJO CORONA, Real Party in Interest

(Opinion by Richardson, J., with Tobriner, Mosk, Newman, Kaus and Broussard, JJ., concurring. Separate concurring opinion by Bird, C. J.) [30 Cal.3d 194]

COUNSEL

George Deukmejian, Attorney General, Robert H. Philibosian, Chief Assistant Attorney General, Arnold O. Overoye, Assistant Attorney General, Arthur G. Scotland, Joel Carey and J. Robert Jibson, Deputy Attorneys General, H. Ted Hansen, District Attorney, Ronald W. Fahey, Roger W. Pierucci and Mark L. Musto for Petitioner.

No appearance for Respondent.

Terence K. Hallinan, Michael A. Mendelson, Isaiah B. Roter and Roy J. Van Den Heuvel for Real Party in Interest.

OPINION

RICHARDSON, J.

Following reversal of his conviction on 25 counts of first degree murder because of his trial counsel's incompetence and conflict of interest, defendant Juan Corona was permitted to relitigate his earlier unsuccessful challenges to two search warrants which had produced evidence leading to his conviction. The People (hereinafter petitioner), protesting relitigation of the search issues, and contending in any event that the search warrants were properly obtained and executed, seek a writ of mandate to set aside the trial court's order suppressing much of the evidence seized pursuant to these two warrants. . . .

During oral argument, defense counsel stipulated to the admission (subject to possible relevancy objections) of a portion of the evidence seized during execution of the first warrant (namely, six rounds of nine millimeter ammunition found in defendant's van), and all of the evidence seized during execution of the second warrant. This stipulation, . . . assertedly based upon counsel's appraisal of the relevance and incriminatory nature of this evidence, was made in furtherance of expediting retrial. On the basis of our review of the complete record and the legal issues therein presented, we accept the stipulation which substantially narrows the issues before us and, accordingly, we do not further consider whether the foregoing evidence was properly seized.

With respect to the remainder of the evidence seized under the first warrant, we have concluded that the writ should issue. While rejecting petitioner's challenge to the trial court's jurisdiction to relitigate the suppression issues, we nonetheless conclude that the court erred in ordering the remaining evidence at issue suppressed. We further conclude that the thoughtful opinion of Justice Grodin for the Court of Appeal, First Appellate District, in this case correctly treats these issues in this prolonged litigation and we adopt a portion of his opinion as our own.

The Court of Appeal opinion, with appropriate deletions and additions,* is as follows:

[] *Procedural Background*

On January 18, 1973, defendant was found guilty and convicted of 25 counts of first degree murder. On May 8, 1978, [the Court of Appeal] set the conviction aside because of inadequate legal representation and conflict of interest on the part of defendant's original trial counsel. . . . The factual background of the case is fully set forth in that opinion . . . and need not be repeated here. The court, in a unanimous opinion authored by Justice Kane, found that "trial counsel in gross neglect of his basic duty, failed to conduct the requisite factual and legal investigation in an effort to develop fundamental defenses available for his client and as a result of his neglect, crucial defenses were withdrawn from the case" . . . thus warranting reversal on the basis of the then-prevailing standard of incompetency. . . . In addition, and as independent grounds for reversal, the court determined that Corona's trial counsel, by obtaining and exploiting literary and dramatic rights to . . . Corona's life story "created a situation which prevented him from devoting the requisite undivided loyalty and service to his client. From that moment on, trial counsel was devoted to two masters with conflicting interests—he was forced to choose between his own pocketbook and the best interests of his client the accused". . . . Without deciding

* Brackets together, in this manner [], are used to indicate deletions from the opinion of the Court of Appeal; brackets enclosing material (other than the editor's parallel citations) are, unless otherwise indicated, used to denote insertions or additions by this court.

whether such a conflict of interest was sufficient in itself to demonstrate denial of the right to effective representation as a matter of law, or whether a showing of actual prejudice was required, the court held that the case met both criteria, and that trial counsel's conduct "constituted not only an outrageous abrogation of the standards which the legal profession has set for itself and upon which clients have a right to rely, but also rendered the trial a farce and mockery calling for reversal of the conviction and requiring a new trial". . . .

The court concluded its opinion by considering several issues relating to the new trial which was to take place. Of these, only one is relevant here. In a proceeding under Penal Code section 1538.5 to suppress certain evidence, the trial court had refused to permit defendant's counsel to call witnesses for the purpose of challenging the accuracy of information contained in affidavits supporting various search warrants. Justice Kane's opinion found this to be error . . . but due to the unavailability of a transcript of the suppression hearing it could not be determined whether the error was prejudicial. The opinion states: "If, on retrial, appellant offers evidence to challenge the factual allegations of the affidavits supporting the search warrants, the court should proceed in accordance with the precepts enunciated in Theodor and as expressed herein". . . .

On March 28, 1979, Corona's present attorneys noticed a motion to suppress all evidence seized under six search warrants. Petitioner opposed the motion on the ground that the court had no jurisdiction to entertain a second Penal Code section 1538.5 motion. . . . Corona's attorneys countered that certain significant arguments had not been made at the original section 1538.5 motion, and that prior counsel's incompetency and conflict of interest had prevented full determination at that time.

Judge Patton, a distinguished and experienced jurist who tried the original case, presided at the new hearings which began April 25, 1979. At first he expressed doubt about the propriety of hearing the issues . . . to be presented by Corona's attorneys, but reserved judgment on that question and insisted on hearing the mandated Theodor aspects first. After doing so, however, he decided that the hearing would encompass all issues raised.

Almost nine court days were required to hear that matter, in the course of which twenty-five witnesses were sworn and testified. At the conclusion of the hearing the court issued a 44-page written opinion suppressing part of the evidence seized under the first warrant on the ground that the affidavit did not establish probable cause to search a specific building, and all of the evidence seized under the second warrant on the ground that the warrant was overly broad. The People stipulated that no evidence seized under the third through sixth warrants would be used [and, as noted above, defendant has now stipulated to the admission of all evidence seized under the second warrant]. Consequently the validity of those warrants [] is not an issue here. . . .

As Justice Kane's opinion noted . . . the constitutional right to effective counsel "includes the requirement that the services of the attorney be devoted solely to the interest of his client undiminished by conflicting considerations." And, as that opinion observed, "some cases take the view that a conflict of interest is so inherently conducive to divided loyalties as to amount to a denial of the right to effective representation as a matter of law". . . . By that view the conflict of interest found to exist on the part of Corona's original counsel necessarily involved denial of the right to effective representation in all of the original proceedings, not just the trial itself, and by itself would warrant the determination that Corona should be entitled to assert anew his new constitutional rights under section 1538.5.

Justice Kane's opinion also noted an alternative view, that the defendant "must affirmatively establish that he has suffered some actual prejudice" resulting from the conflict (ibid.), but refrained from deciding which view was correct. Rather, the opinion stated that the case met both criteria . . . and went on to discuss specific examples of prejudice as demonstrated by the record. While trial counsel's performance at the suppression hearing was not among the examples given, that omission is perhaps explainable by the fact (as the court noted) that no transcript of the suppression hearing was available.

[We need not here resolve the question whether actual prejudice must be shown in a conflict of interest situation such as occurred here. That question has been neither briefed nor argued in the present case.] If there is a general requirement that prejudice be shown from conflict . . . in interest, perhaps that requirement ought not to apply in a situation such as this where the defendant is hampered in presenting evidence as to what occurred in the original proceeding by the absence of any transcript thereof. Justice Kane in his opinion makes reference to unsuccessful efforts by the court to acquire "this important transcript," and to the consequent impossibility of determining whether denial of a hearing on defendant's Theodor motion constituted prejudicial error. . . . We can only speculate as to the reasons for the absence of such a transcript, but whatever the reason the result is defendant is deprived of the best evidence as to what actually occurred.

But assuming that a finding of prejudice is necessary, it was in fact made. Judge Patton expressly determined in the proceedings after remand that Corona's trial counsel "had not fully and adequately represented [Corona] in reference to the search warrants and that the entire matter should be reviewed." Moreover, the finding was amply supported under all the circumstances. The nature of trial counsel's conflict of interest was such that his economic interests were likely to be served by proceeding to trial with all the lurid evidence that the prosecutor could produce, rather than attempt to exclude legally inadmissible evidence on the basis of "technical" assertions of constitutional right. The hearing on the original suppression motion together with hearing on various discovery motions lasted only a total of 4 hours and 35 minutes, and the points and authorities filed by original counsel for Corona did not address themselves to the particular issues which were advanced at the second hearing and which formed the basis for the rulings complained of. Judge Patton, of course, was in a position to know what occurred at the first hearing, since he conducted it; and while it would have been preferable from the standpoint of appellate review for the record to reflect more precisely the basis for his determination that Corona's interests were not then fully and adequately represented, the constitutional rights at stake require that we give considerable weight to his view of the matter. We conclude that the trial court had jurisdiction to hear Corona's section 1538.5 motion on the validity of the search warrants due to the effective denial of any meaningful opportunity for a full determination of the merits. We conclude also that Judge Patton did not abuse his discretion in deciding to hear the matter fully, a decision grounded—in part—upon considerations of fundamental fairness with which we agree.

2. The First Warrant.

On May 20, 1971, the body of Kenneth Whitacre was discovered buried on the Kagehiro Ranch, a ranch neighboring the J. L. Sullivan Ranch. The victim had been stabbed in the chest and had a severe hacking wound in the back of his head. Evidence suggested he had been killed recently and buried on May 19, 1971, some time between 10 a.m. and about 6 p.m.

On the morning of May 25, 1971, a body was found buried on the Sullivan Ranch, apparently the victim of similar violence. Between 4:30 p.m. and 10:45 p.m. on May 25, 1971, seven additional victims were unearthed from graves on the Sullivan Ranch. All the victims had similar stabbing and hacking wounds.

At 2:38 a.m. on May 26, 1971, a warrant issued authorizing the search of various buildings and vehicles for "Knives, axes, machetes, shovels or any other cutting or stabbing instruments or weapons"; bloodstained clothes, vehicles, or weapons of any sort; the personal effects of any of the victims; and "any other evidence including but not limited to payroll and employment records associating Juan V. Corona, or any other person" with the death of the victims. . . .

Among the places authorized to be searched was a building described in the warrant, and in the affidavit for the warrant, as a "single family residence dwelling located fartherest [sic] to the north in the complex of buildings known as the J. L. Sullivan Ranch, loading station and labor camp otherwise known as 4817 Live Oak Highway, Sutter County, California together with the premises surrounding said residence and any and all out buildings and appurtenances thereof." Although not so described in the affidavit or the warrant, the "single family residence dwelling" was in fact a mess hall for farm workers, and was also used by Corona as an office for occasional sleeping purposes. Search of that building yielded an awl or ice pick, a double-bladed axe, two hunting knives, a 9 [millimeter] automatic pistol and ammunition, a pair of tin snips, business receipts, Sullivan Ranch payroll check stubs, and credit cards in Corona's name.

The trial court ordered this evidence suppressed on the ground that the affidavit for the warrant did not establish probable cause for the search of the mess hall.

[*a. Probable Cause to Search Mess Hall*]

[3] On review, we bring to bear the same standard which governed the trial court: the magistrate's order issuing the warrant may be set aside only if the affidavit, as a matter of law, does not establish probable cause. . . . In making that determination all of the facts and circumstances of the case must be considered. . . .

The affidavit contained allegations of certain circumstantial evidence linking Corona to the crimes. Corona was a farm labor contractor, and contracted farm labor for both the Kagehiro and Sullivan ranches; he thus had access to the locations where the nine bodies were discovered; from the manner in which each of the victims had been killed and buried, it appeared they were probably killed by the same person; two receipts issued in Corona's name by a local company were found in the grave of one of the victims; and one of the victims was last seen alive entering a vehicle owned by Corona.

The applicable constitutional test is "whether the affidavit states facts that make it substantially probable that there is specific property lawfully subject to seizure presently located in the particular place for which the warrant is sought". . . . Thus, the issue is whether the affidavit, in addition to linking Corona to the crimes, contained sufficient facts linking Corona to the building to be searched, so as to make it probable that he had stored or secreted items named in the search warrant there. . . . An otherwise insufficient affidavit cannot be rehabilitated by evidence concerning information possessed by the affiant when he sought the warrant but not disclosed to the issuing magistrate. . . .

The affidavit recites that at approximately 9 p.m. on May 25, 1971 (the night the affidavit was prepared and the warrant issued), officers began surveillance of Corona's van. The van was observed to go into Marysville with two occupants, a Mexican male and a female. Then, after about 45 minutes, the vehicle with its two occupants travelled to . . . the Sullivan Ranch and parked "near the house in the northeast portion of the camp" for approximately 15 minutes. Thereafter, the vehicle travelled to a residence at 768 Richland Road, the address of Corona's residence. At this point, according to the affidavit, a female was seen to leave the vehicle and enter the residence.

The trial court reasoned that so far as appeared from the affidavits Corona's connection to the mess hall building consisted (1) of his status as a labor contractor at Sullivan Ranch, and (2) of the fact that his vehicle was seen parked near the building for 15 minutes on the night of the day that 8 bodies were discovered buried on the ranch property. Petitioner contends that the affidavit yields additional inferences which support the magistrate's finding of probable cause.

First, petitioner contends that it is a reasonable inference from the affidavit, not only that Corona is a labor contractor at the Sullivan Ranch, but that he operated a labor camp there, in the complex of buildings of which the mess hall was a part. The affidavit referred to the "complex of buildings known as the J. L. Sullivan Ranch, loading station and labor camp." It also referred to "a bus apparently converted from a school bus currently parked on the above-described Sullivan property and bearing the painted name on its side of Juan Corona and designating him as a labor contractor". . . .

The trial court, in evaluating the particularity of the first warrant's description of items to be seized, expressed the view that Corona was a labor contractor "whose business it was to provide other men to work for farmers, including transportation to and from the farm site," and that Corona was the type of labor contractor who "feeds and houses the laborers (at a labor camp)."

In addition, petitioner contends that it is a fair inference that a labor contractor who operates a labor camp has access to the buildings in the labor camp complex, at least for the purpose of caring for the farm workers; and that he is likely to use buildings within the labor camp as a place to maintain records incident to his business.

Finally, petitioner contends that it is reasonable to infer from the facts regarding the surveillance of Corona's van on the night of May 25, 1971, and its presence outside the mess hall building for approximately 15 minutes at 10 p.m., that Corona in fact entered the mess hall that night, and that he did so either in furtherance of his business relationship as the farm labor contractor or to transfer, conceal, or dispose of criminal evidence in the van or at the crime scene. On either premise, petitioner contends, it was reasonable for the magistrate to conclude that there was a substantial probability that property described in the affidavit would be found there.

Petitioner calls our attention also to the extreme urgency of the situation: the affidavit was prepared, and the warrant was issued, during the course of an ongoing investigation into what appeared, at least, to be the work of a homicidal maniac on the loose; there was thus a heightened risk, petitioner contends, of loss of evidence or further homicide which demanded immediate action. . . .

[] The affidavit, hastily prepared, leaves more to inference than was desirable, or even necessary. We cannot say, however, that the inferences . . . suggested by petitioner are so attenuated that they could not reasonably have been accepted by the issuing magistrate. The magistrate could have reasoned that Corona was in his car on the night of May 25, 1971; that he went to the Sullivan Ranch that night for some reason; and that the reason related to the ongoing discovery of victims on the Sullivan Ranch and the probable existence of incriminating evidence in the mess hall building. In deference to the principle that doubtful or marginal cases should be largely determined by the preference to be accorded warrants, we conclude that the affidavit for the first warrant supplied probable cause to search the mess hall, and that the trial court therefore erred in suppressing evidence from that building. [End of Court of Appeal opinion.]

b. *Seizure of Nine Millimeter Automatic Pistol and Ammunition at Mess-Hall*

[5] Defendant contends that, even if there was probable cause to search the mess hall pursuant to the first warrant, it did not authorize the seizure of guns or ammunition, only "Knives, axes, machetes, shovels, or any other cutting or stabbing instruments or weapons." According to defendant, the trial court properly suppressed the gun and ammunition found in defendant's desk at the mess hall because, "at the time the warrant was issued no victims had been shot; therefore, no nexus existed between the gun and criminal activity." (Italics in original.)

The People correctly observe, however, that the warrant also authorized seizure of "any other evidence . . . associating Juan V. Corona, or any other person," with the death of the victims, as well as seizure of "bloodstained weapons of any sort." (Italics added.) The pistol and ammunition were discovered in a desk whose contents bore defendant's name. These items were lying beside a hunting knife; the gun was cocked, loaded and appeared to have either bloodstains or rust on its barrel. Although most of the victims seemed to have been stabbed to death, it was not unreasonable under the circumstances to conclude that the gun (and its ammunition) had been used to facilitate some of the murders, and that these items thus constituted evidence associating defendant with the victims' deaths. We conclude that the trial court erred in suppressing the gun and ammunition found at the mess hall. Having so concluded, we need not resolve the People's additional contention that seizure of these items was also justified under the "plain view" doctrine. . . .

Let a peremptory writ of mandate issue directing the respondent court to vacate its order of May 30, 1979, and to hold such further proceedings as may be consistent with our opinion.

Tobriner, J., Mosk, J., Newman, J., Kaus, J., and Broussard, J., concurred.

APPENDIX 2

Excerpt from Rodney Alcala's appeal before the United States Court of Appeals, argued February 6, 2003

334 F.3d 862

RODNEY J. ALCALA, Petitioner-Appellee,

v.

JEANNE S. WOODFORD, Warden, of the California State Prison at San Quentin, Respondent-Appellant.

RODNEY J. ALCALA, Petitioner-Appellant,

v.

JEANNE S. WOODFORD, Warden, of the California State Prison at San Quentin, Respondent-Appellee.

No. 01-99005.

No. 01-99006.

United States Court of Appeals, Ninth Circuit.

Argued and Submitted February 6, 2003.

Filed June 27, 2003. . . .

Jeanne Woodford, Warden of California's San Quentin State Prison ("California"), appeals the district court's conditional grant of habeas relief to petitioner Rodney J. Alcala. Alcala was sentenced to death following his conviction for first-degree murder. He is currently in prison.

California argues that the district court (1) incorrectly found that Alcala's trial counsel had been constitutionally ineffective in presenting Alcala's alibi, (2) improperly found that the state trial court committed constitutional error in excluding the testimony of defense witness Dr. Ray London, (3) erred in concluding that the state trial court's denial of Alcala's request for an independent medical examination of prosecution witness Dana Crappa violated the Sixth Amendment, and (4) erroneously aggregated non-constitutional errors in its cumulative error analysis.

Alcala cross-appeals, challenging the district court's conclusions that (1) Alcala's constitutional rights were not violated when the state trial court admitted Crappa's prior testimony; (2) the exclusion of defense witnesses Tim Fallen, Gerald Crawford, and Raul Vasquez did not deny Alcala a fair trial; (3) the admission of the two sets of knives seized from Alcala's home did not deny him a fair trial; (4) trial counsel did not render ineffective assistance in failing to investigate and rebut crime scene evidence, failing to investigate and present evidence of the value of a pair of earrings found in Alcala's possession, and calling David Vogel as a witness without preparation; and (5) these failures to investigate were not constitutional deficiencies that could be included in the cumulative error analysis.

We conclude that Alcala's trial suffered from multiple constitutional errors that had a substantial and injurious effect on the jury's determination of guilt. Accordingly, we affirm the district court's conditional grant of Alcala's habeas petition.

FACTUAL AND PROCEDURAL BACKGROUND

This case concerns the 1979 death of twelve-year-old Robin Samsoe after her sudden disappearance in the area of Huntington Beach, California. Samsoe left the Huntington Beach apartment of her friend, Bridget Wilvert, just after 3:00 p.m. on June 20, 1979, to attend a ballet lesson. She never arrived at her dance class and none of her family or friends saw her alive again. Police discovered Samsoe's partially decomposed body in a remote mountain ravine about fifty miles away from her home almost two weeks after she disappeared. The state of her remains prevented the coroner from determining the cause of death or whether Samsoe suffered sexual molestation.

Police also found Samsoe's beach towel within a mile of where authorities recovered her remains. A criminalist testified that blood stains on the towel indicated "wipe marks," suggesting that someone had used the towel to wipe clean a bloody instrument such as a straight-edged weapon. Detectives also uncovered a knife caked with mud and covered in debris in the same general location as Samsoe's body; the criminalist found a very small spot of human blood on the knife. The test for human blood consumed the entire sample of blood, precluding more specific blood typing.

Various pieces of circumstantial evidence prompted police to arrest Alcala on July 24, 1979, a little more than one month after Samsoe's disappearance. Alcala was convicted of first degree murder and sentenced to death. The California Supreme Court reversed this conviction based on the erroneous admission of Alcala's prior offenses and granted Alcala a new trial. . . .

In 1986, nearly seven years after Samsoe disappeared, California retried Alcala before a different judge. It is this trial that is at issue before us. Again a jury convicted Alcala of first degree murder; he again was sentenced to death. The Supreme Court of California affirmed his conviction. . . .

The prosecutor relied on various forms of circumstantial evidence in securing both of Alcala's convictions; no physical evidence directly connected him to Samsoe's death. This circumstantial evidence that Alcala murdered Samsoe included various eyewitness identifications. Two young women, Lorraine Werts and Patty Elmendorf, testified that on the afternoon of June 20, 1979, a man approached them at Sunset Beach, a few miles north of Huntington Beach, and asked if he could photograph them for a class contest. Werts consented. Police later discovered a slide photo of Werts in a Seattle storage locker that Alcala rented a few weeks after Samsoe disappeared. At trial, Elmendorf identified Alcala as the Sunset Beach photographer.

Samsoe and Wilvert also spent June 20, 1979, at the beach. They were at Huntington Beach at approximately 2:00 or 3:00 that afternoon when a man asked if he could take their pictures for a school contest. They agreed, and he took one photo each of Samsoe and Wilvert and one of the two of them together. As the man photographed them, an adult neighbor, Jackelyn Young, mistook Samsoe for her niece and approached the group. The man hurried away as Young got close. Wilvert and Young helped police prepare a composite sketch, which, according to the district court, bore a "moderate resemblance to Alcala." Wilvert never identified Alcala as the man at Huntington Beach. Although Young could not identify Alcala in a photographic lineup just one week after Samsoe's disappearance, she unhesitatingly identified him as the Huntington Beach photographer at trial seven years later. She testified that he was wearing a striped, collarless shirt, and at the first trial she also had stated, in addition to this description, that it was a long-sleeved shirt.

In addition, Richard Sillett, a city surveyor, contacted police after Samsoe's disappearance. He informed them that he, too, had been at Huntington Beach on June 20, 1979. After Alcala was arrested, Sillett identified him as the man he saw taking photographs there that day. Before this identification, Sillett had seen the composite sketch created with the help of Wilvert and Young, as well as pictures of Alcala in the local media and in a police interview. He testified that he was certain that the man had been wearing a blue Hawaiian shirt and had the impression that the man had on cut-off shorts and sandals.

Two other young women, Joanne Murchland and Toni Esparza, testified at trial that they were at Huntington Beach the day *before* Samsoe's disappearance, when a man sought their permission to take photographs of them for an alleged bikini-of-the-month contest. The man left when the young women declined to give him their phone numbers. Both Murchland and Esparza told police that the composite drawing of the suspect in Samsoe's disappearance depicted the man who took their pictures. Only Murchland selected Alcala's photograph out of a photo lineup. At trial, however, both women positively identified Alcala as the man from the beach. Neither woman could remember what Alcala's car looked like when they testified at the second trial. A police officer who interviewed the women during the investigation testified that Murchland described Alcala's car as "an older red car" and Esparza said it was "an older bigger car," unlike Alcala's one-year-old blue Datsun F-10.

The prosecution also introduced evidence that Alcala straightened his hair three days after Samsoe's disappearance, cut his hair a few days after that, and planned to move away from the Southern California area. In defense, Alcala presented evidence that his girlfriend had been pressuring him to change his hairstyle consistently for about a month before he straightened his hair. He also offered testimony that he had purchased the necessary products for straightening his hair before Samsoe disappeared.

In the Seattle storage locker that Alcala rented after Samsoe disappeared, police found, in addition to the slide photo of Werts, a pair of gold-ball earrings that Samsoe's mother testified belonged to her. The defense rebutted with evidence that Alcala usually wore one earring that a co-worker identified as "exactly like" the ones police found in the locker.

Also at trial, jailhouse informant Freddie Williams testified that Alcala claimed to have kidnapped and killed Samsoe. The defense attempted to rebut this contention with the testimony of David Vogel, who also had been in jail with Williams. Vogel testified that Williams was desperate to testify against someone—anyone—in order to secure a deal with the prosecutor. Vogel significantly undermined his own credibility, however, when he admitted that he, too, once had told police that Alcala confessed to kidnapping and murdering Samsoe.

The testimony of prosecution witness Dana Crappa proved most damaging to Alcala's case. Crappa, a twenty-year-old forest service worker, met with the authorities twelve times before testifying at Alcala's first trial. During this time period, her knowledge about the crime evolved from volunteering nothing at all about the murder to placing Alcala at the crime scene with Samsoe, visiting the decomposing body twice at night, and "interacting" with the corpse twice before the police discovered the remains.

At Alcala's second trial, Crappa testified that she did not recall the kidnapping, her visits to the crime scene and Samsoe's body, or even testifying against Alcala at his first trial. The trial court denied Alcala's motion for a court-appointed, independent psychiatric evaluation of Crappa, found Crappa unavailable as a witness, and allowed the prosecutor to read Crappa's prior testimony into the record. The trial court then refused to allow Alcala to put on Dr. Ray London, who would have testified that Crappa's knowledge of the murder may have been the product of suggestive interview techniques.

After his second conviction and death sentence, Alcala unsuccessfully pursued direct appeals and state post-conviction remedies. In 1994, Alcala sought federal habeas corpus relief. The district court conducted an evidentiary hearing on his claims, and in 2001 conditionally granted his petition, issuing a writ ordering California to release him or grant him a new trial.

STANDARD OF REVIEW

Because Alcala filed his federal habeas petition in 1994, the Anti-Terrorism and Effective Death Penalty Act of 1996 (AEDPA) does not apply to his petition....

Although less deference to state court factual findings is required under the pre-AEDPA law which governs this case, such factual findings are nonetheless entitled to a presumption of correctness unless they are not fairly supported by the record....

DISCUSSION

I. Alcala's Trial Counsel's Presentation of the Knott's Berry Farm Alibi

The district court found merit in Alcala's claim that his counsel provided ineffective assistance in failing to present an alibi defense adequately, determining that this error both prejudiced Alcala and should be included in the cumulative error analysis. To show ineffective assistance, Alcala first "must show that counsel's performance was deficient.

. . . Second, [he] must show that the deficient performance prejudiced the defense". . . . Alcala must prove all facts underlying his claims of ineffective assistance by a preponderance of the evidence. . . . We agree that Alcala has met his burden and that deficiency and prejudice are both present here.

A. Facts

Alcala's trial counsel attempted to show that, on the afternoon of June 20, 1979, Alcala was seeking freelance photography work at Knott's Berry Farm, a theme park in Buena Park, California, and therefore could not have been in Huntington Beach at that time. Trial counsel presented the testimony of four witnesses, all employees of Knott's Berry Farm, who established only that Alcala had visited their office sometime in the afternoon of a day in late June, around the middle of the week. One of these witnesses, Carolyn Carey, testified that she would have seen anyone who entered the office, and that she did not see Alcala, but that on a day that she "assume[d]" was June 20 she and other managers left Knott's Berry Farm between 2:30 and 3:30 p.m. for a tour of other local theme parks.

In closing argument, the prosecutor made every effort to highlight the alibi witnesses' failure to establish the time or date of the Knott's Berry Farm visit:

[Defense counsel] told you that people put him, the defendant, at Knott's Berry Farm on June 20th of 1979. And it absolutely is not true. . . .

I kept waiting. We had four people. . . . [T]hree live people, and one stipulated witness where we agreed what she would say about Knott's Berry Farm. . . .

But recall what the testimony was? Four people came in here and talked about Knott's Berry Farm. People who have worked there. And counsel wrote it up there on his chart as a proven fact.

The defendant was at Knott's Berry Farm, I think, at 3:15 to 3:45, on the afternoon of June 20th, 1979. He wrote that up as if: Hey, that's proven, four people. Terry McDowell was here in person, Robin Humphrey was a stipulation, Joanne Sutch was here in person, Carolyn Carey was here in person.

Carolyn Carey and Joanne Sutch add zero to the alibi. . . .

They never saw Rodney Alcala in their life at anytime before they came to court. . . .

I am left scratching my head: What the heck are they calling them as defense witnesses for? They don't know anything about this case. They never saw this man before.

Robin Humphrey, who wasn't here, but again we stipulated to what she would say—she worked at Knott's Berry Farm.

Sometime during the week of June 20th, which is the 18th, 19th, 20th, 21st, and 22nd, sometime during that week, she saw somebody who looked something like the defendant. No time of day, no date. . . .

The last one, Terry McDowell. And I think she's the one counsel said puts him there. . . .

She said he was there—she's pretty sure this was the guy, and he was there sometime during the week.

Now, what kind of alibi is that? That he was at Knott's Berry Farm? They are assuming that that's been proven. . . .

There's nothing. There's not a doggone thing in terms of alibi at Knott's Berry Farm. . . .

And those are the only four people who came in here and told you anything about Knott's Berry Farm. And they don't help him a bit. . . .

There's no evidence that he was at Knott's Berry Farm on June 20th, 1979. There is zero evidence of that.

The California Supreme Court also noted the lack of a specific date and time for the alibi:

[Alcala] presented an alibi defense, attempting to establish that he was at Knott's Berry Farm in Buena Park during the early to midafternoon of Robin's disappearance, seeking employment as a photographer. . . . [S]everal employees of Knott's Berry Farm testified that they remembered seeing [Alcala] at the park near the date of Robin's disappearance, *although none could testify specifically to having seen him there on June 20*. . . .

We doubt that the alibi helped Alcala's case.

Alcala's counsel did in fact have access to evidence of the date and time, which would have placed Alcala at Knott's Berry Farm on the afternoon of June 20, 1979. At the evidentiary hearing before the district court, Alcala introduced the statements of Tina Dodwell, another Knott's employee, and various business records in Carey's possession. Dodwell told police that Alcala arrived at her office in Knott's Berry Farm on the day of the managers' tour around 2:30 or 3:00 p.m. and that the tour departed around 3:00 or 3:30 p.m. She gave the same information to a defense investigator, who tape-recorded the interview with her consent. After the interview, she called the investigator and stated that Alcala *might* have been there at 1:30 p.m. Carey's records established that the managers' tour occurred on June 20, sometime after 2:10 p.m. The district court found that the failure to introduce this evidence constituted ineffective assistance of counsel.

B. Deficient Performance

Alcala's trial counsel's presentation of the alibi was plainly deficient; Alcala has "show[n] that counsel's representation fell below an objective standard of reasonableness" . . . . Even when we "indulge a strong presumption that counsel's conduct falls within the wide range of reasonable professional assistance," we conclude that Alcala has "overcome the presumption that, under the circumstances, the challenged action 'might be considered sound trial strategy' " . . . .

Trial counsel made a sound strategic choice to present an alibi defense, but nonetheless failed in his duty to present that defense reasonably and competently. The district court found that Dodwell's testimony and Carey's records would have been far more helpful than the testimony of the alibi witnesses who did testify. This finding is not clearly erroneous, and it compels the conclusion that a competent attorney would have presented this evidence unless the attorney was unaware of its existence or had a reasonable strategic reason for not doing so.

We recognize that "[f]ew decisions a lawyer makes draw so heavily on professional judgment as whether or not to proffer a witness at trial" . . . but trial counsel here offered no strategic reason for failing to call Dodwell or to present Carey's records. The record shows that trial counsel identified Dodwell as a trial witness and intended to call her. At the evidentiary hearing, he reaffirmed that "we fully intended to call her," but could not recall why she was not called. The record also discloses that Carey told a defense investigator that her personal calendar, one of the documents submitted at the evidentiary hearing, might be of use in establishing the date of the managers' tour at Knott's Berry Farm. Although trial counsel's lack of recollection as to why he did not present this evidence does not, in and of itself, rebut the presumption that counsel acted reasonably. . .neither does it compel us to conclude that his actions were reasonable where all of the other record evidence suggests otherwise. . . .

California suggests that Dodwell's equivocation about Alcala's arrival time at Knott's motivated trial counsel's decision not to call her, and that we must therefore defer to the decision as a strategic choice. Not only is this argument contrary to our caselaw, because it would have us find a strategic basis for trial counsel's actions in the absence of any evidence, it is inconsistent with the evidence in the record. Dodwell's alleged "recantation" occurred long before Alcala's second trial and long before trial counsel told the trial court that he intended to call Dodwell. Further, even if she had testified that Alcala was in the office around 1:30 p.m., her prior identification of the time as 3:00 p.m. would have been admissible under California law as a prior inconsistent statement . . . and her testimony still would have been far more useful than that of the witnesses who did testify. Finally, this argument does not address the failure to introduce Carey's business records. We will not assume facts not in the record in order to manufacture a reasonable strategic decision for Alcala's trial counsel.

Even if Alcala's trial counsel did offer a basis for his decision not to present alibi evidence, that basis would be unreasonable if it were unsupported by objective evidence because Dodwell's testimony and Carey's records were consistent with the alibi defense that counsel chose. . . . Absent an objectively reasonable basis to undermine the credibility or utility of Dodwell's testimony and Carey's records, "a competent attorney would not have failed to put" on this evidence. . . .

When defense counsel undertakes to establish an alibi, but does not present available evidence of the time or even the date of the alibi, or offer a strategic reason for failing to do so, his actions are unreasonable. Alcala has overcome the presumption that his trial counsel's actions were reasonable strategic decisions. Trial counsel's failure to call Dodwell or to present information regarding the date and time of the managers' tour was deficient.

C. Prejudice

We agree with the district court that Alcala was prejudiced by trial counsel's deficient presentation of his alibi because the alibi would have challenged the eyewitness identification placing Alcala with Samsoe. [W]e find prejudice because "there is a reasonable probability that, but for counsel's unprofessional errors, the result of the proceeding would have been different"; the deficient presentation of the alibi "undermine[s our] confidence in the outcome." . . . Considering "the totality of the evidence" before the jury . . . we conclude that the case against Alcala was "only weakly supported by the record" and therefore "more likely to have been affected by errors than one with overwhelming record support". . . .

We agree with the district court that the prosecution's case was far from compelling. The evidence that Alcala murdered Samsoe was entirely circumstantial. . . . Apart from the dubious testimony of Dana Crappa, discussed at length below, the only eyewitness to testify that she saw

Alcala with Samsoe was Jackelyn Young, who said that she saw them at Huntington Beach around 3:00 p.m. on June 20, 1979.

Alcala has met his burden of proving that the absence of the alibi evidence prejudiced his case. The fact that Dodwell was under subpoena to testify is sufficient to establish, by a preponderance of the evidence, that she could have been called to testify, and the interviews submitted at the evidentiary hearing were sufficient to establish what her testimony would have been. If this testimony had been presented along with Carey's records, the alibi defense would have accounted for Alcala's whereabouts during a critical period of time. The travel time between Huntington Beach and Buena Park would have required at least a half-hour each way, in addition to any time actually spent at the Knott's Berry Farm office. Dodwell's statements and Carey's records suggest that Alcala was present at Knott's Berry Farm around 2:30 or 3:00 p.m., and thus would not have been able to return to Huntington Beach until after 3:00 p.m. at the earliest. In contrast, Young stated that she saw Alcala on the beach with Samsoe around 3:00 p.m., and Bridget Wilvert stated that Samsoe left her house around 3:10 p.m.

The alibi evidence would have given the jury a choice between believing the testimony of apparently disinterested employees of Knott's Berry Farm or that of Young. Although Young's identification was confident at trial, it was not unimpeachable. Prior to the first trial, Young had been unable to identify Alcala from a photo lineup, and Young's description of Alcala's clothing was inconsistent with other witnesses' testimony. Furthermore, Wilvert, who was present with Samsoe when Young allegedly saw the girls with Alcala, never identified him.

If trial counsel had presented the evidence establishing that Alcala was at Knott's Berry Farm, in Buena Park, on June 20, 1979, around

3:00 p.m., there is a reasonable likelihood that the jury would have discounted Young's testimony and concluded that Alcala could not have encountered Samsoe as she left Wilvert's house at 3:10 p.m. Such conclusions would have significantly weakened, if not wholly undermined, the prosecution's case.

Not only was the deficient presentation of the alibi far less helpful than a competent presentation would have been, it was probably actually harmful to Alcala's case. Trial counsel told the jurors that he would prove that Alcala was at Knott's Berry Farm on the afternoon of June 20, 1979, and utterly failed to do so, harming the credibility of Alcala's entire defense. The prosecutor's rebuttal highlighted the weakness of the alibi evidence; indeed, the prosecutor devoted more of his closing argument to the alibi than Alcala's trial counsel did.

The district court did not err in finding prejudice from the deficient presentation of the alibi and in granting the writ on this basis.

II. The Exclusion of Dr. Ray London's Testimony

The trial court also found constitutional error in the exclusion of defense expert Dr. Ray London, a psychologist who would have testified that Crappa had been hypnotically influenced in various interviews with police investigators. We agree that the exclusion of Dr. London's testimony violated Alcala's due process right to a fundamentally fair trial and to present crucial witnesses in his defense.

A. Facts

Dana Crappa was the prosecution's key witness. In 1979, she was a twenty-year-old firefighter with the United States Forest Service. Her knowledge and memory of the murder continuously evolved. Crappa's

Forest Service crew discovered Samsoe's body on July 2, 1979, near Mile Marker 11 on Santa Anita Canyon Road. Crappa volunteered nothing about the crime or the corpse at that time. One month later on August 2, 1979, after being shown photographs of Alcala, Samsoe, and Alcala's Datsun F-10, Crappa told the police that she did not recognize either Alcala or Samsoe. She claimed that she had nearly collided with the Datsun while driving near Mile Marker 11 between 9:30 and 10:00 p.m. on the night that another firefighter had prepared a pizza dinner, either June 7 or June 14. Five days later, she revised her story, asserting that she had seen the vehicle on the evening of June 21. At the preliminary hearing in September 1979, Crappa revised her story a third time, testifying that she saw the Datsun parked on the side of the road around 10:00 or 10:30 p.m. Crappa testified that she did not see anyone in or near the car.

Five months later on February 7, 1980, Crappa was introduced to Art Droz, who unbeknownst to her was a police detective trained in hypnosis. Droz claimed that he could help Crappa deal with the incredible stress she was experiencing if she told him her dreams and anxieties. Crappa related a similar story about seeing the Datsun on June 21, 1979, adding that there was a full moon that night and that her dreams were like movies that she saw a little more of each time she awakened. Crappa told Droz that in one of her dreams she saw a man, who may have been wearing Levis and a white shirt, sitting on a wall near the Datsun F-10. She emphasized, however, that she did not "know if I really saw it or if I just think I saw it." Crappa also told Droz that on the night of June 29, 1979, she had seen the decomposed body of a child near Mile Marker 11, with clothes strewn about the area, a "crusty" knife in a hole, and six .22 caliber bullet casings on the ground that she picked up and threw away. During this interview, Crappa was under the misimpression that the police had established the cause of death.

Four days later, on February 11, 1980, Crappa again met with Droz, who was accompanied this time by psychologist Larry Blum. Both men encouraged Crappa to discuss her "feelings," "impressions," and "dreams." In doing so, she could not recall seeing a child near the Datsun F-10 or having seen Samsoe and remained unsure about whether she had seen a man next to the car. Crappa confirmed, however, that she saw six .22 shells that were still "pretty" and not rusted next to the body and a knife "in the hole" near the body. When Crappa insisted that she could not recall anything further, Blum warned Crappa "when you start talking and then say I don't know, I know that's B.S. You understand that, I know that's B.S." Crappa also explained that one of the investigators even assured her of Alcala's guilt, saying that he was "a hundred percent sure this guy is guilty, a hundred percent without any doubt."

On February 15, 1980, Crappa met with prosecutor Richard Farnell and police officer Craig Robison, both of whom were trained in hypnosis. Although Crappa had told the police that she had not seen the Datsun F-10 prior to June 21, 1979, she revised her story a fifth time. In the recorded portion of the interview, Crappa claimed that on June 20, the day before she almost collided with the Datsun, she saw the same car parked on the side of the road and a man nearby "pushing" or "steering" a young blond-haired girl into the ravine. She stated that the man was wearing a white t-shirt and Levis and that she thought he was "the same guy that's . . . suspected of killing the little kid." Crappa claimed that she never told anyone about this incident because she "just felt guilty like [she'd] done something wrong." Crappa also reiterated that she had gone to the murder scene on the night of June 29, 1979, and had seen a knife and children's clothes near the corpse.

Eleven days later on February 26, 1980, Crappa met with Robison again, revising her story a sixth time. Crappa had told investigators that she never saw Samsoe's corpse before June 29, 1979, but Robison told her that he found this contention implausible. Because Crappa could not account for her activities on the evening of June 25, 1979, Robison suggested that she visited the scene that night; he proceeded to paint a hypothetical picture of what the scene would have looked like at that time, suggesting that the body would have "smelled foul" and been easy to find. Crappa denied having visited the scene on June 25 the first few times Robison asked her about it, but eventually stated that, "Well, it's a real possibility" that she visited the corpse prior to June 29 as well.

Crappa continued to talk to investigators before trial. On March 19, 1980, at Alcala's first trial, Crappa testified that she saw a man "forcefully steering" a girl with long blond hair towards the ravine. He was wearing a white t-shirt and Levis and was near a vehicle that resembled Alcala's car. Crappa further testified that she saw that same vehicle parked nearby at the side of the road on June 21. This time she claimed that she saw the Datsun between 8:00 and 8:30 p.m. and that her earlier estimate of 10:00 or 10:30 p.m. had been mistaken. According to Crappa, there was a man standing near the vehicle, again wearing Levis and a white t-shirt that "appeared to be sort of dirty or have a stain."

Crappa also repeated her story that she visited Samsoe's corpse on the night of June 29, 1979. Unlike in her previous versions of this event, Crappa denied seeing a knife near the corpse, although she repeated her earlier statement that she picked up six .22 shells and discarded them. She said that this visit took place around 7:00 p.m. Crappa also testified for the first time at trial that she had made another nocturnal visit to the murder scene on June 25, 1979, that it "smelled pretty foul," and that she saw a child's tennis shoe and some clothing near the body. She also testified that she saw Samsoe's corpse and that it was "cut up pretty bad."

On April 30, 1986, the prosecution called Crappa as a witness in Alcala's second trial. Four days earlier, however, Crappa had told the prosecutor that she could no longer remember any of the facts or circumstances relating to Samsoe's murder. She had told them she could not even recall testifying at the first trial. The prosecutor advised the trial court:

Miss Crappa, who would be the People's next witness, is present outside in the hallway ready to testify under subpoena. However, she has essentially informed me that she . . . is not going to testify because she doesn't have any recollection about the events in this case, essentially. . . .

She has further told me, in response to my direct question essentially, I have asked her, is it a situation where you can't remember, or you don't want to remember. And essentially it seems to be a situation where she just doesn't want to remember so she is going to say she doesn't remember. But it's not a situation where she can't remember.

The prosecutor argued that Crappa was thus unavailable as a witness and requested admission of Crappa's testimony from Alcala's first trial. Crappa then testified, first to the court outside the presence of the jury and then before the jury, that she could not remember testifying at Alcala's first trial or any of the events relating to the case against him.

Between Alcala's two trials, the California Supreme Court found hypnotically-induced testimony inherently unreliable, and thus, per se inadmissible. . . . Accordingly, Alcala wanted to offer Dr. London at his second trial to prove that investigators had hypnotized Crappa. In determining the admissibility of Crappa's testimony . . . the trial court made a preliminary finding of fact that Crappa had not been hypnotized, which is a question for the court, not the jury, under California law. . . . Alcala did not offer Dr. London solely for the purpose of proving that Crappa was hypnotized . . . however, but also to impeach Crappa's testimony as tainted and unreliable. Dr. London's testimony was offered to demonstrate the influence that hypnotic and suggestive techniques had on Crappa's memory as well as Crappa's adoption of investigators' suggestions, her increasingly certain memory over time, and her purported amnesia at Alcala's second trial.

Dr. London had reviewed all of the transcripts of police interviews with Crappa preceding Alcala's first trial and listened to the available tape recordings. He concluded that Crappa was hypnotized at the interviews on February 7 and 11, 1980, and that she may have been hypnotized on February 15. Dr. London found that Detective Droz and others used specific techniques and suggestions to put Crappa into a hypnotic state and to aid Crappa in "remembering" what she saw in the mountains.

He opined that Crappa adopted the investigators' suggestions. For example, Crappa originally told police that she never saw Alcala and Samsoe together. During the course of the investigation, however, detectives encouraged Crappa to piece different clues together, such as the man she saw on the mountain road and the girl who was kidnapped. Crappa ultimately adopted this suggestion and, at the first trial, testified that she saw Alcala "forcefully steering" Samsoe into the ravine on June 20. Crappa also adopted the investigator's suggestions that she saw Samsoe's body prior to June 29, 1979.

Dr. London testified that people who undergo hypnosis commonly experience progressively increased certainty in their recollections, much like Crappa's evolving confidence in her memory. He added that Crappa's behavior at Alcala's first trial, including substantial pauses in her testimony and rocking her body back and forth while speaking, suggested a hypnotic trance. Other behavior indicated "dissociation," or separation from reality, and "vivification," or making an image or dream so real that it seems to take place presently—both of which indicate an altered state of consciousness. Additionally, Dr. London took note of negative post-hypnotic suggestions, which communicated to Crappa that she should not remember the content of or techniques used in the interviews. He also pointed out that Crappa's certainty in her testimony waned between the February 15 interview and a March 12 conversation with an investigator, explaining that hypnotically-induced suggestions must be reinforced with some frequency to last. This phenomenon explained Crappa's amnesia at Alcala's second trial. . . .

B. Error

In weighing the importance of evidence offered by a defendant against the state's interest in exclusion, the court should consider the probative value of the evidence on the central issue; its reliability; whether it is capable of evaluation by the trier of fact; whether it is the sole evidence on the issue or merely cumulative; and whether it constitutes a major part of the attempted defense. A court must also consider the purpose of the [evidentiary] rule; its importance; how well the rule implements its purpose; and how well the purpose applies to the case at hand. The court must give due weight to the substantial state interest in preserving orderly trials, in judicial efficiency, and in excluding unreliable or prejudicial evidence. . . .

The weight of the . . . factors compels us to conclude that the trial court's exclusion of Dr. London violated Alcala's duc process rights. First, Dr. London's testimony was highly probative because of its remarkable impeachment value. It would have emphasized the suggestive nature of police interview tactics, the evolution of Crappa's testimony and its vulnerability to and incorporation of investigators' suggestions, and Crappa's increased certitude. This impeachment testimony would have explained Crappa's bizarre and disturbing demeanor at Alcala's first trial, her subsequent amnesia, and the parallel relationship between her testimony and both the prosecution's theory and the physical evidence.

Second, California did not object to Dr. London's expert qualifications or the bases for his conclusions, giving us no reason to question its reliability. That prosecution witnesses disagreed with Dr. London's conclusion that Crappa was hypnotized does not make his expert opinion unreliable; rather, it provides the very basis for admitting and relying on Dr. London's testimony—the presentation of the defense theory of the case. Third, California does not assert that the jury could not evaluate Dr. London's testimony and consider it with the totality of the evidence. Fourth, Dr. London provided the sole evidence for impeaching Crappa on the basis of hypnosis, suggestion, brainwashing, cajoling, or improper influence; his testimony was not cumulative but was critical to Alcala's case.

Finally, the testimony of Dr. London proved integral—vital even—to Alcala's case. His testimony would have provided a formidable defense tool because his expert opinion would cast serious doubt on the most damning portions of Crappa's testimony and on its overall believability. As the star prosecution witness, Crappa was the only person to place Alcala at the murder scene with the murder victim close in time to the theorized murder date. The district court's compelling analysis demonstrates the import of Dr. London's testimony to Alcala's case:

[W]ithout Dr. London, the defense was prevented from rebutting the prosecutor's claim that Crappa's inconsistencies were attributable to the traumatic nature of the events that she was describing (and had allegedly witnessed). Without Dr. London, the defense was precluded from presenting evidence that the substance and evolution of Crappa's testimony at the first trial, and subsequent claim of amnesia, were indicative of hypnosis. Without Dr. London, the defense was precluded from proving that hypnosis could instill a greater degree of certainty and that the hypnotic subject was incapable of distinguishing implanted memories from actual recollection. Without Dr. London, the defense could not dispel the aura of credibility that Crappa's testimony received by virtue of its consistency with the remaining evidence. Through Dr. London, however, the defense proposed to offer an explanation for this "fit"—because the memories had been constructed through hypnosis, Crappa's testimony had been manufactured to fit.

In short, Dr. London provided the only available means for Alcala to impeach Crappa's testimony with a coherent theory. This theory would not only have undermined Crappa's accounts of what she saw, but also would have diminished the overall weight, if any, the jury afforded her testimony.

California's interest in excluding Dr. London does not outweigh Alcala's strong interest in the admission of his testimony. The trial court excluded Dr. London's testimony under California Evidence Code § 352, finding that presentation of this evidence, though probative, would confuse the issues and waste an undue amount of time. While the policy underlying this rule is to allow the exclusion of otherwise probative evidence if an undue consumption of time or confusion of the issues would *substantially outweigh* its relevance, that is not the case here. We cannot conclude on the record before us that Dr. London's testimony would consume even a considerable amount of time, let alone an undue amount of time, or that it would confuse the jury.

The balance of these factors supports a conclusion that the trial court unconstitutionally excluded Dr. London. Therefore, we must consider whether the exclusion was prejudicial. . . . We agree with the district court that it was.

Crappa's testimony provided the bedrock of the prosecution's case by placing Alcala and his distinctive car at the murder scene with the victim just hours after she disappeared. Dr. London's testimony, if accepted by the jury, would have damaged Crappa's credibility severely. It also would have helped place the cold transcript of Crappa's testimony in context by showing the dramatic evolution of her purported recollections. Thus, the exclusion of Dr. London likely had a substantial and injurious effect or influence on the jury's verdict.

III. The Trial Court's Denial of Alcala's Motion for an Independent Medical Examination of Dana Crappa

The district court held that the trial court's denial of Alcala's motion for an independent medical examination of Crappa constitutes a violation of the Sixth Amendment's Compulsory Process Clause. We disagree. While the Compulsory Process Clause guarantees a criminal defendant the right to present relevant and material witnesses in his defense . . . the trial court never barred Alcala from exercising this right.

A. Crappa's Alleged Unavailability

The prosecution asserted that Crappa was "unavailable" because of her purported amnesia. After hearing Crappa's testimony on April 30, 1986, the trial court observed that Crappa appeared to be suffering from an "existing . . . mental illness or infirmity" and, therefore, "probably qualifie[d] under unavailability, in view of [her] present mental status."

When Alcala requested additional time to consider Crappa's purported claim of amnesia, the trial court set a hearing for May 5, and informed Alcala,

But I really think you gentlemen can do all the research in the world, and everybody knows I am never hampered by the law anyway.

Basically, what we are going to do is put her on, let her have her say-so, give it a shot, and get into the reading. . . .

And there won't be anything further until tomorrow. And then you have the rest of the night to show me I am wrong, and everybody knows I never am.

On May 5, Alcala filed a motion asking the trial court "to appoint, for the information of the court, a mental health professional to conduct a clinical interview of [Crappa]." Alcala argued that due process required the trial court to perform an independent medical examination of Crappa's current mental condition before ruling on Crappa's unavailability.

Two witnesses testified at the hearing: Dr. Anthony Staiti, a psychiatrist called by the prosecution, and Superior Court Judge Phillip Schwab, who had presided over Alcala's first trial. Dr. Staiti had met with Crappa three times for a total of two to three hours to assess whether "she was capable of returning to her position as a police dispatcher." Dr. Staiti explained that his "working diagnosis" of Crappa was that she was suffering from "post traumatic stress disorder chronic delayed."

The defense called Judge Schwab. He commented that Crappa's demeanor during Alcala's first trial was "unusual," and often punctuated with long delays of one minute or longer between questions and answers. Judge Schwab also testified that Crappa's behavior was peculiar and that he even conferred with the parties about the possibility of terminating her testimony.

At the close of the hearing, the trial court denied Alcala's motion for an independent medical examination and ruled that Crappa was "unavailable" because of a "pre-existing mental infirmity." The court based its decision on, *inter alia*, "the history of the case" as well as the "obvious frailties of the witness."

Accordingly, Crappa was excused from testifying in person and the prosecution was permitted to read a transcript of Crappa's previous testimony to the jury.

B. Alcala's Right to Compulsory Process

The right of an accused to have compulsory process for obtaining and calling witnesses in his favor is guaranteed under the Sixth and Fourteenth Amendments. . . . "Just as an accused has the right to confront the prosecution's witnesses for the purpose of challenging their testimony, he has the right to present his own witnesses to establish a defense. This right is a fundamental element of due process of law." . . . . Alcala's right to compulsory process was violated if he was barred by the trial court from presenting "testimony [that] would have been relevant and material, and . . . vital to [his] defense." . . .

At the hearing on Crappa's purported unavailability, Alcala was never barred from presenting any witnesses or evidence, nor did Alcala ever request an opportunity to examine Crappa with his own medical experts. Alcala points out that if the prosecution was permitted to present a medical expert, due process requires that the defense be allowed to do the same. But, Alcala never requested such an opportunity; he only asked that the trial court appoint a mental health professional to conduct an independent medical examination of Crappa for the court's benefit in assessing her unavailability.

If the trial court had barred Alcala from presenting defense witnesses or from conducting a medical examination of Crappa, Alcala would be correct in arguing that his constitutional rights were violated. . . . However, that did not happen here. Rather, the trial court merely refused to exercise its discretion to appoint an expert to conduct an independent investigation of a disputed matter.

While Alcala's suggestion was probably the more prudent path for the trial court to adopt, the court's decision not to perform an independent investigation of the facts cannot be characterized as a violation of the Sixth Amendment. . . . California law defines a "mental infirmity" as "a defect of personality or weakness of the will". . . . In order to establish the existence of a mental infirmity, expert medical testimony, while potentially relevant, is not essential. . . .

At any point between April 30, when Crappa informed the court of her amnesia, and May 5, when the court found her unavailable, Alcala could have requested that he be allowed to examine Crappa with a defense expert or, if additional time was needed, moved for a continuance. Alcala offers no explanation as to why he never made such requests.

Accordingly, we hold the district court erred in granting Alcala's claim that his Sixth Amendment rights were violated by the trial court's denial of his motion for an independent medical examination.

IV. The Admission of Crappa's Previous Trial Testimony

The district court rejected Alcala's claim that the admission of Crappa's previous testimony violated his rights under the Confrontation Clause of the Sixth Amendment. In his cross-appeal, Alcala argues that Crappa's testimony was not sufficiently reliable to be deemed admissible as evidence.

The Sixth Amendment's Confrontation Clause, made applicable to the states through the Fourteenth Amendment, provides that, "In all criminal prosecutions, the accused shall enjoy the right. . . to be confronted with the witnesses against him" . . . .

Crappa's demeanor during Alcala's first trial was odd, if not bizarre. Her conduct was so peculiar that it is next to impossible *not* to question the trustworthiness of her testimony. The record is replete with examples of Crappa behaving in a manner that calls into question her credibility, mental stability, psychiatric health, and veracity as a witness.

- Crappa waited up to one minute or more before answering certain questions and, at times, did not answer questions unless they were repeated multiple times. Judge Schwab testified that, "There were, at least in portions of her testimony, substantial delays between the question and an answer, sometimes running perhaps close to a minute, perhaps even longer."

- At one point during her testimony, Crappa was "rocking back and forth, her eyes closed. . . ." for several minutes. According to Alcala's trial counsel, Crappa "seem[ed] to be undergoing some kind of psychiatric or psychotic break."

- For one period lasting fifteen minutes, Crappa's only responsive utterance to the prosecutor's questions was to mutter repeatedly, "It was a."

- The prosecution asked Crappa to describe what she saw on the evening of June 25, 1979, multiple times. Crappa, however, either remained silent, muttered unresponsively to the questions, or would continue to rock her body back and forth without speaking. It was only after the trial court called for a recess and Crappa spoke with Robison, a police officer and trained hypnotist, during the break, that she was able to return to the witness stand and testify in a somewhat coherent fashion about having seen Samsoe's corpse on the evening of June 25.

- Judge Schwab, a veteran California state trial judge with more than twenty years of experience on the bench, agreed that Crappa's behavior was "unusual." In particular, the length of time it took for her to begin responding to a question after it was asked was not normal. Judge Schwab even called counsel into chambers to discuss whether it was appropriate for Crappa to continue testifying. Although he said this was not the only time he had considered terminating a witness's testimony, he could not recall any other specific cases where he had done so.

- Judge Schwab advised Crappa of her constitutional right to assert her privilege against self-incrimination and consult an attorney, after it was suggested to him that Crappa was committing perjury.

Crappa's behavior as a witness was so extraordinarily odd that it strikes at the very core of her reliability as a witness. Moreover, reading the cold transcript of her testimony may have had the effect of transforming an incredibly bizarre performance into a credible presentation.

We are asked to determine whether, under these unusual circumstances, Crappa's past trial testimony nonetheless bears sufficient indicia of reliability to have been admissible. California argues that the reliability of prior trial testimony given under oath and subjected to cross-examination should be inferred without further inquiry because such testimony is recognized as a firmly rooted exception to the hearsay rule. We do not opine on whether prior trial testimony is a firmly rooted hearsay exception, although we acknowledge some indications in the case law that it is. . . . In any event, the Supreme Court has noted that in "extraordinary cases," further inquiry into the reliability of prior trial testimony may be required. . . .

Although this may be such a case where further inquiry would be appropriate, we ultimately need not decide whether Crappa's testimony bears adequate indicia of reliability. The trial court's other constitutional errors, combined with the ineffectiveness of Alcala's trial counsel, are more than sufficient to warrant the denial of California's appeal and the granting of Alcala's petition. Accordingly, we decline to rule on this issue as it is unnecessary in our ultimate assessment of the merits of Alcala's petition.

V. Cumulative Error

The district court granted Alcala's habeas petition in part due to cumulative error. We hold that the district court did not err in finding that the combined prejudice of the multiple errors committed in this case deprived Alcala of a fundamentally fair trial and constitutes a separate and independent basis for granting his petition.

California contends on appeal that some of the purported errors considered by the district court in its cumulative error analysis were not constitutional errors and that others were not prejudicial. Alcala argues that the district court erred in failing to find error in the exclusion of certain defense witnesses, holding that his trial counsel's failure to investigate the crime scene was not deficient, and in ruling that some adverse evidentiary rulings were not sufficiently prejudicial to grant the petition on those grounds alone.

A. The Exclusion of Certain Defense Witnesses

The prosecutor theorized that Alcala kidnapped Samsoe on the afternoon of June 20, 1979, some time after she left Wilvert's home and before she should have arrived at her ballet class. Crappa's testimony placed Alcala in the mountains with Samsoe later that very day, suggesting that Alcala killed Samsoe on the same day that he kidnapped her, June 20, 1979.

The testimony of Tim Fallen would poke at least one hole in this theory. Fallen testified at Alcala's first trial that he saw Samsoe in Huntington Beach on June 21, 1979—the day after she disappeared. A police detective showed Fallen a picture of Samsoe on June 21 and asked if he had seen her. Fallen told the detective that he had seen Samsoe just minutes before the detective's arrival. He offered, without prompting, that she was riding a yellow, ten-speed bike. When Samsoe left Wilvert's home the day before, she had borrowed her friend's yellow ten-speed.

Late the next night, on June 22, 1979, police officer Gerald Crawford saw a car parked at a turnout just north of Mile Marker 11 on the Santa Anita Canyon Road, about 100 feet from where authorities ultimately found Samsoe's remains. Crawford then saw Raul Vasquez walking toward the car. Crawford questioned Vasquez about his purpose for being in the area. He responded that he had relieved himself in the woods while waiting for his girlfriend. When Crawford asked Vasquez his girlfriend's name, he either did not know her name or did not respond.

Crawford patted Vasquez down and found a pair of heavy pliers in his back pocket. Crawford questioned Vasquez about the tool, and he responded, "you never know what can happen up here in these mountains." Crawford also searched Vasquez's car, where he found a towel or blanket in the back seat and a six pack of beer on the floorboard of the front seat. Crawford noted that a passenger window was shattered, and broken glass lay strewn across the back seat. Crawford testified that Vasquez seemed upset, extremely nervous, and very shaky; he acted as if he were hiding something.

Alcala wanted to offer Crawford and Vasquez to advance his theory that someone other than Alcala kidnapped Samsoe on June 21—after Fallen saw her—and that Vasquez murdered Samsoe on June 22. Crawford would have testified, as he did at Alcala's first trial, to his encounter with Vasquez, while Vasquez would have testified that he was on parole from a murder conviction.

At Alcala's first trial, Fallen had identified a photograph of a different young blond girl as the one he saw; the prosecutor argued at the second trial that Fallen's testimony was neither probative nor reliable. Despite Alcala's arguments to the contrary, and considering only Alcala's offer of proof and the prosecutor's objection, the trial court excluded Fallen's testimony as confusing and irrelevant.

The trial court also excluded the testimony of Crawford and Vasquez. After stating on the record that "[criminals] usually stay away from the scene of the crime," which would be inconsistent with Vasquez "go[ing] back on the 22nd to see if he did a good job," the trial judge found that "the probative value of this type of evidence is zero" and that presenting it would be "a waste of time."

Even if the trial court erroneously excluded Fallen, Crawford, and Vasquez as a matter of state law, we cannot afford him habeas relief unless the exclusion violated his due process right to a fair trial. . . . We employ a balancing test for determining whether the exclusion of testimony violates due process. Courts should weigh the probative value of the evidence, its reliability, whether the trier of fact can evaluate the evidence, whether the evidence is cumulative, and whether the evidence proves integral to the defense theory in evaluating whether admissible evidence was unconstitutionally excluded. . . . In addition, we must consider California's interest in excluding the evidence. . . .

i. Exclusion of Fallen's Testimony

While California concedes that the trial court erred in excluding Fallen's testimony, some analysis of whether this exclusion violated Alcala's due process rights is helpful. First, Fallen's sighting of the girl he believed to be Samsoe is probative to a central issue in this case: whether Alcala kidnapped and killed Samsoe on June 20. Fallen's testimony could create reasonable doubt that Samsoe was kidnapped and killed on June 20, the day on which eyewitnesses claimed to have seen Alcala at Huntington Beach, rather than June 21, the day Fallen claimed to have seen Samsoe. Fallen could also rebut Crappa's testimony placing Alcala with the victim close to the murder scene.

Fallen's testimony also bears indicia of reliability. He identified the girl he saw within five or ten minutes of viewing her; his memory was recent. He also volunteered that the girl was riding a yellow ten-speed bicycle, before the officer could indicate that Samsoe was riding such a bike when she disappeared. Moreover, that the prosecutor impeached Fallen at the first trial did not make his testimony unreliable but instead raised questions about his credibility and the weight his testimony should be accorded. These are issues to be weighed by the jury, not the judge. . . .

No question exists that the jury could evaluate Fallen's testimony. His insistence that he saw Samsoe the day after the prosecutor argued that she was kidnapped introduces an alternate exculpatory theory. The evidence is inconsistent with the prosecutor's case, but that it conflicts is the very point of presenting Fallen's testimony. If courts prohibit the introduction of any evidence that conflicts with the prosecution's case because it might "confuse" the jury, the right of the accused to present a defense would exist only in form. In addition, Fallen's testimony was not cumulative; it provided the only evidence that Samsoe was seen alive after June 20.

Lastly, Alcala focused on a misidentification theory via his efforts to rebut the various eyewitness identifications, to undermine Crappa's credibility, and to put on an alibi defense. Fallen's testimony would have facilitated this theory by allowing Alcala to undermine the prosecution's assertion that Samsoe was kidnapped and killed on June 20. In other words, if Samsoe were kidnapped on or after June 21, and the prosecution could not link Alcala to the area on June 21, Alcala could further his misidentification defense.

The trial court excluded Fallen because his testimony was both confusing and irrelevant. These concerns do not outweigh Alcala's interest in putting on this testimony. That Fallen's testimony weakened the prosecution's case made it probative, not confusing, and that it contradicted California's theory demonstrates its great relevance.

Because the factors weigh in Alcala's favor, the trial court committed constitutional error in excluding Fallen's testimony. This error likely affected the jury's verdict. Fallen's testimony would have given the defense an eerie coincidence for the jury to weigh against the many bizarre coincidences that the prosecution presented. It also would contradict the prosecution's theory that Alcala kidnapped and murdered Samsoe on June 20. Regardless of whether this error was sufficiently prejudicial in itself to grant Alcala's petition, the district court correctly included this error in its cumulative error analysis.

ii. Exclusion of Crawford's and Vasquez's Testimony

The exclusion of Crawford's and Vasquez's testimony is subject to the same balancing test. . . . Their combined testimony about the events of June 22, 1979, is arguably more probative than Fallen's testimony to the central issue: Alcala's guilt. Vasquez was found in a remote mountain area, after he literally emerged from the bushes 100 feet from where authorities ultimately discovered Samsoe's body. Crawford testified that Vasquez was upset, nervous, and shaky and acted like he was hiding something. Vasquez provided Crawford with a flimsy excuse for his presence in the area. He possessed a heavy tool, which he suggested he would use as a weapon if necessary.

This testimony also is reliable. Crawford was a police officer with no motive to lie. Indeed, he was called by the prosecution to testify about finding the body. As for Vasquez, his testimony only concerned his prior homicide conviction. Even if he did testify to the events of the night of June 22, 1979, California has suggested no reason that Vasquez would lie about that night in order to incriminate himself.

Just as Fallen's testimony was capable of evaluation by the trier of fact, so too was the testimony of Crawford and Vasquez. Again, their testimony presented an alternate explanation for Samsoe's murder that the jury could accept or reject. Again, their testimony would not have been cumulative; it provided the sole evidence that Vasquez may have murdered Samsoe.

Finally, the exclusion of testimony from Crawford and Vasquez precluded Alcala from presenting a third-party culpability defense; he instead relied on a misidentification theory. Crawford and Vasquez would have helped Alcala pursue a third-party culpability defense, a theory not inconsistent with the defense presented and which—had the evidence been admitted—would have proven a strong defense theory.

The trial court excluded Crawford's and Vasquez's testimony as irrelevant and a "waste of time," and suggested Alcala's third-party culpability theory was untenable. Even still, the above factors clearly weigh in favor of Alcala's interest in having the testimony admitted. The testimony was relevant, and no record evidence indicates that it would have consumed an undue amount of time.

This evidence helps demonstrate reasonable doubt as to Alcala's guilt by suggesting that Vasquez may have murdered Samsoe. The exclusion of this evidence prejudiced Alcala and belongs in the cumulative error analysis.

B. The Admission of the Kane Kutlery Knives

As mentioned above, police discovered a knife obscured by some vegetation and covered with debris and caked mud in the same general area as Samsoe's remains. The prosecutor theorized that Alcala used the knife as the murder weapon because of blood found on the knife, wipe marks on Samsoe's towel, and Crappa's testimony that the body was "pretty cut up."

To support this hypothesis, the prosecutor admitted into evidence two complete, unused sets of kitchen knives that police seized from Alcala's home where he lived with his mother and stepfather. Kane Kutlery manufactured both these knives and the carving knife found in the ravine near Samsoe's remains. Alcala's mother testified that the knife sets were gifts from her husband's former employer. She also asserted that her husband's employer never gave her a separate knife like the carving knife found near Samsoe's body, that she was not missing any knives from her kitchen pantry, and that the alleged murder weapon found in the ravine differed from the knife sets she owned.

The trial court judge remarked on the many differences between the knife sets and the purported murder weapon. He noted the difference in the studs on the handles, the type of wood used for the handles, and the shape of the knives. He stated that "[t]here's no way that this particular weapon could be tied in [ ] the remotest to any of these particular sets [seized from Alcala's home]—I mean, the whole knife set is not even close to the knife [found in the ravine]." To buttress its murder weapon theory, the prosecutor called Clella Schneider, a Kane Kutlery representative, as a witness. Schneider testified that although the two knife sets seized from Alcala's home and the alleged murder weapon both were distributed through Kane Kutlery to the same six western states and marketed around the same time, the knives differed in design. Schneider also testified that during a period of five years, Kane Kutlery sold about 15,000 of each of the two knife sets in six western states and about 4,000-5,000 of the individual carving knives in the same general geographic area. She further testified that the carving knife found in the ravine was sold separately from the seized knife sets and that all of the knives in question were sold at major supermarket chains and drug stores.

The trial court admitted the knives and Schneider's testimony over Alcala's objection that they were irrelevant and highly prejudicial.

A conclusion that the admission of the Kane Kutlery knife sets violated Alcala's right to a fundamentally fair trial requires that the knife sets and Schneider's testimony were irrelevant to the prosecution's case and that the "erroneously admitted evidence was of such quality as necessarily prevents a fair trial". . . . "Evidence is considered irrelevant if it fails to make any fact of consequence more or less probable". . . . Moreover, "[o]nly if there are *no* permissible inferences the jury may draw from the evidence can its admission violate due process". . . .

The knife sets, and the accompanying testimony of Schneider, are irrelevant. The evidence showed that two unused sets of Kane Kutlery knives were found in Alcala's home. These knives belonged to Alcala's mother and stepfather and had been given to them by a former employer; they were not found in Alcala's direct possession, nor did he purchase them. Furthermore, even as the trial court admitted, the knife sets differed in many material respects from the knife found at the murder scene.

The jury could draw no permissible inference from this evidence. To infer that Alcala used the knife in the ravine to murder Samsoe, the jury would have had to speculate—and could have done no more than speculate—that because the purported murder weapon and the unused knife sets shared the same brand name, Alcala was connected to the murder weapon. That the same company manufactured both the purported murder weapon and the knife sets fails to make any fact of consequence to the prosecution's case more or less probable.

California argues that the knife sets were relevant to show that Alcala had access to or familiarity with Kane Kutlery. The fact that Alcala's home contained substantially different types of knives of the same brand as the purported murder weapon, however, does nothing to advance the argument that Alcala had special or increased access to Kane Kutlery knives. As Schneider testified, both the knife sets and the carving knife were readily available by the thousands in major supermarkets and drug stores in six western states. This evidence fails to show that Alcala had any more access to Kane Kutlery knives than any other person in the general public with access to stores that sold this brand of knife. Admittedly, the fact that Alcala's mother and stepfather had Kane Kutlery knives in their kitchen may show that Alcala was familiar with this particular brand. This purported familiarity, however, does not tend to make any fact of consequence to California's case more or less probable. Alcala's general access to or familiarity with Kane Kutlery has no relevance to connecting Alcala to the alleged murder weapon.

The admission of the knife sets amounts to constitutional error, and the prejudicial effect of this evidence likely influenced the jury. California's entire case rested on "strange coincidences." That the alleged murder weapon and the knives seized from Alcala's home were both of the Kane Kutlery brand fits neatly into that "strange coincidences" theme, and the prosecutor spent a good deal of his closing argument—more than three pages of the court reporter's transcripts—framing the issue that way. Thus, there is a reasonable likelihood that some jurors linked Alcala to the knife in the mountains based on brand commonality with the seized knives. Because this evidence caused some prejudice to Alcala, the district court properly included it in its cumulative error analysis.

C. Ineffective Assistance of Counsel

As noted above, one of the grounds on which the district court granted Alcala's petition was that his trial counsel had been ineffective in presenting his alibi. The district court also included this deficiency, along with the deficient preparation of defense witness David Vogel, in its cumulative error analysis. Alcala suggests that, in addition to these deficiencies, his counsel was deficient in failing to investigate the crime scene and in failing to investigate the value of the gold-ball earrings found in Alcala's storage locker. California argues that none of these acts and omissions amounts to deficient performance.

We agree with the district court's inclusion of the deficient presentation of the alibi in the cumulative error analysis. We further agree that counsel was deficient in failing to prepare Vogel and that the prejudice resulting from this deficiency was properly included in the cumulative error analysis. In addition, the district court should have included in the cumulative error analysis trial counsel's deficiency in failing to investigate the crime scene. Finally, the district court correctly concluded that there was no deficiency in failing to investigate the value of the earrings.

i. Preparation and Presentation of David Vogel

Vogel's testimony, which was intended to discredit jailhouse informant Freddie Williams's testimony, was completely undermined by the prosecutor on cross-examination. Vogel, who had himself acted as a jailhouse informant in several previous cases, denied ever giving police or prosecutors false information about another inmate. He then admitted talking to the police about Alcala, with whom he had also been in jail, but claimed that he did not remember what he told the police. The prosecutor then confronted him with an interview he had given to the police in 1979, in which Vogel stated that Alcala had confessed to him that he murdered Samsoe. Vogel ultimately testified that he had lied to the police about Alcala's confession to him, but that he was not lying in his testimony under oath, in part because he had converted to Christianity in the interim.

In addition to this evidence, the district court made several factual findings to support its conclusion that Alcala's trial counsel's performance was constitutionally deficient; none of these findings is clearly erroneous. First, trial counsel knew about Vogel's 1979 police interview prior to putting Vogel on the stand. Vogel was a former client of Alcala's trial counsel, and when the prosecutor sought to play a tape of the interview at trial, trial counsel volunteered, "Your honor, I have a transcription of the tape. . . . If the court wishes we can Xerox this. It's my understanding this was prepared by . . . the district attorney's office, back in 1979."

The district court also found that "prior to testifying at trial, Vogel had given little thought to the fact that he had previously reported that Alcala had made incriminating statements." Vogel's own testimony, in which he stated that he could not remember telling police that Alcala had confessed to him, supports this finding.

Finally, the district court found that Alcala's trial counsel failed "to forewarn Vogel that this topic would likely be covered during cross-examination" and failed "to ascertain for himself how Vogel would likely respond." Again, Vogel's own testimony is evidence of a lack of preparation. Furthermore, at the evidentiary hearing, trial counsel confirmed that his general practice was not to interview witnesses himself—let alone prepare them for specific topics of cross-examination—but merely to say a few words to them in the hallway immediately prior to calling them.

Given these facts, we must determine whether Alcala's trial counsel's conduct "falls within the wide range of reasonable professional assistance". . . . Although an attorney's performance is generally entitled to a strong presumption of competence. . . . deference to the attorney's strategic decisions is diminished where the attorney has not done the preparation necessary to make informed decisions; in particular, the decision not to call a witness is entitled to less deference if the attorney has not interviewed the witness. . . . The same holds true for an attorney's decision to call a witness whom he has not interviewed or otherwise prepared.

Here, we fail to see, and California fails to explain, how the decision to call Vogel without preparing him for cross-examination could possibly "'be considered sound trial strategy' " . . . . Any competent attorney would have made an effort to find out what Vogel would say when asked about his statements to the police incriminating Alcala. There is no suggestion that trial counsel had limited access to Vogel before the trial; indeed, Vogel was his former client. We need not determine whether, after proper preparation, the decision to call Vogel might have been a reasonable exercise of professional judgment. In the absence of such preparation, Alcala's trial counsel's performance was clearly deficient.

We agree that this deficiency prejudiced Alcala and should be included in the cumulative error analysis. If Alcala's trial counsel had adequately prepared Vogel to testify, two outcomes are likely: either Vogel would have been forthright in his testimony about his 1979 interview with the police, or trial counsel would have realized that the 1979 interview was a serious liability and elected not to call Vogel at all. Either way, we can assume that Vogel's initial evasive answers, which greatly damaged his credibility, were likely the result of defense counsel's incompetence. . . .

We have no trouble concluding that Alcala would have been better off if Vogel had either not testified at all or testified credibly. If Vogel had not testified, his statement to the police that Alcala had confessed to murdering Samsoe would not have been admitted. If he had testified candidly, he would have been more useful as an impeachment witness against Williams, lessening the impact of Williams's testimony that Alcala had confessed to him. Because a "defendant's own confession is probably the most probative and damaging evidence that can be admitted against him" . . . either of these outcomes would have been more favorable than the damaging testimony that Vogel actually gave. The district court properly included the prejudice from this deficiency in the cumulative error analysis.

ii. Failure to Investigate the Crime Scene

At trial, two expert witnesses testified for the prosecution about the crime scene and Samsoe's remains: a criminalist, Margaret Kuo, and a pathologist, Dr. Sharon Schnittker. Kuo testified that she found a single, tiny drop of human blood on the blade of the knife recovered from the scene. As noted above, the prosecutor used this testimony, along with Dana Crappa's testimony that Samsoe's body was "pretty cut up," to argue that the knife was the murder weapon. Schnittker testified that there was no evidence of knife wounds on the skeletal remains but stated that it was possible for fatal stab wounds to leave no mark on a skeleton.

Alcala claims that his trial counsel was ineffective for failing to investigate the crime scene and to introduce competing expert testimony to show that Crappa's observations were factually impossible. He suggests that a full investigation by a forensic pathologist and a criminalist would have revealed additional details to impeach Crappa and discredit the prosecution's theory. The district court found that Alcala's trial counsel was not deficient in failing to investigate the crime scene. We disagree and, contrary to the district court, include the prejudice resulting from this deficiency in our cumulative error analysis.

Alcala has met his burden of demonstrating that an adequate investigation could have resulted in additional evidence favorable to the defense. At the evidentiary hearing, Alcala presented the testimony of a forensic pathologist that, due to the condition of Samsoe's skeleton, "it is highly unlikely that Robin Samsoe died as a result of multiple stab wounds," as well as a criminalist, who testified that the condition of the knife was inconsistent with its purported use as a murder weapon. The criminalist noted that, even after disassembly, there was no blood in any crack or crevice of the knife as would typically be found if it had been used as a murder weapon. Moreover, the spot of blood on the knife was consistent with a blood splatter rather than a wipe or smear mark.

Although it may have been reasonable for trial counsel not to retain specific experts, such as a pathologist or a criminalist, it cannot have been reasonable for him not to investigate the crime scene at all. . . .

Here, by contrast, trial counsel apparently had decided that evidence to impeach Dana Crappa *would* be of help; he went to the trouble of calling an astrophysicist to refute Crappa's testimony as to the phase of the moon on one of the nights in question. Impeaching Crappa was central to Alcala's defense, and without an investigation, trial counsel could not reasonably have known whether the crime scene evidence was consistent with her testimony.

[T]he prosecution's case against Alcala rested largely on the credibility of Dana Crappa. The prosecution's own witnesses established that there was no physical evidence to establish the cause of death as testified to by Crappa, and Alcala's trial counsel elected "simply to rely on" the prosecution's investigation as "the sole source of information on the subject" . . . . He could not have made an informed decision about whether the inability to establish a cause of death and other objective crime scene evidence should be used to impeach Crappa's testimony. . . .

[W]e hold that the failure to investigate the crime scene was deficient. Alcala has shown some prejudice resulting from this deficiency, suggesting that if his trial counsel had investigated the crime scene, he would have retained the services of a criminalist and a forensic pathologist. The resulting evidence would have helped to discredit Crappa's testimony and the prosecution's inferences drawn therefrom. The district court should have included the prejudice flowing from this deficiency in the cumulative error analysis, and we will do so here.

iii. Failure to Investigate the Value of the Earrings

At trial, the prosecution presented evidence that a pair of gold-ball earrings had been seized from a storage locker rented by Alcala. Marianne Frazier, Samsoe's mother, testified that the earrings were similar to a pair of cheap $3 earrings that she owned and that Samsoe sometimes wore, earrings that she had not seen since Samsoe's disappearance.

Alcala urges that his trial counsel was constitutionally ineffective in failing to call an expert gemologist to demonstrate that the earrings found in the storage locker were not cheap $3 earrings, such as those that Samsoe's mother testified that she had owned, but instead were mid-priced custom jewelry with a higher gold content. Alcala presented the testimony of a gemologist at the evidentiary hearing to establish the gold content and value of the earrings. This testimony was inconsistent with Frazier's testimony, substantially undercutting the assertion that the earrings found in the storage locker were taken from Samsoe. Although the district court recognized the potential impact of an expert gemologist's testimony in "neutraliz[ing] the damaging inferences the jury might otherwise draw from the similarity between the earrings in Alcala's storage locker and Ms. Frazier's lost earrings," the district court found no deficiency because trial counsel had no way of knowing that the earrings were inconsistent with Frazier's description.

We agree with the district court's conclusion that this alleged deficiency was properly excluded from the cumulative error analysis. Alcala's trial counsel reasonably could have expected that if the earrings were more valuable than Frazier suggested, Alcala, as the owner of the earrings, would have informed him of this fact. . . . There is no indication in the record that Alcala did so, or that competent counsel would have realized that the earrings were more valuable than the earrings described by Frazier. Trial counsel's performance was not deficient, and the prejudice from the failure to investigate the value of the earrings cannot be included in our cumulative error analysis.

D. Cumulative Prejudice

We now turn to the issue of whether the cumulative effect of these errors had "a substantial and injurious effect" on the jury's verdict. . . . We agree with the district court that the cumulative effect of these errors "operated to deprive Alcala of a fundamentally fair trial." The district court correctly weighed all of the errors together in order to assess their cumulative impact on Alcala's constitutional rights. "[E]ven if no single error were [sufficiently] prejudicial, where there are several substantial errors, 'their cumulative effect may nevertheless be so prejudicial as to require reversal'". . . .

Here, the cumulative impact of these errors goes to the heart of the prosecution's theory of the case and undermines every important element of proof offered by the prosecution against Alcala. Indeed, after reviewing the errors in this case, we are left with the unambiguous conviction that the verdict in this case was not the result of a fair trial.

The trial court precluded Alcala from effectively challenging or excluding the testimony of the prosecution's key witness—Dana Crappa. The trial court's exclusion of Dr. London's expert testimony deprived Alcala of an important opportunity to discredit the only eyewitness who allegedly could place Alcala with Samsoe at the scene of the crime on the evening of June 20. Had Dr. London been permitted to testify, the jury may have discounted Crappa's testimony as not credible in light of the fact that it was obtained through improper and dubious means, as well as the obvious and apparent instability of Crappa's mental condition. Dr. London's expert testimony, combined with Crappa's bizarre demeanor, would have seriously called into question her reliability as a witness. Had the credibility of the prosecution's star witness been effectively challenged, the case against Alcala would have been undoubtedly weaker.

Second, aside from Crappa, the only witness who could place Alcala with Samsoe was Jackelyn Young, who claimed to have seen Alcala with Samsoe at Huntington Beach on the afternoon of June 20 at 3:00 p.m. Had Alcala's counsel adequately presented Alcala's Knott's Berry Farm alibi, Alcala could have directly challenged Young's testimony. Alcala's alibi also would have challenged the theory that Alcala abducted Samsoe after she left Wilvert's house at 3:10 p.m.

Third, Fallen's, Crawford's, and Vasquez's testimony would have further weakened the prosecution's theory of the case. The combined testimony of these witnesses would have challenged Crappa's version of the events and presented a colorable third-party culpability theory for the jury to assess.

Fourth, the erroneous admission of the Kane Kutlery knives seized from Alcala's home permitted the jury to draw an impermissible connection between Alcala and the purported murder weapon—the key and *only* piece of physical evidence discovered at the scene of the crime that could be linked to Alcala. The prosecution's placement of undue emphasis on this link compels us to conclude that the jury's verdict was tainted by the admission of this evidence.

Fifth, Alcala's trial counsel presented a fatally impeachable witness, Vogel, without first assessing how Vogel would respond on cross-examination to evidence that he told police that Alcala confessed to him. As a result, Vogel actually served to reinforce the informant's tale that Alcala confessed to murdering Samsoe. Trial counsel's performance not only deprived Alcala of a potentially meritorious defense, but his actions and omissions also substantially impaired Alcala's efforts to demonstrate reasonable doubt.

Lastly, Alcala's trial counsel completely failed to conduct any investigation of the crime scene. This failure likely resulted in the loss of an opportunity to challenge Crappa's purported observations as inconsistent with the objective evidence.

Therefore, we conclude that the cumulative impact of these errors is more than sufficient to demonstrate prejudice. The cumulative weight of the above errors deprived Alcala of a fundamentally fair trial.

CONCLUSION

We conclude, as did the district court, that the deficient presentation of Alcala's alibi and the exclusion of Dr. London's testimony was each on its own an error sufficiently prejudicial to grant Alcala's petition. When combined with the erroneous exclusion of Fallen, Crawford, and Vasquez, the erroneous admission of the Kane Kutlery knives, the deficient failure to prepare Vogel to testify, and the deficient failure to investigate the crime scene, the cumulative impact of these errors severely undermines our confidence in the jury's verdict. We affirm the conditional grant of Alcala's petition.

AFFIRMED.

APPENDIX 3

Excerpt from John Wayne Gacy's appeal in the United States Court of Appeals, Seventh Circuit, argued March 4, 1993.

994 F.2d 305

61 USLW 2665

JOHN WAYNE GACY, Petitioner-Appellant,
v.
GEORGE WELBORN, Warden, Menard Correctional Center, and Roland W. Burris, Attorney General of Illinois, Respondents-Appellees.

Nos. 92-3448, 92-3965.

United States Court of Appeals,
Seventh Circuit.

Argued March 4, 1993.
Decided April 12, 1993.
Rehearing and Rehearing En Banc
Denied May 7, 1993.

John Wayne Gacy is a serial killer. Between 1972 and 1978 he enticed many young men to his home near Chicago for homosexual liaisons. At least 33 never left. Gacy tied up or handcuffed his partners, then strangled or choked them. Twenty-eight of the bodies were dumped into the crawl space under the Gacy residence; one was entombed under the driveway; the rest were thrown into the Des Plaines River. Gacy, who operated a construction business, had his workers dig trenches and throw lime into the crawl space. Gacy's wife complained about an "awful stench." But the slaughter continued until the disappearance of 15 year old Robert Piest on December 11, 1978. Piest vanished after telling his mother that he was going to see a building contractor about a summer job. The presence of Gacy's truck outside the place where Piest was to meet his potential employer led to Gacy's arrest within two days.

The discovery of so many skeletons, several with rags stuffed in the victims' mouths, created a national sensation. Gacy regaled the police with stories about his exploits, which he attributed to "Jack," an alternative personality. A jury convicted Gacy in March 1980 of 33 counts of murder, rejecting his defense of insanity. The same jury sentenced Gacy to death for 12 of these killings, the only 12 that the prosecution could prove had been committed after Illinois enacted its post-Furman death penalty statute. The Supreme Court of Illinois affirmed. . . . Opinions in this case already exceed 200 pages. We spare readers further recapitulation and turn directly to the four arguments Gacy has culled from more than 100 raised at one or another stage of this litigation, now 14½ years old. Gacy has in this sense already escaped the 12 judgments of execution, for judge and jury cannot decide whether a murderer will die, but only how soon.

*Illinois commits the capital sentencing decision to the jury. If the jury convicts a defendant of a capital offense, there is a sentencing proceeding. At this proceeding the prosecution bears the burden of establishing the existence of defined aggravating circumstances. If the jury unanimously decides that there is at least one aggravating circumstance, the defendant becomes eligible for a death sentence. . . .

If the jury determines unanimously that there are no mitigating factors sufficient to preclude the imposition of the death sentence, the court shall sentence the defendant to death.

Unless the jury unanimously finds that there are no mitigating factors sufficient to preclude the imposition of the death sentence the court shall sentence the defendant to a term of imprisonment under Chapter V of the Unified Code of Corrections.

The second paragraph means that a single juror's belief that the defendant has demonstrated the existence of a single mitigating factor precludes the death sentence. Such a rule surprises some judges, who are accustomed to telling jurors that decisions must be unanimous. . . .

* At the close of Gacy's penalty proceeding, Judge Garippo instructed the jury:

If, after your deliberations, you unanimously determine that there are no mitigating factors sufficient to preclude the imposition of the death sentence on the Defendant, you should sign the verdict form directing a sentence of death. If, after your deliberations, you are not unanimous in concluding that there are no mitigating factors sufficient to preclude imposition of the death sentence, you must sign the verdict form directing a sentence of imprisonment.

As Judge Grady, who denied Gacy's petition for a writ of habeas corpus, remarked: "This written instruction is completely accurate." The jurors had this instruction, like the others in the three-page charge, during their deliberations. Unfortunately, Judge Garippo did not read the instruction to the jury as written—or at least the court reporter did not take down the same words that appear in the written instructions. The transcript has it that the second sentence of this instruction was delivered as: "If, after your deliberations, you unanimously conclude there are mitigating factors sufficient to preclude the imposition of the death penalty, you must sign the verdict form directing a sentence of imprisonment" . . . .

Gacy's jury was told that if it is unanimous in finding a mitigating circumstance, it must return a verdict of imprisonment. The oral version of the instruction is accurate, as far as it goes. But the instruction did not give the jury the whole truth, because it did not tell the jurors what to do in the event of disagreement. . . .

Judge Garippo opened the sentencing phase of Gacy's trial by describing to the jurors the findings they would need to make. The judge said, among other things:

If you cannot unanimously agree that there are no sufficient mitigating factors to preclude the imposition of the death penalty, you will sign that verdict so indicating, and the Court will sentence the Defendant to imprisonment.

The final instructions came close on the heels of the preliminary set, for the jury did not receive fresh evidence; instead the lawyers presented arguments based on the evidence at the five-week trial. Defense counsel emphasized during these arguments that unanimity was unnecessary:

[T]he only way that you can impose the death penalty on Mr. Gacy, and His Honor will instruct you, it is a unanimous decision, all 12 of you have to agree to give Mr. Gacy the death penalty. If there is just one of you who feels that he was acting under an emotional disturbance, or if there is just one of you who feels it would not be the right thing to do, if there is one of you who feels that he should be studied for any reason at all, if there is one of you, then you must sentence him or direct the court to sentence him to a term of imprisonment.

This argument, an accurate statement of Illinois law, was presented without objection from the prosecutor. For his part, the prosecutor did not urge the jury to seek unanimity on mitigating factors.

What we have, in sum, is a slip of the judicial tongue. No one noticed at the time; defense counsel did not object to the misreading of the written instruction. The complete, and completely accurate, instructions were available to the jurors during their deliberations. The text was short; vital information did not drown in a sea of words. If the jurors wondered about the consequences of disagreement, they had correct answers at their elbows. Within two hours, the jurors brought back death verdicts on all 12 counts. This is too little time to reach unanimous agreement on aggravating factors and beat down even a single holdout on mitigating factors. So the question at hand probably did not arise in the jury's deliberations; they must have been in agreement from the outset. These circumstances "rule out [any] substantial possibility that the jury may have rested its verdict on the 'improper' ground". . . .

B

Gacy's remaining arguments require less discussion. Each received extended treatment by Judge Grady, whose opinion withstands all challenges.

*Because comment in the media was especially intense in Chicago, the court chose a jury in Rockford. During the four days devoted to screening potential jurors, the court put many questions to candidates. The judge asked, for example, whether the pretrial publicity made it impossible to approach the subject with an open mind, and whether Gacy's homosexuality (and the sexual nature of the crimes) would affect their judgment. The judge declined, however, to ask members of the venire exactly what they had read in the papers and exactly what they thought about homosexuals. Gacy contends that the judge's refusal to ask the questions his lawyer proposed deprived him of a fair trial. . . .

Before the trial began, court and counsel compiled an index of what had appeared in the media. The judge asked the jurors what they watched and read. This information, combined with the index, enabled Gacy's lawyers to know the allegations to which each juror had been exposed. As Judge Garippo concluded, it could have been counterproductive to require each juror to repeat the details, because this could have summoned up information that the juror otherwise would have forgotten—and in the process contaminated other members of the venire. The index, the questioning, and drawing the venire from Rockford were adequate to select an unbiased jury. . . .

Gacy contends that the judge's questions about homosexuality were inadequate. Judge Garippo asked general questions, such as: "Now, does the fact that the Defendant is charged with homosexual conduct prevent you from being fair to either side?" and "Could you put aside any feeling that you might have regarding homosexuality in rendering your verdict in this case?" These are inadequate, Gacy submits, because they invited bland "yes" or "no" answers and thus hid any subtle signs of bias. The questions his lawyer proposed, by contrast, called for potential jurors to describe their feelings about homosexuals. It may well be that the kind of questions proposed by the defense would have afforded greater entree into the jurors' attitudes, but Morgan does not require them. That case tells judges to ask about specific areas of bias rather than asking a general question such as "can you be fair and impartial?" Judge Garippo did what Morgan requires. To do more would have extended the jury-selection process considerably and left many jurors flustered and resentful, which in the end may have worked against the defendant. Defendants' safety lies in the size of the jury and in cautions from the court, not in extra questions posed in advance of trial. A long series of probing questions can anesthetize or offend the panel rather than enlighten judge and counsel. Experienced judges accordingly prune the list, omitting some that may look appropriate in isolation. Judge Garippo did just that—and proceeded to follow up with more pointed questions when appropriate. Judge Grady's opinion details several of these sequences, which we need not repeat.

Moreover, as Judge Grady pointed out, general questions about attitudes toward homosexuality were beside the point. Gacy admitted killing many persons. His defense was insanity. Gacy's lawyer did not ask the judge to propound questions along the line of "Do you believe that homosexuals are more likely than heterosexuals to be sane?" or "Are you disposed to convict an insane person whose murders were related to homosexuality, although the law and the evidence require acquittal?" Of course questions this blunt would have been useless, but Gacy's lawyer also did not propose ways to get at these subjects indirectly. Which is not to fault his lawyer: the subjects are not easy to broach. Even in hindsight it is not clear what more counsel, or the court, could have done. All that we need hold is that the trial judge was entitled to resist the invitation to turn voir dire into a trial of jurors' attitudes about homosexuality.

Gacy presented his defense of insanity through six expert witnesses: four psychiatrists and two psychologists. Judge Garippo declined to allow Gacy's lawyers to use these witnesses to relay to the jury verbatim statements Gacy made to them, ruling that these were hearsay when offered for the truth of the matter asserted. Gacy did not testify at trial, and the prosecutor used the hearsay objections to prevent Gacy from getting the more favorable portions of his story before the jury indirectly. The trial judge nonetheless permitted the expert witnesses to recount the substance of what Gacy had said. The prosecutor did not hesitate to ask these six witnesses, and the state's own experts, about Gacy's incriminating statements. These came in as admissions of a party opponent. Gacy contends that this one-sided use of his words violated his rights under the due process clause.

Without detracting in any way from the care Judge Grady lavished on this issue, or the correctness of his decision that any error was harmless, we hold that there was no error at all—no constitutional error, that is. Anderson was based on state law. Beyond explicit rules such as the privilege against self-incrimination and the confrontation clause, none of which applies here, the Constitution has little to say about rules of evidence. . . . The hearsay rule and its exception for admissions of a party opponent are venerable doctrines; no serious constitutional challenge can be raised to them.

C

At last we reach the inevitable attack on trial counsel. It is, as Judge Grady concluded, unpersuasive. Gacy received a skillful, vigorous defense by lawyers who were prepared to the nines. Gacy's lead counsel, Sam Amirante, is now a judge of the court that conducted his trial.

For this appeal, Gacy's current legal team has discarded all but two objections. First comes the argument that Amirante raised the insanity defense over Gacy's objection, depriving him of the ability to control decisions vital to the defense. Second, Gacy insists that Amirante's loyalties were compromised by his pursuit of revenues from a book and other publicity. The lure of lucre led him to induce Gacy to confess, the argument goes, the better to get an interesting story—but with devastating effect on the defense. Although such claims could in principle raise problems, they fail for want of proof.

Let us start with the latter claim. Amirante filed an affidavit denying that he was pursuing profits from publicity. No book by Amirante or any of his associates appeared after the trial. Although an investigator may have leaked some tape recordings to Tim Cahill, author of *Buried Dreams* (1985), Amirante denied authorizing or knowing of this misconduct. A tape recording of a conversation between Gacy and Amirante 10 months before trial contains a brief discussion of publication possibilities. Amirante offered to refer Gacy to another lawyer to pursue that possibility—exactly the right thing to do, and the antithesis of a conflict of interest. All that remains is one paragraph in an order entered by the trial court requiring Gacy's lawyers to continue their work at public expense (Amirante had been retained privately at the outset):

That, over the objection of Defense Counsel, it is hereby ordered that Attorneys Amirante and Motta reimburse Cook County to the extent of fees received for services rendered from any royalties received as a result of book or movie rights hereafter acquired, excluding any professionally oriented works, lectures, treatises, or the like.

The record does not reveal who raised the subject of royalties (the prosecutor, the judge, or defense counsel), or the basis of the objection. For all we know, only the judge had movies on his mind. So Amirante asserted in his affidavit. In the absence of any contrary evidence, this is a blind alley.

As for the contention that counsel barged ahead with an unwanted insanity defense: again the evidence gets in the way. Gacy cooperated with extended interviews and tests by six experts for the defense and another six for the state, not the behavior you would expect of a person who wanted to stand on a plain denial of guilt. In mid-trial, Gacy threatened to stop cooperating with his attorneys, complaining: "I'm not running the trial." When the judge asked what the problem was, Gacy continued: "I was against the insanity defense from the beginning." This assertion, never heard again during the trial, has become the foundation for the attack on counsel. In an affidavit dated July 25, 1990, Gacy at last furnished a reason: "I couldn't believe that anyone could go insane 33 different times and then run a successful business, [and] if I didn't believe it how could [Amirante] expect 12 jurors to believe that". Good question—but how did Gacy expect to persuade the jury to disregard his confessions, plus the damning evidence of the 28 skeletons under his house, a 29th under his driveway, and 4 more recovered from the river, not to mention the testimony of witnesses who barely survived their encounters with him? His current story, that he was out of town on every occasion, is unsupported by evidence and less plausible than his insanity defense.

As Judge Grady remarked, Gacy's only real choice was between an insanity defense and a guilty plea. It may be that Gacy could have obliged Amirante to desist from the insanity defense and conduct a defense limited to guilt, trying (as Amirante did not) to suppress the confessions and fob off the significance of the human remains. We say "it may be" because several of Gacy's experts testified that he was not competent to assist in his defense. Although Judge Garippo rejected that position and ordered Gacy to stand trial, the duties of counsel representing a client of borderline competence are not so clearly established as the duties of counsel representing a normal defendant. However that may be, Gacy did not tell Amirante to stop. A statement such as "I was against the insanity defense from the beginning" is some distance from "I directed Amirante to drop that defense, and he refused." Being "against" a defense at the outset is consistent with yielding to the judgment of those who know better. Even the affidavit of 1990 does not assert that Amirante refused to carry out any direct instructions from his client. There is consequently no material dispute requiring an evidentiary hearing.

AFFIRMED.

SOURCES

1. JUAN CORONA

Caldwell, Earl. "Corona's Defense Calls No Witnesses." *New York Times*, January 4, 1973.

Caldwell, Earl. "Corona's Lawyer Says a Homosexual Committed the 25 Killings." *New York Times*, October 4, 1972.

Caldwell, Earl. "Prosecution Opens the Corona Case." *New York Times*, September 30, 1972.

Caldwell, Earl. "Trial of Mass Murder Suspect Opens on Coast." *New York Times*, September 12, 1972.

"Corona's Attorney, Criticizing Prosecutor, Seeks a New Trial. *New York Times*, January 28, 1973.

"Corona Guilty—Convicted of All 25 Murders—Courtroom Stunned by Verdict." *Los Angeles Times*, Jan. 18, 1973, p. 1.

Cray, Ed. *Burden of Proof: The Case of Juan Corona*. New York: Macmillan, 1973.

"Jury Finds Corona Guilty of Slaying 25 Workers." *New York Times*, January 19, 1973.

Kneeland, Douglas E. "Coast Man Seized in Dozens of Killings," *New York Times*, May 27, 1971.

"Mild Heart Attack Suffered By Corona." *Los Angeles Times*, Jun. 30, 1971.

Turner, Wallace. "Conviction Reversed in Migrants' Murder." *New York Times*, May 9, 1978.

2. DEAN ALLEN CORRL, ELMER WAYNE HENLEY, AND DAVID OWEN BROOKS

Capote, Truman. Truman Capote papers regarding Houston Diary. http://archives.nypl.org/mss/24831

Chriss, Nicholas C. and Rawitch, Robert. "Corll's Portrait: Polite, Quiet, Neat, 'Always With Young Boys.'" *Los Angeles Times*, August 19, 1973.

"8 Bodies Found in Houston Lot." *New York Times*, August 9, 1973.

Hollandsworth, Skip. "The Lost Boys." *Texas Monthly*, April 2011.

Montgomery, Paul L. "Houston Finds Murder Ring Random, Enigmatic Intrusion." *New York Times*, July 21, 1974.

Montgomery, Paul L. "Juror Hears Officers Describe Finding 27 Bodies Near Houston." *New York Times*, July 9, 1974.

"Parents of 2 Boys Missing in Houston Criticize the Police." *New York Times*, August 13, 1973.

Sterba, James P. "Police Find Four More Bodies." *New York Times*, August 11, 1973.

"Texan Said to Admit Role in 25 Killings." *New York Times*, August 10, 1973, p. 63

"Texas Man Convicted of Torture Slayings." *Washington Post*, June 28, 1979.

3. RODNEY ALCALA

Buettner, Ross. "Judge Cries During Sentencing of Serial Killer Rodney Alcala." *New York Times*. January 7, 2013.

Eisenberg, Larry. "Serial Murderer Charged with Two Killings in the 1970s." *New York Times*, January 27, 2011.

Esquivel, Paloma. "Jury Gets Alcala Case; Convictions in Earlier Trials Were Overturned." *Los Angeles Times*, February 25, 2010.

Esquivel, Paloma. "Rodney James Alcala Gets the Death Penalty." *Los Angeles Times*, March 10, 2010.

Hicks, Jerry. "Alcala Asks Jury to Spare Him, Insists He Isn't Murderer." *Los Angeles Times*, June 19, 1986.

Hicks, Jerry. "Alcala Given Death Sentence in Slaying of Girl, 12." *Los Angeles Times*, June 21, 1986.

Hicks, Jerry. "Death Ordered for Alcala." *Los Angeles Times*, June 21, 1986.

Jarlson, Gary. "Man Arrested in Girl's Murder." *Los Angeles Times*, July 27, 1979.

Jarlson, Gary. "Suspect in Girl's Murder to Be Arraigned." *Los Angeles Times*,

July 26, 1979.

Reyes, David. "Alcala Found Guilty at Retrial in Killing of 12-Year-Old Girl." *Los Angeles Times*, May 29, 1986.

Sands, Stella. *The Dating Game Killer*. New York: St. Martin's True Crime, 2011

Esquivel, Paoma. "Suspect in 5 Killings Acts as His Own Attorney." *Los Angeles Times*, February 3, 2010.

Weinstein, Henry. "New Trial, New Charge in Old Cases." *Los Angeles Times*, June 28, 2003.

4. EDMUND KEMPER

Kleinfield, N. R. and Goode, Erica. "Coast Man Guilty in Eight Murders." *New York Times*, November 9, 1973.

Kleinfield, N. R. and Goode, Erica. "Retracing a Trail: The Sniper Suspects: Serial Killing's Squarest Pegs: Not Solo, White, Psychosexual or Picky." *New York Times*, October 28, 2002.

Kleinfield, N. R. and Goode, Erica. "Slayer of 8 Gets Life in California." *New York Times*, November 10, 1973, p. 9.

Lunde, Donald T. *Murder and Madness*. New York: Simon & Schuster, 1975.

5. DAVID BERKOWITZ

"Killer to Cops: 'I'll Do It Again.' Taunting Note is First Solid Clue. *New York Daily News,* April 19, 1977.

Klausner, Lawrence D. *Son of Sam*. New York: McGraw Hill, 1981.

McFadden, Robert D. "The '77 Blackout: Writing by Candlelight." *New York Times,* July 10, 2007.

McQuiston, John T. "Columbia Coed, 19, Is Slain on Street In Forest Hills." *New York Times*, March 9, 1977.

Perlmutter, Emanuel. "Fourth Woman Slain by Same Gun." *New York Times,* April 18, 1977.

Saxon, Wolfgang. "Woman Dies in Mystery Shooting." *New York Times,* January 31, 1977.

Schram, Jamie and Musumeci, Natalie. "Son of Sam: I've Found My Life's Calling." *New York Post*, June 22, 2016.

Schumach, Murray. "Adolescent Sought as Student's Killer." *New York Times*, March 10, 1977

"Son of Sam Fires Four Shots into Double-Parked Car in the Bronx, Killing One. *New York Daily News*, July 30, 1976.

"Son of Sam Kills a Woman Sitting Next to Her Boyfriend in Car." *New York Daily News,* January 31, 1977.

6. TED BUNDY

Rule, Ann. *The Stranger Beside Me*. New York: W. W. Norton & Co., 1980.

Nordheimer, Jon. "All-American Boy on Trial." *New York Times*, December 10, 1978.

7. VAUGHN GREENWOOD

"California Suspect Indicted in Killing of 11 By Slashing." *New York Times*, January 24, 1976

"Escaped Convict Sought on Coast In 'Slash' Deaths." *New York Times*, February 2, 1975.

8. HERBERT MULLIN

Lunde, Donald T. *Murder and Madness*. New York: Simon & Schuster, 1975

Lunde, Donald T. and Morgan, Jefferson. *The Die Song*. New York: W. W. Norton & Co., 1980.

9. THE ZEBRA KILLERS

"4 Whites Killed by Roving Gunmen—At Least one Other Injured in San Francisco Area." *The New York Times*, January 30, 1974

Lembke, Daryl. "Alioto Sticks to Claim on Death Angels Killings." *Los Angeles Times*, May 3, 1974.

Lembke, Daryl. "4 Found Guilty in S.F. Zebra Murder Spree." *Los Angeles Times*, March 14, 1976.

"Police Seize 7 in Zebra Killings." *Chicago Tribune*, May 2, 1974.

Turner, Wallace. "Hundreds of Coast Blacks Frisked in Hunt for Killers." *New York Times,* April 18, 1979.

Turner, Wallace. "7 Arrested Men Tied to Muslim." *New York Times*. May 4, 1974

10. KENNETH BIANCHI AND ANGELO BUONO

"Apparent 13th Victim of Hillside Strangler Found." *Los Angeles Times*, February 18, 1978.

"Bianchi Sentenced to Six Life Terms for Five Slayings." *Los Angeles Times*, October 23, 1979.

"Buono Charged in Ten Hillside Strangler Killings." *Los Angeles Times*, October 19, 1979.

Cannon, Lou. "Police Say Actor Is Not Strangler." *Washington Post*, February 10, 1978.

"Hillside Strangler, Angelo Buono, 67, Dies." *New York Times*, Sepetmber 23, 2002.

Kistler, Robert and Rosenzweig, David. "Bianchi's Cousin Emerges as a Central Figure in Hillside Strangler Murder Case." *Los Angeles Times*, May 10, 1979.

Lindsey, Robert. "California Agrees to Take Over Prosecution of Suspect in Stranglings." *New York Times*, July 29, 1981.

Lindsey, Robert . Jury Given Lesson in Hollywood Life. *New York Times*, December 5, 1982.

Lunde, Donald T. *Hearst to Hughes: Memoirs of a Forensic Psychiatrist*. Bloomington, IN: AuthorHouse, 2007.

"Reward Offered in 10 LA Stranglings." *Los Angeles Times*, December 1, 1977.

Townsend, Dorothy. "Defense to Escape Strangler Outlined." *Los Angeles Times*, December 2, 1977.

"2 Arrested as Hillside Stranglers After a Confession." *New York Times*, October 20, 1979.

11. PATRICK WAYNE KEARNEY

Cannon, Lou. "California Murder Cases Seen as Setback for Gay Rights." *Washington Post*, July 17, 1977.

Crewdson, John M. "Coast Killings: Bizarre Case Widens." *New York Times*, July 11, 1977.

Lindsey, Robert. "Californian's Silence Frustrates Investigation of Mass Murders." *New York*, August 12, 1977.

"Man Guilty in 'Trash Bag' Deaths Is Charged in 21st Murder Count." *New York Times*, February 19, 1978.

"Pair Arraigned in 2 Trash Bag Murder Cases." *Los Angeles Times*, July 6, 1977.

12. CORAL EUGENE WATTS

Coral Eugene Watts, 53; Murderer Claimed He Had Killed 80. *Los Angeles Times*, September 23, 2007.

Easton, Pam. "Serial Killer's Pending Release Disquiets Families, Survivors." *Detroit Free Press*, August 19, 2002.

Flanigan, Bryan. "Watts Admits Killing Writer." *Detroit Free Press*, August 21, 1982.

King, Wayne. "Suspect in Texas Slayings Was Under Police Surveillance in 2 States." *New York Times*, August 11, 1982

Kurth, Joel. "Parole Date Reignites Fear: Task for to Retrace Deaths Tied to Killer." *Detroit Free Press*, November 24, 2002

Leung, Rebecca. A Deal with the Devil?" 60 Minutes, October 14, 2004. https://www.cbsnews.com/news/a-deal-with-the-devil-14-10-2004.

"The Man Who Murdered Women: Coral Watts Stalked Them in Michigan and Texas. His Toll: At Least 13." *Detroit Free Press*, August 22, 1982.

"Watts Clears Convict." *Detroit Free Press*, August 18, 1982.

Witsil, Frank. "Witness Tells of Watching 1979 Killing in Ferndale." *Detroit Free Press*, November 11, 2004.

13. WILLIAM BONIN

Bonin, William George. California Department of Corrections and Rehabilitation Executed Inmate Summary. https://www.cdcr.ca.gov/capital-punishment/inmates-executed-1978-to-present/william-george-bonin/

Ellingwood, Jr., Ken, Moehringer, J. R., Trounson, Rebecca. "'Freeway Killer' William Bonin Is Executed: Sadistic Slayer Confessed to 21 Murders." *Los Angeles Times*, February 23, 1996.

Farr, Bill. "Two Men Charged in 'Freeway Killer' Case." *Los Angeles Times*, July 30, 1980.

Lindsey, Robert. "Coast Killings Tied to Homosexuality." *New York Times*, September 21, 1981.

People v. Bonin (1988). https://scocal.stanford.edu/opinion/people-v-bonin-30935.

People v. Bonin (1989). https://scocal.stanford.edu/opinion/people-v-bonin-30907.

14. JOHN WAYNE GACY

The author drew extensively for this chapter from the following resources:

- Circuit Court of Cook County, Criminal Division. The People of the State of Illinois vs. John Wayne Gacy. Official transcripts. January 10, 1979, to March 21, 1980.
- Louis B. Garippo, Judge, (Retired) Circuit Court of Cook County, Illinois.
- William J. Kunkle. First Assistant State's Attorney, Cook County, Illinois, and former Circuit Court Judge, Cook County, Illinois.
- Robert Egan, Assistant State's Attorney, Cook County, Illinois.
- Greg Bedoe, Investigator, Cook County State's Attorney's Office.
- Michael Ficaro, Assistant State's Attorney, Cook County, Illinois, and Assistant Illinois Attorney General.
- *Chicago Tribune*. December 23, 1978 to December 17, 2018.
- *Chicago Sun-Times*. December 23, 1978 to October 15, 2019.

Bazerghi, Alice. "Property Where John Wayne Gacy Killed Most of His Victims Is on the Market." *Chicago Sun-Times*, October 15, 2019.

Dudek, Mitch. "Where John Wayne Gacy Buried the Bodies, More; Key Sites Tied to Serial Killer." *Chicago Sun-Times*, December 14, 2018.

Fritsch, Jane. "Youth Tells of Grappling with Gacy." *Chicago Tribune*, February 12, 1980.

Kifner, John. Gacy, Killer of 33, Is Put To Death as Appeals Fail. *The New York Times*. May 11, 1994.

Rumore, Kori. "Timeline: Suburban Serial Killer John Wayne Gacy and the Effort to Recover, Name His 33 Victims." *Chicago Tribune*, December 17, 2018.

Smith, Sid. "John Wayne Gacy, The Country's Worst Serial Killer." *Chicago Tribune*, December 22, 1978.

INDEX

A

Agnos, Arthur C., 103
Aguilar, Melinda, 127
Aguirre, Frank, 29
Alcala, Rodney
  background and appearance of, 32, 33–35
  The Dating Game and, 32–33
  parole and, 35, 36, 46
  sexual molestation by, 33, 34, 37–39, 42
  trials and penalties, 36–37, 38–39, 40–41, 42–43
  victims, 33, 37, 38, 39, 40, 42, 43–46
Alcala-Buguor, Rodrigo Jacques. *See* Alcala, Rodney
Alioto, Joseph, 98, 99, 100, 101, 102
Allen, Paul B., 12
Amirante, Sam, 147, 150, 155
Anderson, Ward, 105
Atkins, Susan, 6

B

Bambic, John, 104
Barca, Charles, 98
Barcomb, Jill, 40, 45
Barker, Glen, 141
Barr, Ann Marie, 80
Beame, Abraham, 67, 68
Beck, George N., 85
Bedoe, Greg, 146, 152, 162
Beierman, Sigurd E., 11–12
Berger, John, 34–35, 41. *See also* Alcala, Rodney
Berkowitz, David
  arrest, plea, and sentence, 67–68, 69, 70
  background and appearance of, 69
  health, 69
  notes and letters by, 57, 58–61, 62–63
  victims, 54–55, 56, 64, 66
Berkowitz, Nathan, 69
Berkowitz, Pearl, 69
Bertuccio, Ilario, 103
Bianchi, Kenneth
  background, 110–111, 112
  pleas and sentences, 114–115, 116, 117
  testimony against Buono, 112, 116
  victims, 111–113, 114
Blair, Jerry, 80
Boling, Tommy, 154
Bonafide, Sam, 13
Bonin, William G., 134, 135, 141, 142. *See also* Freeway Killer murders
Bonnin, Michael L., 153
Borrelli, Joseph, 58
Borstein, Leon, 42
Bowman, Margaret, 77
Bowman, Matthew, 154
Boyd, Kerri Kaye, 111
Brauer, Harry F., 51
Breckinridge, Paul G., Jr., 124
Breslin, Jimmy, 61, 62, 63–64
Brisbon, Henry, 160
Briseno, Francisco, 40
Brody, Earl C., 86–88
Brooks, David Owen, 21–23, 26, 27–28, 31
Bryant, Anita, 123
Bundy, John, 74
Bundy, Louise, 74
Bundy, Theodore Robert
  arrested and released, 72–73
  background, 74, 78–79
  escapes by, 75–76
  execution of, 80
  Rule and, 73–74
  trials and sentences, 79

victims, 71–72, 74–75, 77–78, 79, 80
Bundy, William George, 165
Bunton, Paul, 126
Buono, Angelo
background, 114
Bianchi and, 111, 112, 116
death, 117
marriage, 117–118
trial, 116–117
Burden of Proof: The Case of Juan Corona (Corona and Cray), 18
Burger, John, 36. *See also* Alcala, Rodney
"Butcher Baker," 170–171
Butkovich, John, 153
Butts, Vernon, 132, 135–136. *See also* Freeway Killer murders

C

Camacho, Chris, 34
Campbell, Caryn, 75
"The Candyman," 20. *See also* Corll, Dean Allen
Capote, Truman, 24–25
Card, Brian, 90
Carrol, William, Jr., 153
Carter, Jimmy, 107
CBS News, 44
Cepeda, Dolores, 113
Chandler, Karen, 77
Chicago Sun-Times, 149
Chicago Tribune, 148, 149
Chi Omega House of Florida State, 77
Clark, Bernard, 120
"Classified Ad Rapist," 170
Clinton, Bill, 107
Clyne, Jeanne, 128
Cobble, Cary, 21
Cobble, Charles Ray, 29
"Co-ed Killer," 48. *See also* Kemper, Edmund, III
Cooke, Dan, 110
Cooks, Jessie, 102. *See also* "Zebra Murderers"
Corll, Arnold, 27
Corll, Dean Allen, 19–20, 26–27. *See also* Henley-Corll murder competition
Corona, Gloria, 9
Corona, Juan Vallejo
appeals, 17–18
background, 3, 4, 7, 10
book deal, 17–18
death, 18
health, 7, 10, 13, 15
lawyer, 9–10
parole and, 18
trials and sentence, 14, 15–17, 18
victims, 2, 3, 4, 10–13
writing samples from, 14–15
Corona, Natividad, 3, 18
Corona, Pedro, 9–10
Cottle, Chris, 92
Crappa, Dana, 36
Cray, Ed, 18
Crilley, Cornelia, 42, 45
Culture of 1960s-1970s
assassinations, 5
hitchhiking, xii, 8, 25
homosexuality, 123, 151–152
as portrayed on television, 8–9
Vietnam War protests, 4–5
Cupp, Edward M., 13

D

Dahlstedt, Arthur, 83, 86
Dahmer, Jeffrey, 170
Daily News. See *New York Daily News*
"Damsel of Death," 169
Dancik, Paul Roman, 103
Dansie, Feliciana, 15
DaRonch, Carol, 71–72, 74
Davis, Edward M., 84, 85
Davis, Ross, 79
Dean, Robin, 149
DeAngelo, Joseph James, 172
Death Angels, 101, 102, 105–106
Delone, Johnnie, 29
DeMartini, Theresa, 103
Deukmejian, George, 116
Dial, Preston, 29
Diaz, Tony, 9
Diel, John, 56
The Die Song: A Journey into the Mind of a Mass Murderer (Lunde), 96
DiMasi, Donna, 55
Ditnes, Bruce, 41–42

DNA, xi, 37, 39, 40, 44, 167, 168
Dreibelbis, Mark, 90
Dutcher, Helen, 130, 131

E
Eder, Carl A., 83
Egan, Robert, 155, 164
Enger, Linda Lou, 102
Erakat, Saleem, 103
Esau, Alexander, 56
Evans, Dan, 78, 79

F
Falco, Richard David. *See* Berkowitz, David
Farnell, John, 37
Federal Bureau of Investigation, xii–xiii, 35, 76, 80, 167, 172–173
Fleming, Charles C., 11
Fort, Joel, 50–51
"44-caliber killer," 57, 61. *See also* Berkowitz, David
Fox, Frank Dennis, 139, 141–142
Foy, Joseph, 130–131
Francis, Damion, 90
Francis, Kathleen, 90
Francis, Michael, 90
Franich, Charles, 91
Frazier, Marianne, 38
Freeway Killer murders, 132–133, 135, 138–142
Freund, Christine, 56
Frias, George, 87
The Frozen Ground, 171

G
Gacy, John C., 157, 158
Gacy, John Wayne
background, 144–145, 146, 157–158, 161
death, 161–164
health, 155–156, 157, 158–159, 161
homosexuality, xii, 155
trial and sentence, xiii, 150–151, 152, 155–158, 160
victims, xii, 144, 148, 149, 150, 152–155, 164–165
Gacy, Marian, 157–158
Gallego, Gerald and Charlene, 171
Ganzon, Donita, 155
Gao Chengyong, x
Garcia, Homer, 29
Garippo, Louis B., 150, 152, 159–160
Gates, Daryl F., 112
Gatlin, Ronald, 140
"The General" (Patton), 14, 17, 18
"Genesee River Killer," 171
George, Ronald M., 116
Gianera, Jim, 89
Gianera, Joan, 89
Gilroy, Robert E., 154
Girolamo, Marietta Di, 103
Glassman, Craig, 67
Godzik, Gregory, 153
Goethals, Thomas, 38
"Golden State Killer," 172
Gore, Bob, 118
Grabs, Marcus, 135, 138
Graham, William, Jr., 86
Green, Larry C., 101–102. *See also* "Zebra Murderers"
"Green River Killer," 168
Greenwood, Vaughn
arrest of, 84
parole and, 87–88
trial and sentences, 85–86
victims, 82, 84, 86–87
Grossman, Jay, 124
Guilfoyle, Mary, 90, 93

H
Haakenson, James, 164
Hagen, Chris, 76. *See also* Bundy, Theodore Robert
Hague, Quita, 102
Hague, Richard, 102
Haines, Donald, 34
Hallet, Sally, 49
Haluka, John J., 11
Halvonik, Paul, 99
Hamill, Pete, 65
Hankins, J. J., 9
Hansen, Robert Christian, 170–171
Harris, Anthony C., 102
Harris, Anthony Cornelius, 105–106
Hatten, William, 28
Hawk, Richard E.
appeals, 17–18
book deal, 17–18
career, 9–10
Corona and, 13–17
Diaz and, 9
jailed, 14–15, 17
Hay, Clyde C., 87

Hayes, Albert L., 13
Hearst, Patty "Tania," 106–107
Hearst to Hughes: Memoir of a Forensic Psychiatrist (Lunde), 112
Henley, Elmer Wayne. *See also* Henley-Corll murder competition
  background, 26
  Corll and, 19, 20, 21–22
  health, 28, 29
  in jail, 27–28
  parole and, 31
  trials and sentence, 28–31
  victims, 29
Henley, Mary, 22, 29
Henley-Corll murder competition
  as homosexual torture/murder ring, 24
  victims, 20, 21, 22, 26
Hensley, Ann, 150
Hill, Byron, 122
Hill, David Douglas, 119–120, 121–122
Hilligeist, David, 21
Hillside Strangler, 108, 109, 110, 114
Hitchhiking, xii, 8, 25, 30, 37, 49–50, 134
Hocking, Clarence, 12
Hoff, Carole, 158–159
Holly, Jane, 104
Holmes, John B., Jr., 127
Homosexuality. *See also* Freeway Killer murders
  Bonin, Butts, and Miley, 133, 134, 135, 136–137
  Freeway Killer murders, 132–133, 135, 138–142
  Gacy, xii, 148, 155
  Henley-Corll murder competition, 23
  Kearney and Hill, 120, 123
  Natividad Corona and, 18
  runaways and, 134–135
  views about, 151–152
Hornberg, Benjamin, 84, 86
Hosler, Mildred, 104
Houston Chronicle, 81
"Houston Diary" (Capote), 24
Hover, Ellen Jane, 35–36, 41–42, 45
Howard, James W., 12
Hoyt, Monique, 37–38, 46
Hudspeth, Cindy Lee, 110, 113
Huff, Rebecca Greer, 126
Hughes, John, 124
Hyden, Donald Ray, 139

I

In Cold Blood (Capote), 24

J

Jackson, Charles, 83, 87
Jackson, James, 92
Jackson, John H., 13
Jack the Ripper, x, xi–xii
Jacobson, Walter, 164
Jamison, J. B., 29–30
Johnson, Sonja, 113
Johnston, Rick, 153
Jones, Marty Ray, 21, 29

K

Kagehiro, Goro, 1
Kahan, Andy, 129
Kamp, William Emery, 12
Kasabian, Linda, 6
Kastin, Elissa Teresa, 113
Kearney, Patrick Wayne, 119–124
Keenan, John L., 68. *See also* Berkowitz, David
Keene, William, 141
Kelley, Warren J., 11
Kemper, Edmund, 48
Kemper, Edmund, III
  background and appearance of, 48, 52
  health, 50–51, 52
  parole and, 50, 53
  surrender to police, 48–49
  trial and sentence, 50–51
  victims, 47, 48
Kemper, Maude, 48
Kendrick, Darin Lee, 139
Kent, Debra, 72

Kerley, Tim, 20
Kindred, William, 154
King, Evelyn Jane, 113
King, Sean, 140–141
Kistler, Robert, 100
Kizuka, Christine, 117–118
Kleiner, Kathy, 77
Krenwinkel, Patricia, 6
Kunkle, William J., 147–148, 150, 152, 163–164

L
LaBianca, Bianca, 6
LaBianca, Leno, 6
Lake, Leonard, 171–172
LaMay, John Otis, 121, 123
LaMay, Patricia, 121
Lamb, Charlotte, 40, 45
Landingin, Frank, 154
Lang, Sanford, 85
Lanza, Adam, x
Lauria, Donna, 54–55, 62, 64
Lawrence, Billy, 29
Leach, Kimberly Ann, 79
Lee, Harper, 24
Levy, Lisa, 77, 79
Lister, Lori, 126–127
Little, Samuel, 167–168
Liu, Alice, 49
Lomino, Joann, 55
Long, Bobby Joe, 170
Lorre, Catherine, 115
Los Angeles Times, 14, 16, 33–34, 40, 48, 50, 82, 85, 109, 114, 115
Luchessa, Anita, 49
Lunde, Donald T., 52, 93, 95, 96, 111–112, 172–173
Lundgren, Thomas, 140
Lupo, Salvatore, 64

M
"The Machete Murderer," 3. *See also* Corona, Juan Vallejo
Maczak, Joseph, 13
Mandic, Karen, 111, 114
Marino, Michael, 164
Marquez, Arturo, 122, 123
Martin, Kimberly Diane, 109, 113
Martinez, Bob, 80
Mass murderers, x
Mazzara, James, 154
McCabe, James, 136, 138–139
McCoy, Timothy Jack, 158, 164
McMillan, Roxanne, 104
Melder, Charles, 29
Miley, Gregory Matthew, 136
Miller, Judith Lynn, 113
Miranda, Charles, 133, 135, 136, 138
Misner, Kenneth, 77. *See also* Bundy, Theodore Robert
Moore, Manuel, 101, 102. *See also* "Zebra Murderers"
Moskowitz, Neysha, 69
Moskowitz, Stacy, 66, 67, 69
Mosley, Howard Ware, 128
Mowery, John, 154
Moynihan, Neal, 103
Muchache, Raymond, 13
Mullin, Herbert W.
background, 93–94
health, 92, 93, 94–95
parole and, 96
trial and sentence, 91–93
victims, 89–91
Munro, James M., 136, 138. *See also* Freeway Killer murders
Murder and Madness (Lunde), 52, 93
"Murdermobile," 115
Murdoch, Rupert, 65–66
Murillo, David, 139
Myers, Marlene, 157–158

N
Naslund, Denise, 74–75
Nelson, Russell, 154
Newsom, Gavin, 45
New York City blackout, 65
New York Daily News, 54, 55, 57, 61, 65, 66
New York Post, 65–66
New York Times, 3, 10, 41, 42, 55–56, 57, 64, 65, 67, 78
Ng, Charles, 171–172
"Night Stalker," 172

O
"Officer Roseland," 71–72
Oliker, David, 90
O'Rourke, Timothy, 154, 155

O'Shea, John, 24
Ott, Janice, 74

P
Parenteau, Jill M., 37, 38, 40, 46
Parker, Kenneth, 164
Patton, Richard E., 14, 17, 18
Pegelow, Edwin, 30
Pendergast, Donna, 129
Perez, David, 86
Perez, Fred, 90
Pesc, Mary Ann, 49
Peterson, Pete, 11–12
Piest, Robert, 145, 146–148, 154, 155–156,
Piest family, 145–146, 157
Placido, Judy, 64
Prestidge, John S., 153
Puente, Dorothea Montalvo, 168–169
Pugh, William Ray, 137

R
Rainwater, Thomas, 104
Ramirez, Richard, 172
Reffett, Randall, 153
Ressler, Richard, 173
Richmond, Gloria, 126
Ricker, Kenneth, 86
Ridgway, Gary Leon, 168
Riley, Elbert J. T., 12
Rivera, Albert, 123
"Rochester Strangler," 171
Rose, Frances, 103
Rugh, Russell, 141
Rule, Ann, 73–74, 80, 81
Runaways, 25
Russell, David, 84, 87

S
S., Tali, 34, 45
Sample, Melford, 11
Sampson, Darrell, 153
Samsoe, Robert, 40–41
Samsoe, Robin Christine, 33, 36, 38, 46
Santucci, John, 56
Schall, Cynthia Ann, 49, 50
Schmuki, Warren, 115
Schwab, Philip E., 37
Schwartz, Amital, 99
Searles, Suzanne, 127
Sexual molestation
  by Alcala, 33, 34, 37–38, 39, 42
  by Bundy, 77
  Corona killings, 16
  Henley-Corll murder competition, 20, 21
  by "Zebra Murderers," 99
Shannahan, Robert (Tex), 86–87
Sharp, Lawrence, 141–142
Shaver, Doug, 127–128, 129
Shawcross, Arthur, 171
Sheaman, Jeff, 44
Sherman, Jerome M., 128
Shields, Mark Beverly, 13
Shields, Nelson, 105
Shields, Nelson T., IV, 98
Short, Herman, 25
Simon, J. C., 101, 102. See also "Zebra Murderers"
Sizelove, Steve, 1, 2
Skid Row Slasher, 82. *See also* Greenwood, Vaughn
Small, Shirley, 126
Smallwood, Johan R., 12
Smith, Agnes O'Brien, 101
Smith, Donald Dale, 11
Smith, Tana, 104
"Son of Sam," 57, 61. *See also* Berkowitz, David
Speck, Richard, x, 5, 150
Spector, Robert, 90
Springer, Ken, 95–96
Stapleton, Samuel, 153
Steele, Gloria, 126, 131
Story, Linda, 105
Strandberg, Clarenell, 49
The Stranger Beside Me (Rule), 73–74, 80
Strawinski, Casimir, 86
Suarez, Samuel, 87
"Summer of Sam," 61
"Sunday Morning Slasher," 125–126. *See also* Watts, Coral Eugene
Suriani, Valentina, 56
Szyc, John A., 153

T
Talsma, David, 154
Tate, Sharon, 6
"Ted," 74. *See also* Bundy, Theodore Robert
Teja, G. Dave, 13, 17
Tevrizian, Dickran, 124

Texas Tower Sniper, 6
Thomas, Cheryl, 78
Thornton, Kathy, 43–44
Thornton, Mary Ann, 44
Thornton family, 43–44, 46
Thorpe, Rosalind, 49–50
Tomei, Henri, 91, 92
"The Trashbag Killer," 119, 121, 122, 123
Turner, Harry Todd, 140

U
Underwood, Naomi, 17

V
Valenti, Jodi, 54–55
Vance, Carol S., 28, 30–31
Vance, Cyrus R., Jr., 41
Van de Kamp, John, 114
Van den Heuvel, Roy, 9, 18
Victims
  Alcala's, 33, 37, 38, 39, 40, 42, 43, 45–46
  Berkowitz's, 54–55, 56, 64, 66
  Bianchi's, 111–113, 114
  Bundy's, 71–72, 73, 74–75, 76, 77–78, 79, 80
  Corona's, 2, 3, 10–13
  Dahmer's, 170
  Freeway Killer's, 132–133, 135, 138–142
  Gacy's, xii, 144, 148, 149, 150, 152–155, 164–165
  Gallego's, 171
  Greenwood's, 82, 83, 84, 86–87
  Hansen's, 171
  Henley-Corll murder competition, 20, 21, 22, 26, 29
  Hillside Strangler's, 108, 109, 110, 114
  Kearney's, 121, 122, 123, 124
  Kemper's, 48, 49–50
  Lake and Ng's, 171, 172
  Little's, 167–168
  Long's, 170
  Mullin's, 89–91
  Puente's, 169
  Ridgway's, 168
  Speck's, 5
  Watts's, 126, 127, 128, 130, 131
  Whitman's, 5–6
  Wuornos's, 169
  "Zebra Murderers," 98, 99, 101–102, 103–105
Vietnam War, 4–5
Violante, Robert, 66, 67
Voskerichian, Virginia, 56

W
Wagner, Lauren Rae, 113
Wallis, Georgia, 17
Washington Post, 24
Watkins, Charles, 6
Watts, Coral Eugene
  deal made by, 125, 127, 128–129
  death, 131
  health, 128
  sentence, 125, 128
  victims, 126, 127, 128, 130, 131
Weckler, Kristina, 113
Wells, Steven, 136, 138, 140
Wenzel, Lloyd W., 13
Whitacre, Kendall, 2, 10
Whitaker, Roy D., 4, 13
White, Lawrence, 90, 93
White, Terry, 105
Whitman, Charles, 5–6
Wilder, Diane, 111, 114
Williams, Bartley, 15–16, 17
Williams, James F., 85
Williams, Rhonda, 20
Winch, Robert, 154
Wipf, Richard, 118
Wittner, Bonnie G., 42–43
Wixted, Georgia, 39, 45
Wollin, Vincent R., 104
Woo, Aiko, 49
Wood, Steven, 140
Wuornos, Aileen, 169

Y
Yakanak, Moses August, 83, 86
York, Ned, 109–110

Z
"Zebra Murderers"
  sexual molestation by, 100
  trial, 102, 105–106
  victims, 98, 99, 101–102, 103–105

IMAGE CREDITS

Alamy: Everett Collection: 54

AP: AP File Photo: 19, 23, 68, 82, 94, 108, 113; Ross Dolan/Glenwood Springs Post Independent: 75; Hugh Grannum/Detroit Free Press Pool: 125; Sacramento Bee: 1

Courtesy Des Plaines Police Department: 143

Courtesy FBI: 71

Getty Images: Bettman: 99, 132, 135; Tony Korody/Sygma: 119, 122; New York Daily News Archive: 63, 64

Courtesy Santa Cruz Police Department: 47, 89

Courtesy San Quentin State Prison: 32

Wikimedia: 105, 160, 163

ABOUT THE AUTHOR

Jane Fritsch is a journalist who was a reporter and editor at *The New York Times*, where she was a finalist for the Pulitzer Prize. She was also a reporter for *The Los Angeles Times*, *Newsday*, and *The Chicago Tribune*, where she covered the trial of the serial killer John Wayne Gacy. She was an assistant professor at The Greenlee School of Journalism and Communication at Iowa State University.